ADDITIONAL PRAISE

"An amazing, powerful story. You validate the line in the big book: '...our members find that they have tapped an unsuspected inner resource which they presently identify with their own conception of a Power greater than themselves.' A fascinating, enlightening read."
—Ray Wylie Hubbard, Texas troubadour and recording artist

"I've long admired Don McLeese as a trusted, professional music critic who rarely wrote about his own life. But now I realize he was just saving it for the book! We rarely read about the functioning alcoholic because he or she hides their true lives so well. But here it comes barreling out, a life lived in the clouds. If you think you might have a problem with alcohol you almost certainly do."
—Michael Corcoran, Austin music journalist, author, *Ghost Notes: Pioneering Spirits of Texas Music*

"In recovery, we are told, 'Don't compare, identify!' I identify with Don McLeese so much that reading this book I felt that the only distinction between his story and my story is that I like the Mets and he is a Cubs lifer. His candid, eloquent book tells a story of alcoholism and recovery with the self-awareness, honesty and humor that has characterized his life as a newspaper guy, music critic, college professor, and family man. His book is at the top of the pyramid of journalistic memoirs of bouncing back from the bottom of an empty bottle that include Pete Hamill's *A Drinking Life* and Caroline Knapp's *Drinking: A Love Story*."
—Wayne Robins, author, *A Brief History of Rock, Off the Record* and adjunct professor at St. John's University in Queens, NY

"Rock journalist McLeese (*Kick Out the Jams*) chronicles his road to sobriety in this uninhibited saga ... charts in hurtling vignettes a new identity for himself free from the pressure of his addiction. The author's fans will bask in the storytelling."
—*Publishers Weekly*

Slippery Steps

Rolling & Tumbling Toward Sobriety

Don McLeese

Ice Cube Press, LLC
North Liberty, Iowa, USA

Slippery Steps: Rolling & Tumbling Toward Sobriety

Copyright © 2022 Don McLeese

ISBN 9781948509350

Library of Congress Control Number: 2022931825

Ice Cube Press, LLC (Est. 1991)
North Liberty, Iowa 52317
www.icecubepress.com steve@icecubepress.com
Check us out on Facebook & Twitter

No portion of this book may be reproduced in any way without permission, except for brief quotations for review, or educational work, in which case the publisher shall be provided two copies. The views expressed in *Slippery Steps: Rolling & Tumbling Toward Sobriety* are solely those of the author not the Ice Cube Press, LLC.

The paper used in this publication meets the minimum requirements of the American National Standard for Information Sciences—Permanence of Paper for Printed Library Materials, ANSI Z39.48-1992.

Made with recycled paper.

Manufactured in Canada

Author photo—Paul Jensen
Bear illustration—Jon Dee Graham
Cover art and design—John Soss, Maxine and Hans.

For Maria, Kelly and Molly
And for Mike B

Part I: Falling Down Again

1. It was a drunk and stormy night

THE FLASHLIGHT SHOT THROUGH MY stupor like a laser beam to the skull, sparking the first faint glimmers of consciousness. Above me, a male voice, with calm authority, asked, "Are you all right, sir?"

His concern was impersonal—I could tell before opening my eyes that I didn't know him, and that he didn't know me. He had been summoned in some official capacity. He was probably half my age.

Was I all right? I suppose I was, still breathing, semiconscious, feeling no pain. So I mumbled something in the affirmative, likely unintelligible. But I really had no conception of what "all right" might mean. I wasn't exactly sure who I was, where I was, or why. I had no idea how long I had been there. It was very dark out, and it was still pouring, but was it 10 at night or 4 in the morning? There was lightning, and there was thunder. It was a hot August night in West Des Moines. I was lying on the grass, immobile, soaked.

So the stranger's question made little sense to me and neither did his presence. But the fact that he was talking to me—that he was there at all—suggested that something was very wrong. And likely to get worse. Who *was* I? I was the guy who lived in the house that had this fenced backyard, which I had awakened to vaguely recognize. For some reason I was on the ground, my predicament witnessed by someone I didn't know, someone who didn't belong here. Not that I belonged here, on the ground, in the downpour.

As the fog in my head continued to clear, here's what I remembered: I had taken Rosie, our Cavalier King Charles puppy, out into the rain. She had been scared of the thunder, and wouldn't go on her own. When I followed her down the soaked steps, I didn't feel like I'd had too much to drink—almost a bottle of wine at dinner, then a cigar, followed by a full snifter or two of brandy. I knew what drunk felt like, and I wasn't. Or hadn't been. If I'd returned inside, I likely would have felt the need for another glass, or a joint, or both, before I could fall asleep. Or, more accurately, pass out, as was my nightly ritual.

But *something* had happened. When Rosie was done, quickly, she had run up the stairs to the deck, and I had followed her. Or attempted to. My legs wouldn't move the way my foggy brain had told them to. I had tried and failed repeatedly to navigate the three wooden steps that rose from our backyard to the deck outside the backdoor. I simply couldn't maintain my balance long enough, or move my legs well enough, to climb three slippery steps.

Eventually, I had decided on a different approach. I would crawl up the stairs on my hands and knees, figuring that a lower center of gravity might help (actually intuiting; I wasn't thinking clearly, or rationally). But I could no more crawl up those stairs than climb them. I'd make it up one, and then slip back while trying to hoist myself, balancing on my forearms, up the second. In retrospect, I must have looked like a slapstick Sisyphus, but it was no laughing matter at the time. I was becoming increasingly desperate. And wet. It was starting to rain even harder.

I have no idea how long I kept trying, failing, and humiliating myself, before I gave up. Felt like an hour or so; could have been five or ten minutes. Long enough that my knees and elbows had bloody scrapes, and that I would have visible scars on my arms for days afterward. It was late, hot summer, and I was wearing shorts and a T-shirt.

At some point, as I lay semicomatose, my wife Maria had come out and shrieked, "Donald, what are you doing?" The dog had come upstairs and I hadn't, but it wasn't just that. Most nights I stayed downstairs for a while after Maria and Rosie had both gone up. If I were to drink as much as I'd like, it was easier to do so without Maria monitoring me. And then I'd slip into bed after she'd fallen asleep, if I hadn't passed out on the couch. Or the chair. But maybe the thunder and rain had alarmed her, so she came down to look for me, and when she didn't find me on the couch, she went outside.

She's the only one who ever calls me "Donald," and often when she's mad at me. It was hard to tell whether she was mad, or scared or both. And I didn't know how to respond. What *was* I doing? I supposed I'd taken a rest, or a break, figuring that if I couldn't crawl onto the deck right then, I would be able to later, after I'd gathered my energies. Or the stairs had become less slippery. Or something. So I'd lain in the wet grass, in the pouring rain. Until I was so rudely, briefly, interrupted.

"I'm just resting," I had groaned. As if it were perfectly normal to take a quick nap outside in the middle of a severe thunderstorm. She later told me that she feared I'd been hit by lightning. And that was why she made the call to 911 that had summoned the disembodied voice. And reinforcements—both EMS and the police had responded.

But what I mainly remembered was that male voice of authority, which remained disembodied to me. I've blotted out all visual detail, couldn't tell you whether he was taller or lighter than me. I don't remember what kind of uniform he wore. He and another guy helped me up, took me by the arms, supported me up the steps. I remember us sitting in the three-season porch, between the deck and the kitchen.

I think he wanted to measure my blood alcohol level, and I know he asked me if I wanted to go to the hospital. I have no memory of the results of the former, but know that I adamantly resisted the latter. In my mind, what had happened was over, and what remained was gaper's block. *Move along, nothing to see here.* It was time to go to bed.

My most indelible memory of the night, other than trying and failing to navigate those damn steps, was hearing him tell my wife, "I hope he gets some help. For your sake." He wasn't talking to me, and I wouldn't have listened. I didn't need help. This was an aberration, an accident. Could have happened to anyone.

I had been drinking for decades, nightly, and, yes, progressively more and more. There had been other incidents, but spaced far apart. A couple of years earlier, I had tumbled down a flight of stairs and had been rushed to the hospital, fortunate that I hadn't cracked my head open. Maria had called 911 then as well. In retrospect, I know I could have died, but at the time it was no big deal—a wake-up call that perhaps I might temper my alcohol consumption, watch myself, take it easy. Such resolutions didn't last long. I continued to drink nightly without visible consequences and had soon surpassed my former levels of consumption.

Since then, a few times I had found myself on the floor rather than the couch where I had been lying, with no idea how I had gotten there. The scariest were the times when I awoke gasping for breath, as if I were suffocating on the Grand Marnier I had overserved myself before passing out. Often half of the last glass would have spilled, drenching my shirt or the couch or both.

But, to me, these were flukes, not a pattern that would be cause for concern. They concerned Maria, who thought I had a drinking problem. I thought I had a nagging problem. I was a full-grown man, a good father and husband, a responsible breadwinner who had never lost so much as a day of work, let alone a job, to alcohol. I worked hard; I played hard; I deserved my reward. I never had a drink before dinner, though increasingly I had a lot more once I had started.

I figured this was my business, a preference, not a problem. I could do what I liked, as long as I wasn't harming anyone. I liked to drink. That's why I drank so much.

Yet this night would prove tougher to rationalize. Not that Maria wanted to hear anything from me anyway. She had already gone to one of the spare bedrooms, with our daughters off to college, and had locked the door.

The two men continued to help me up the steep steps to our bedroom, the ones I had tumbled down two years earlier. I staggered into the bedroom, peeled off my shirt, and realized that the front was caked with vomit. Even after all that rain! I had absolutely no recollection of throwing up on myself, something I'd usually remember, and something that made the encounter with the strangers summoned to help even more embarrassing.

But this was nothing compared to taking off my shorts, when I was stunned to discover that there was excrement in my underwear, smeared up and down the back of my legs, and now on the sheet of the bed where I'd been getting undressed. Again, no memory whatsoever, but now the stench was overpowering, and more degrading than anything I'd ever felt in my life. Drunk or sober, I'd never done this, at least not since diaper days.

Through the decades, my drinking had passed through many phases, as the self-image I hoped to present to the world had changed.

I had been a teenage high-school rebel sneaking beer and cigarettes, a college kid who shared pitcher after pitcher, a young adult who liked to push boundaries and live on the edge, and then an older sophisticate who planned not only dinners but vacations (Napa, Tuscany, the south of France) around fine wines that provided the lubrication—and the reward!—for the life well lived.

Never once had I pictured myself as the kind of drinker who couldn't control his bowels, and wasn't even aware of it. So, yes, now I had to admit I had a problem, and I knew I had to confront it. There was no more rationalizing it away.

When Maria woke up, I vowed that I would make things right. I resolved that I would make a huge change—*no more drinks after dinner.* I'd limit myself to two glasses of wine a night. That should fix it.

2. The Morning After

You know that cliché about how today is the first day of the rest of your life? It offered no comfort. That morning looked dismal, blacker than bleak, and so did the rest of my life. That night had been a turning point, and this was definitely a turn for the worse.

Yet I still thought I had some wiggle room. All I wanted to do was make things right, whatever that might mean. I'd promise to cut back on my drinking, drink sensibly, like normal people. Maybe a glass or two of wine at dinner, a promise I'd made before. And I'd always kept it, for a little while, though soon relying on bigger glasses, filled to the top. I could finish a whole bottle with two glasses. But I wouldn't. I'd always leave a little, or split the bottle with Maria (usually finishing her half glass along with the rest). Because, in my mind, drinking a whole bottle by myself might mean I was an alcoholic.

And, once again, absolutely no more drinking after dinner. At least for a while. This was another vow I'd made and broken, more than once. Because I'd soon interpret it as no more drinking *nightly* after dinner. I'd make exceptions for special occasions, and it wouldn't be long before more and more nights would feel special to me. A restaurant meal. A trip out of town. A weekend. And when nothing particularly bad happened on those occasions, I'd be back to considering this a choice to be made every night. When I allowed myself that choice, I'd always choose to drink, maybe a third of a bottle of cognac to still my mind so I could go to sleep.

After all, I was the one who made the rules. And I could always change them. In interpreting the law, I was a very lenient judge, particularly after that first drink.

Those days were over. Had to be. I knew it. We obviously needed to negotiate something—something significant, something radical, something with teeth. But, while I'd been asleep, Maria had started without me, pouring every opened bottle into the sink. And bringing her suitcases out. She was still sleeping while I was stumbling myself awake—hungover, groggy, humiliated—but it was obvious that the terms of negotiation had already escalated. And that whatever bargaining position I'd imagined I'd occupied had plummeted in the process.

I'd long maintained that I was innocent—of problem drinking, of "using it as a crutch," as Maria often charged, turning my personal preference into a character weakness. After last night's degradation, I knew that the best I could do was plea-bargain. I had to plead guilty, admit that I had a problem, one that the officers the night before had recognized and most likely even smelled. Maria was right, and I was wrong. I was ready to submit to a resolution. On whatever terms Maria might want, at least in the short term.

What I hadn't expected to face was the maximum, the death penalty—for our marriage. The suitcases showed she had reached her own turning point. When Maria woke up, she barely acknowledged my presence. She had no interest in talking about last night or hearing however I might propose to make it up to her. We'd been together a quarter century, and I'd never seen her so silently steamed. So I pulled out my ace in the hole, something I never had previously considered.

"I'll quit drinking," I promised. Cold turkey. No more. That's it. At least until the heat was off, and we could reach some accommodation.

"I don't care what you do," she responded, her voice flat, deadly devoid of emotion. This was way worse than yelling, or nagging. "I'm finished."

And, for her, that was it. We had nothing more to discuss. There would be no negotiation. We'd been fighting this battle, on and off, for more than a decade. Maria was the only one I knew who thought I had a drinking problem. Or at least told me so. Of course, since I had begun to do most of my drinking at home, and never during the day, she was the only one who had any suspicion of how much my drinking had escalated. And since I did much of it after she'd gone to bed, even she didn't know the extent. Except when I fell down the stairs or blacked out in the back yard.

I've long maintained that nobody has any idea what goes on in a marriage except for the two who are married to each other. And even they may only have partial truths, or different truths. But even through my drinking, Maria and I had long agreed that our marriage was better than most. A lot of other people we knew shared similar sentiments about us, even a little good-natured envy. The idea that we could or would split up would come as a shock. It was a shock to me.

It would be like the lip-locked Al and Tipper Gore splitting. So huggy and smiley on the big political stage. So mutually supportive as the Clintons' running buddies. And then splitting and divorcing without explanation after his loss in the election moved them out of the spotlight. See how little we know about anyone else's marriage?

The Maria who had just pronounced our marriage dead wasn't the wife I knew. From decades of experience, I could deal with emotional, impetuous, mercurial Maria. I knew that she responded from the heart while I countered from the head, and that this was one of the many ways in which we complemented each other. She had long been quick to anger and easy to annoy, but her threats were typically short-lived. She wanted things different, so she would let me know in the strongest possible way that she wanted things different.

But now she wanted out, and she was talking and behaving in a way that was really radical, as if her past with me was something she had moved beyond; she had suffered and survived and she was cutting her losses. Whatever happened to me was collateral damage, and so be it. It was my own damn fault. She was getting on with her life, and her life no longer included a man who got so drunk he would shit in his pants, and not even know it. A man whose presence disgusted her.

So, hell yes, she was outta here. Leaving me with the wreckage. Stuck with myself and the mess I had made. After all the threats, all the arguments, she'd given up on us. On me. She thought I wouldn't change, not really, or couldn't change. And if I wanted to rationalize or play games of semantics, I could do it on my own.

I felt blindsided, despite decades of warning. We'd been fighting small skirmishes on so many different fronts that the drinking problem just seemed—to me—like one part of an extensive, perpetual battle. I'm very stubborn and even more defensive. I've never responded well to anyone telling me what to do—parents, bosses, editors, wives. I need to have the upper hand. When I was underage, drinking was an essential part of this rebellious self-image, the rejection of authority.

It had long since become an essential part of my professional identity, as a rock critic for daily newspapers and national magazines, as someone who had not only bought into the myth of unbridled rebellion but helped perpetuate it. I had made my living as a rock critic for decades, and, now that I was teaching, being the rock and roll professor was still part of my identity. Rock had become a huge industry since the formative years when it had shaped my self-image.

It was an establishment unto itself. But it still had that outlaw aura, flirting with taboo, that feeling of making your own rules. Excess was part of the package. As Tom Petty once sang, "Too much ain't enough." Drinking and doping didn't require any self-regulation beyond doing what felt good at the time.

But now they had little to do with feeling good or keeping the party going. They had become a self-medicating coping mechanism. Part of the reason I drank was to get the sleep I needed to get the work done that I needed to do. My brain was otherwise on the hamster wheel, with no shutoff button. Like John Lennon sang, "Whatever gets you through the night, it's all right." What business was it of Maria's?

I wasn't even convinced that my drinking was the major issue on the table, or the real issue. In a lot of marriages, including ours, whatever an argument is ostensibly about—money, sex, where to have dinner, what kind of pizza to order, whether to get another dog (and another and another)—the underlying issues are power and control, about who gets to be, as George W. Bush famously put it, "the decider." I'd say we couldn't afford new carpeting, yet think nothing of spending whatever I wanted on necessities such as cigars, books, CDs. And liquor. Maria felt the same about makeup, jewelry, and other things I dismissed as frivolous.

She had dozens of robes and purses, along with a lipstick assortment that could last several lifetimes. I had hundreds of T-shirts. Maybe thousands? Both of us thought that the way the other spent money was crazy, and it's likely that each of us was right. Our marriage worked fine as long as neither of us got too much in the other's face. She had her issues; I had mine.

There were control issues on both sides. Amid plenty of competition, I think the silliest ongoing argument we had was about my haircuts.

She'd get annoyed when I got a haircut, because she didn't like my hair shorter, and she knew I knew it, so she figured I was having it cut to piss her off. Consciously, I wasn't—it just felt more comfortable, thinned out, but the issue was a nagging irritant for both of us.

Until the morning after the night that my world had collapsed, my drinking seemed like a larger but essentially similar issue to me, an area where she was overstepping her bounds. Overplaying her hand. Maria also liked to drink, just not nearly as much or as often as I did. I was a good husband, a good father; I brought home a good paycheck. I didn't cheat or gamble. I mowed the lawn (though not as often or as well as she preferred). I did my own laundry. Against my own controlling instincts, I tried my best to let her make the decisions that meant a whole lot more to her than they did to me.

But what gave her any right to question how much I wanted to drink? Maria said she was worried about my health, but I didn't buy it. No doctor had ever said that my drinking was causing me any problems (although no doctor had ever been told the truth about how much I drank). My liver was fine.

The best spin I could put on it is that Maria thought I was going to die younger because I drank so much, and she didn't want to deal with that. And I'd often counter that her resolute refusal to exercise (which I had done daily for decades, mainly to clear my head) represented even more of a health risk, and I didn't nag her about that. Until she nagged me. And that's how our marriage proceeded, with an underlying tension, both of us knowing which buttons to push and pushing them often. She hated that I always had a comeback, that I needed to have the last word. And, in those days, I did. I was always pretty defensive.

This may not be everyone's definition of a happy marriage, but we were generally happy in our own pugnacious ways. We loved each other, we needed each other, we balanced each other.

Even that morning, I wasn't convinced that I had a major drinking problem, though I knew I had a very serious marriage problem. I'd thought I had a prodigious thirst—for life and its pleasures—and an exceptional capacity to hold my liquor. Except, apparently, when I tumbled down stairs or shit my pants. So, yes, I had plainly exceeded that capacity, but I figured I could dial it down, rein it in.

And now, Maria had called it quits. A quarter-century together can turn molehills into mountains that no longer feel worth the climb. Prior to falling in love with Maria (at first sight, and pretty much every sight since then), I'd had a shelf life of about ten years. My first marriage (when I was so young that most are surprised to learn of it) lasted ten years. I spent ten years at the first newspaper that hired me (*Chicago Sun-Times*) and then ten years at the second (*Austin American-Statesman*). These transitions seemed to happen not only every ten years, but at the turn of a decade. Which, for a guy born in 1950, also coincided with a milestone birthday.

So Maria had been a real trouper, sticking around well beyond my ten-year shelf life. Now that both of our daughters were away at college, we had both speculated on what big change the next decade would bring—new job, new home, whatever. I'd be turning 60 in 2010, a big change in itself, for a guy who still showed some symptoms of perpetual adolescence.

But now she'd jumped the gun, deciding that whatever happened for each of us would be without the other. *This* would be the next big change in our life together—that we wouldn't have one. I needed to have the last word? Maria was now telling me fine, go ahead. Talk all you want. To an empty house. "I don't care what you do." What terrible freedom. What a hollow victory.

Plainly, this drinking thing had been a bigger deal to Maria than I'd suspected, as deep in denial as I was. In her mind, Maria had been giving me a choice between our marriage and my drinking. And I (in her mind) had chosen to continue to drink—progressively and excessively more. She suspected I loved drinking more than I loved her. And though I never would have framed things that way, I couldn't face the possibility that it might be true. What a wretched person that would be—a guy who preferred to drink himself into solitary oblivion rather than truly share a life with the woman he loved.

I couldn't bear to be that person. Whether or not there was a chance that this marriage could be saved (a la the *Ladies Home Journal* column that I'd long loved and ridiculed), I needed to show that I was serious about quitting. And changing. Whatever extreme measures or extravagant gestures might demonstrate this commitment, I'd embrace them. I had something to prove to myself, if not to Maria.

So, the first thing I did was call our family doctor, make an appointment to see him that morning. I asked for a prescription for Antabuse, the drug that was said to make you very sick if you ingested the slightest bit of alcohol. I didn't know whether or not I'd succumb to the compulsion to drink without it, but I was positive I wouldn't be tempted if I knew that a drink would make me violently ill. Since my doctor knew I drank daily (but with no idea how much), he had occasionally raised this as a potential issue, and he had no problem prescribing.

The second thing I did was Google Alcoholics Anonymous (AA).

3. One Day at a Time

EVERYONE KNOWS ALCOHOLICS ANONYMOUS, at least the big-picture generalities. In the same way that everyone knows the Salvation Army—something to do with God, maybe a cult, does more good than harm. Yet the Salvation Army is visible—with stores and bells and kettles (at least during the Christmas season) and shelters for the homeless to sleep. If they would come without drugs or drink, if there was enough room. And maybe the Salvation Army has uniforms, or once had.

By comparison, Alcoholics Anonymous, to those not involved with it, seems to operate invisibly, move in mysterious ways. Because alcohol and addiction run rampant in rock music (the beat I had covered) and in journalism (my chosen career), I'd known four people well who had been in AA. One had been a chronic relapser, the other three long sober and seemingly devoted. I probably knew a lot more, but they just didn't talk about it. I knew the program involved attending meetings regularly, even when you were traveling, maybe even more than one a day, but I had no idea what went on in those meetings.

And if I'd been more curious, it still wouldn't have felt right to ask. Because that was the "anonymous" part, right? Like Vegas, without the drinking and carousing. In AA, what happens there, stays there.

I knew there were 12 steps, because AA and others that followed a similar model (for narcotics, sex, gambling, overeating, whatever) were called 12-step programs. It was okay to say you were in a 12-

step program, but anonymity discouraged people from saying they belonged to AA. So how did you become a member? What did it mean to belong? Where did you sign up? Were there monthly dues, a blood oath, a secret handshake? I had no clue.

I just knew that this was the next step for me, that it would show Maria I was serious about quitting drinking. If Maria even cared. She knew no more or less about AA than I did, but another thing we both knew was that it preached abstinence rather than moderation, that it considered alcoholism as a disease, or a condition, or an allergy, or something, for which there was no cure. There was only remission. And you somehow stayed sober, if you did, by going to meetings. And working the steps. Whatever they were. Maybe if I were able to shift the framing of my drinking from moral failing to progressive disease, Maria would shift as well—stop judging me and start taking pity on me.

Maria also knew how much I hated meetings, or any sort of small talk with strangers, or new experiences where I had no idea what to expect. My willingness to try this reinforced my sense of purpose. My comfort level is razor thin, and I'd long used alcohol to fortify it, to close myself off. Being alone didn't bother me—I enjoyed it—but I never felt lonelier than in a crowded room where everyone was connected and chit-chatting. Everyone but me, the oddball, the social misfit, the guy who seemed to have an invisible shield that would repel casual conversation. The guy who was obviously so uncomfortable in his own skin. So I'd head to the bar.

One thing I knew for certain about an AA meeting: There would be no bar.

I began my inquiry on the internet, where everyone starts anything these days. And after typing "Alcoholics Anonymous Des Moines" into the search engine, I was amazed to discover that there was a noon meeting in less than an hour, at a church ten minutes from our suburban home. I guess I'd hoped that there was some meeting, somewhere, that day, but this was one of maybe three dozen meetings throughout the metro area on Mondays alone, from close to daybreak to well into the evening. Who knew? Many were in churches, but there were some in office buildings, mental-health clinics and hospitals, supermarket cafeterias, and a couple of locations I couldn't identify (which turned out to be specifically AA properties). Apparently AA was everywhere, if you knew where to look.

And there were a bunch of meetings from which to choose happening simultaneously at noon. Selecting my first meeting was easy, because I was desperate to show I was serious, and the closer and sooner the better. But did going to this meeting mean I was committing to a specific group to the exclusion of the others? Or were you allowed to be promiscuous in your meetings, date around, try a bunch out, go to as many different ones as you desired?

How long did a meeting last? What went on there? Were there really enough down-and-out drunks in Des Moines to fill dozens of different meetings every day? As I drove to the church, a modern one in a middle-class neighborhood, I suspected that all those options would thin the attendance at any one. I figured I'd find myself in a small room with maybe a half-dozen bleary-eyed brown baggers, the desperate ones who had run out of money and options and self-esteem, and who had somehow staggered their way from under the downtown bridge to suburbia.

Instead, I heard cheerful conversation and even laughter as I walked down the hall toward a large room filled with lively conversation. There were maybe 70 people in this bright, smokeless space (another expectation dashed), and they seemed like a happy, healthy and fairly prosperous lot. At least compared to what I'd expected. It looked like the Rotary Club. In a positive way. (And, no, I don't really know anything about the Rotary Club either, beyond the clichés.)

There were more men than women, but not overwhelmingly so. The age span seemed to run the gamut from early 20s to 80s (or older), with the bulk of them (us?) middle-aged and middle-class. All were white; this was Iowa. (I would subsequently encounter slightly more diversity at other meetings.)

As I sat down in one of the card table chairs, arranged in three rectangular rows, one man in particular took notice of me. Ordinarily I'd resist any interaction with someone I didn't know, but I welcomed the approach of the smiling, friendly stranger, a guy a little younger than me. Everybody else seemed to be talking and comfortable, and connecting with someone, anyone, would make me feel less like an outcast. Though here I was in a room full of outcasts who had somehow made peace with their affliction, their shame, and seemed to be engaged in the sort of normal social interaction that had eluded me even when I was drinking to make myself more comfortable.

This guy seemed to know I was new, though it somehow didn't make me uncomfortable in the way he singled me out. I was already uncomfortable. And the fact that I had somebody to talk with made me feel less conspicuous, like I somehow belonged, in this place where I really had no idea whether I belonged. The fact that we both introduced ourselves as "Don" seemed like it might have been some sort of sign, or at least a funny coincidence. I had arrived knowing no one, and now I knew someone.

He was open and friendly and nonjudgmental. He seemed sincerely interested in what had brought me there, and he didn't seem to be selling any snake oil solution. He laughed easily. He just wanted me to know that I had a friend if I needed one, and that I was in a roomful of friends who understood what I was going through because they'd all experienced and survived, even overcome, a similar affliction. In fact, most of them had done far worse, sunk way lower, before they had found their way to their first meeting.

Many were, as I would learn in the terminology of AA, "low-bottom drunks," the sort who had to sink desperately low and bottom out—losing their health, jobs, homes, whatever—whereas I was what I learned to call a "high-bottom drunk." What I might have once termed a "functioning alcoholic," if I'd been willing to admit I was an alcoholic.

Here's what you'll likely hear from a guy like that, or from someone at a meeting, when you show up for the first time:

You'll never have to be alone with this. And you'll never have to take another drink. There's always a meeting, a phone call, a friend there to help you. You don't have to beat this thing by yourself.

And here are a few other things you'll hear at your first meeting, where you'll likely receive enough attention to feel welcome, but not so much that you'll feel uncomfortable. Inevitably someone, or many people, will call you brave for coming to your first meeting, and they'll say with a laugh that you'll only have to go to your first meeting once. And that everyone there had to do the same, and likely felt the same.

They'll tell you, *You're the most important person in the room.* And they'll mean it, because it's something of a special occasion when someone comes to his first meeting. You'll learn that some of those there have been sober for twenty or thirty years, and that they'll continue to go to meetings as long as they live, that they want to give back—to help others as they were helped. Or even saved. And that the only way to keep the program, to adhere to its principles, to stay sober, is to give it away. You'll also hear, and not understand, that the longer you've been sober, the closer you are to your next drink. So coming to meetings wards off complacency. Nobody there would ever say that they had this thing licked. Some would describe themselves as "recovering alcoholics." None considered themselves cured, or ever expected to be.

I hadn't expected to encounter so many who had been sober for decades and who had long overcome any obsession with alcohol. Or at least it seemed as if they had. I'm not sure what I'd expected, but it was definitely a shorter-term commitment, as far as going to meetings. I figured that after a few weeks or months I'd be sober and want to stay that way, or I'd have returned to drinking but in some controlled manner.

I took "one day at a time" to heart, and I found comfort in it. I was only making this decision for this day. If things changed tomorrow, or next month, or next year—however long it took to take the heat off this and get our marriage beyond the crisis stage—I could reassess and make a different decision. But I knew I didn't want to drink today, I'd already taken a pill that would make me sick if I did so, and this cheery group of people didn't make a day (or a life) without drinking seem like much of a sacrifice.

Here's something else you'll hear at your first AA meeting: *We're not going to tell you that you're an alcoholic. Only you can decide that. But you're probably here because alcohol has caused some problems in your life. We don't get many tourists here.*

Until this morning after the dreadful night before, I would have resisted any suggestion that I was an alcoholic. I hadn't lost any jobs or even any days at work. I didn't drink until dinner. I hadn't ruined my family life (yet) or gotten a DWI. By outward appearances, except to my wife, my life had been fine. But here I was, scarred and broken, at least in comparison with these folks, and I was willing to give it a shot. If they wanted to hear me say, "My name is Don, and I'm an alcoholic," I'd say that. If they wanted me to say I believed in the Easter Bunny, I'd say that.

Another line you'll hear often, if not at your very first meeting: *Our best thinking is what got us here.* If I was as smart as I'd thought I was, why had I been passed out in a thunderstorm, caked in vomit and excrement, my wife with her suitcases packed? And my mind had told me I didn't have a problem? So, by attending my first meeting, I was at least opening myself to the possibility that I'd been in a bit of denial.

Then the meeting started the way almost all of them do, with a "moment of silence for the alcoholic who still suffers," followed by the Serenity Prayer:

> *God grant me the serenity to accept the things I cannot change, the courage to change the things I can, and the wisdom to know the difference.*

I was familiar with the prayer from reading it, but I don't think I'd ever heard it recited aloud. I know I'd never said it before. This time the words sank in, far deeper than the mental version of lip service. The language was so simple, the challenge so difficult, the promise so hopeful.

Things didn't seem quite as bleak as they had before I arrived here.

4. How It Works

From the front table where the meeting leaders sat, there was a series of procedural matters—announcements of AA business and the like. And then birthdays (which were in fact sobriety anniversaries, the celebrant reborn on the day after he had taken his last drink, the birthday recalibrated after any relapse) commemorated with chips, poker-sized medallions with the number of months or years of sobriety on them. Applause and congratulations all around. I was amazed when one man announced that he'd been sober for 37 years today. And he was still going to meetings!

I'd figured that once you got over this thing, or got it under control, or whatever, you'd be done. You'd move on. But I'd soon learn that some of these folks were in this for good, with AA at the center of their existence, encompassing everything from their spiritual lives to their social lives. They had been reborn in AA, and their new life was basically the program. They would say that you needed to make the program the most important thing in your life. I didn't know if I ever could. I still don't.

Then the agenda proceeded to the heart of the matter, the obligatory recitation of "How It Works." Printed on laminate (for it will pass through many hands in years of meetings), it is the text from the first two and a half pages of chapter 5 of "The Big Book," a chapter that is also titled "How It Works."

The Big Book? Nobody in Alcoholics Anonymous ever calls it anything else, though it isn't particularly big in size, and its paperback edition could fit in the pocket of a sports coat (of which there were a few at the meeting) or jeans (there were more). Embossed on the dark blue cover so that it can barely be seen in certain light is the actual title, *Alcoholics Anonymous,* with no author credited.

The Big Book is treated with the reverence throughout AA that Christians reserve for the Bible. Even many of those who have no faith in a conventional God believe that the Big Book was divinely inspired, particularly the first 164 pages that have remained the same, inviolable, through a series of editions. It was mainly written by Bill Wilson, or Bill W., the most prominent co-founder of the program and a man considered something of a secular saint within it (despite his oversized ego, marital infidelities and experiments with LSD, well after he took his last drink).

The rest of the book offers chapters of personal testimony (what some call "drunkalogues," in spoken form). Each edition replaces some of the older stories, in an attempt to keep the program more contemporary, relatable. (The first 164 pages could also stand some updating, but to open that door to debate would be sacrilege.) Newer or older, these stories are very personal, very human and often very inspirational. They offer what members of AA call "experience, strength and hope" by relating "what we used to be like, what happened, what we are like now." Like the Holy Trinity, this program favors the power of three.

But where the stories that change from edition to edition are instructional, testimonies of discipleship, the first 164 pages are scripture, on another spiritual plane entirely. Tenets of faith within the program, shared even by those who are otherwise faithless, include the assumption that we are all connected by (or to) something greater than ourselves, and that only a "higher power" can allow us to overcome our obsession with alcohol—an adversary that is "cunning, baffling, powerful." Only if we "surrender," admit our powerlessness over alcohol, can we be "happy, joyous and free." (Again, the incantatory power of three.)

That opening of "How It Works" offers a litany that many in the room absorb in prayerful or meditative mode, eyes closed as they concentrate on every word, though many have heard this repeated over so many days, weeks, months, decades. Its centerpiece is the 12 Steps, the heart of the program, only one of which even mentions alcohol—the first step—with God or a "higher power" permeating the rest.

A couple of anecdotes you might hear in AA, if you stick around: A guy who has been around long enough to lose the temptation to drink says that he gets everything about the program except for the spiritual part. The response from another guy who has been around a whole lot longer: "The spiritual part is everything. The whole program is spiritual."

The other offers the distinction to which most in AA adhere, the one between religion and spirituality: Religion is for people who don't want to go to hell. Spirituality is for those of us who have already been there and never want to return.

I, of course, was lost in a fog as the ritual proceeded. I had never heard "How It Works" before, never heard the term "Big Book" or had any idea what it contained. I knew there were 12 Steps, but I hadn't known what any of them were. And, as they were read, I figured that there were at least four that fell into the "not a chance" category and a couple more that could stand some editing and concision. I'd been accustomed to gaming the system, whatever that system might be, and I figured I might be able to work this as my personal 8 Step program. Maybe 6.

Once you hear "How It Works" enough to find comfort into it, it seems to seep into you like osmosis. Eventually, I would feel like so many others, that different phrases would jump out at me as if I were hearing them for the first time, and my appreciation for the spiritual implications of its plainspoken cadences would deepen beyond all expectation. Some of what I early dismissed as gibberish clichés became like mantras to me.

It is often said that at an AA meeting you hear what you need to hear, either through the experiences of others or readings that you'd heard as litanies but had hit you differently this time, taking on a deeper meaning. Some say that their version of a "higher power" speaks through them at meetings, that the other members are the embodiment of the spiritual connection that would keep us sober.

Did I want to be sober? Would I, as "How It Works" put it, "go to any lengths to get it?" I wasn't sure. I was mainly shell-shocked, a little numb, trying to absorb the strangeness of it all, yet willing to give it a shot. Today, at least. One day at a time. Though I wanted this experience to work for me, however it worked, I wasn't looking to make a lifetime commitment. I was there to repair my marriage, or to see if that was possible. I knew that, if it were possible to get another chance from Maria, stopping drinking was a necessary first step. But not necessarily a permanent one—maybe a few days or a week or two would be enough.

So the comfort I took in "one day at a time" was that I wasn't making any long-term commitment. This was like the two-week free trial before I signed anything or handed over my spiritual credit card, to pay for the sobriety I'd never previously considered as a way of life.

Further reservations as I listened to "How It Works" for the first time were about what sort of Kool-Aid I'd have to swallow, what leap of faith I'd have to pretend to make, if this program had any chance of working for me. I'd always considered myself someone who didn't much like meetings. Didn't much like people, if you got right down to it. I drank for many reasons, or for no particular reason at all, but I'd certainly used it to make my discomfort in social situations a little more tolerable, or, at home, to isolate and numb myself, drink myself into a sleep that was more like oblivion.

So, it was an unexpected revelation, very early on, to discover that I felt comfortable among these people, that I liked these meetings. These people did seem to have an ease to them, a feeling of being comfortable in their own skins, which I'd never had. I certainly wasn't ready from the start to buy into all of "How It Works"—my mind challenges and overthinks everything, another of the myriad reasons I drank, to shut it off, or at least slow it down—but I'd try my best to deal with what I could understand and ignore what I couldn't accept. I was there to quit drinking, not to pledge allegiance to some cult of sobriety, even if these folks didn't seem very cult-like in their warmth and humor.

Did I want what they had? Was I willing to go to any lengths to get it? I'd let that decision come gradually, one day at a time. But even before the preamble ended and the actual talking—or "sharing"—began, I had softened some, opened the door to possibility. If only for the hour that this meeting would last. Most of these people had been driven to the program by misery—or by court order—and most of them had been more miserable drinking than I had. Now most of them seemed happier than I had been while drinking, when every day led to the same numbness and oblivion. Like Groundhog Day.

In AA, you learn by listening, and one of the first things you learn is that practically everyone introduces his remarks with, "My name is Tom (Dick or Harry), and I am an alcoholic." Most of them know each other's names, maybe even last names, but this is part of the ritual, and it's a comforting one, to the newcomer, because you're not singled out by making an introduction. When it got to me, I had no hesitation about saying, "My name is Don, and I am an alcoholic," even though I'd never called myself that before and still wasn't sure that I was one. But I'd play along.

5. A Daily Reprieve

MARIA CAME HOME AFTER WORK. A good sign, not that we were out of the woods. I knew better than to try to persuade her that I had changed (in a few hours? after one meeting?) or to press her on her plans. The stronger I pushed, the more she would resist. It was an old pattern. Generally, I am uncomfortable without knowing that things are settled, and so I tend to push for resolution while things are still settling. And to make difficult situations even more difficult, I always wanted what the cliché calls "closure." I had no inkling that my need to control situations was connected to my drinking.

Didn't people drink to escape the binds of control? To get loose?

But I had no control over this situation. The only thing I could do was talk, and see how long she would listen. And then maybe I could listen, if she had any interest in talking. I wanted to share with Maria what I'd done since she'd left that morning, what I'd experienced, partly to see if anything would change anything, but mainly because I truly did feel different. At least for now. Having had no idea what to expect at my first AA meeting, I'd also had no idea how I would feel afterward—how much lighter and unburdened, like someone whose great crime had been discovered, or whose great secret had been revealed, and who now felt a great sense of relief along with deep remorse.

This was a physical sensation, because I still wasn't convinced that I had a drinking problem, or any secrets. And I certainly hadn't committed a crime, beyond the embarrassment of unconsciously soiling my underwear. But I definitely felt lighter, as if a great weight had been lifted from my shoulders. And I wanted to share this with Maria, for whatever good it might do.

So I started with the visit to the doctor, and the Antabuse, the pill I'd popped as soon as I'd picked up the prescription. I told her that the medication was supposed to make me violently ill if I had any alcohol. So drinking was off the table, for that day at least, even if she hadn't poured every open bottle of wine, bourbon and cognac down the kitchen sink. And since I planned to take the Antabuse tomorrow and for as long as I felt that I needed protection from my cravings, I would no longer be drinking. (At least as long as we both felt this was necessary, though I didn't think I needed to share this qualification.)

This was a big step and a new one. Throughout our marriage, there had been tensions about the amount I drank and how much was too much. These had intensified since our move from Austin to Des Moines. I had been drinking more in Iowa, and drinking differently—mostly at home, alone, rather than out seeing music or trying to wind down after a deadline. I didn't drink much with friends; I didn't have any.

My defensive belligerence had intensified as well, as she had pushed me to cut down and I'd pushed back. In my mind, there was no problem, except her attempt to try to control my behavior. I didn't cause trouble, miss work, or get mean. I was a quiet, reflective drinker, not a surly one. I had been a good husband and father (by my definition), a good provider and an otherwise responsible citizen. What I did on my own time was my business. And my own time was after dinner, with a book and a cigar, until I fell asleep, with as much drinking as felt right, followed by a marijuana nightcap.

This was my routine, and I was—and remain—a creature of habit. Obsessively so. Drinking would no longer be part of that routine.

How about the rest? Would I still crave the cigar without the drinking that contributed to the after-dinner satiation? Would I still want that daily reading hour without the cigar? Could I still smoke dope if I quit drinking?

How would I get to sleep?

I had no idea about any of this. I couldn't really project even one day at a time at that point. It was more like one minute at a time. Hell, I didn't even know if Maria would be sticking around for more than a minute or two, to pack her bags and split. Maybe we'd already had our last dinner together, our final night. But as long as I kept talking, and she kept listening, all of that was in limbo. And that limbo was preferable to the dead certainty of her decision that morning to leave, and the total disgust toward me she had displayed.

She didn't seem as abrupt and cold as she had been that morning, when she was committed to putting something behind her, and that something was me. She now appeared more receptive as she listened, her resolve softened, and so I continued talking, proceeding to the meeting, telling her more about the AA experience than anyone had ever told me. I explained about Googling the schedule, about the noon meeting at a church fairly close, about how many meetings there were all over the metro, at all hours of the day. I told her about the guy who had been so welcoming to me before the meeting, and about how much I had appreciated the experience, how different it had been from anything I had expected (having gone with no real expectations). Even with all the "God" talk, I knew I'd be going back. Tomorrow, most likely. One day at a time.

The lightness I'd felt, and continued to feel, was the toughest to explain. It really felt palpably physical, like a deadweight had been lifted from my shoulders. I had been concerned, because Maria had been concerned, over how much drinking was too much, how many

I could have, whether I had a problem beyond a wife who wanted to control me.

And now, that part of my obsession seemed gone, for today at least. And for tomorrow, and for as far as I could project. Maybe I was the one who was ready to put something behind me. I was done calculating strategies and counting drinks. I now knew how many drinks was too many: One. My all-or-nothing obsessiveness had been resolved in favor of nothing. There would be no more limiting drinks, sneaking drinks, hiding drinks. I had somehow started again with a blank slate, and I would be adding no tally marks to it, unless I wanted to start counting the days without drinking.

Maria and I talked for an hour or so, or rather I mainly talked and she mainly listened. And if my resolve to stop drinking seemed provisional, so did her decision to stay. Not that she said she was staying, nor did I press her. But she didn't make any move toward leaving, and I wasn't going to give her any more reason to leave. By taking the Antabuse, I had stopped drinking. And by going to AA—attending a meeting with strangers, somehow finding some comfort in putting myself way out of my comfort zone, I had underscored my resolve.

So, we would stay together, today, and maybe tonight. One day at a time, though neither of us articulated this. Now we had five hours or so before we went to bed, and I wish I could give some account of how we filled them. Or how I filled mine, because I was the one for whom everything had changed. I know we had dinner, though I can't remember the meal or the circumstances, or even what I drank, except that it wasn't my usual wine or any other alcohol.

I know I didn't have a cigar after dinner, because I didn't want any triggers, even with the Antabuse. And one of the pleasures of the cigar was the cognac afterward. And then the marijuana after that. I know I also didn't smoke my usual joint that night, though that part of my routine, like the cigar, was simply in suspension as I adjusted to whatever the new routine might be. Maybe I could smoke dope nightly and never be tempted to drink. Maybe I would still appreciate the cigar after dinner, even without drinking.

I didn't even go out to read that night. My after-dinner reading was all tied up with my cigar, which was tied up with the drinking—the wine with dinner and the after-cigar drinking. And reading would have required the sort of concentration that my mind lacked that night. It was as if the entire focus of my existence was "not drinking," a personal prohibition that required constant vigilance after the decades of drinking that came as easy as the next breath.

I had initially typed "sobriety" in that earlier paragraph, but realized that it wasn't accurate. As I would learn from the introduction to every meeting, this program demands "rigorous honesty." It would take months before I would feel sobriety as a natural state, and a couple years before I would appreciate its richness, how much more there was to being sober than just defining yourself by abstention, denial.

But, hell, the previous night I must have drunk so much that it was probably still in my system, certainly in the lingering effects of my hangover. It would take longer for my brain chemistry to change, but my brain itself still seemed foggy that night. I do know that I slept better than I would have thought without drinking and doping myself into oblivion. Because I'd feared I wouldn't sleep at all, and I would remember if I hadn't.

6. A Whole Lotta Firsts

As I started taking baby steps toward sobriety, so much of my experience began to feel fresh and new. Once you commit to quitting drinking—or, in AA parlance, once you "surrender" to the realization that "you are powerless over alcohol"—you'll likely start seeing your life as a series of firsts. The first day without drinking. The first week. First month. Keep going to meetings, don't drink in between them, and you'll likely acclimate yourself to a whole series of firsts, as you settle into a different way of life.

I still felt like I had one foot in, one foot out. I hadn't really even decided if I was done drinking forever, though every day, week or month without a drink would mean that I was feeling better about not drinking. Because, knowing me, if I hadn't been feeling a whole lot better than I had anticipated, I would have returned to drinking and rationalizing my return. At least one day at a time, not drinking felt both way different and way better than I'd ever anticipated. Lighter, existentially, with less to think about and worry about. As long as I stuck to my new routine, I would be fine.

As long as I stuck to my new routine, I'd be less likely to revert to my old one. Yet sticking to that new routine involved a couple of logistical challenges, very early on. A couple more "firsts." My fall semester, just a few weeks into sobriety, would be my first academic sabbatical. On one hand, this would be a huge relief, because I could focus on not drinking, without any stress of class preparation, grading and the 100-mile (one way) commute to Iowa City for half the week.

I wouldn't say I drank because of that stress, but I know I looked forward to my evening dosage of self-medication to take the edge off. One of the many ways that alcohol had functioned for me was as an aid to compartmentalizing, to letting my brain know that it was time to ease back from the overdrive part of the academic life. Alcohol was my "off" switch, sending my brain the signal that it was time to shut it down for the day.

Those in AA would insist it was no mere coincidence that my sabbatical came when my program started, that it was all part of some higher plan. I knew that it would be easier adhering to my new routine than it would have been during a working semester—driving back and forth, living out of a suitcase, always thinking about the next class session or the cyber-stack of papers that needed grading. And I would have had to accustom myself to a whole new schedule of AA meetings in Iowa City.

On the other hand, my semester without teaching carried different responsibilities. "Sabbatical" was actually a word not spoken during the process at the University of Iowa; it didn't reflect the expectation and responsibility. We instead called them Career Development Awards, or CDAs, and the requirement was that we would use the time to research and publish a project that would justify these months off. These awards were supposedly competitive, and actually became more so (as budgets tightened), requiring a proposal of what one intended to accomplish during this period and then a summary report at the end, detailing that accomplishment.

So, contrary to the public perception of a sabbatical as a time to recharge, maybe by traveling or leisure reading or simply relaxing by some pool, our CDAs required documented productivity. In my case, I had two major projects in different stages of development. My book in collaboration with the *New York Times* on arts and culture journalism was in the midst of its final edit (before the last proofreading), with all of the heavy lifting done, and a terrific editor who wouldn't allow me to drift off course. We were right on schedule, with no problems anticipated.

The other project was a different matter, one I was in the very early stages of both researching and writing. It was a critical biography of country-music renegade Dwight Yoakam, a hillbilly throwback who didn't play nice by the standards of the Nashville music industry. It would launch a new "American Music" series, to be published by the University of Texas Press. It would also be the first thing I had ever written (rather than revised, as would be the case with the Times book) without the lubricating aid of alcohol. I had made my living as a drinking writer for more than three decades; now we would see how well I could function as a newly sober one.

Writers are funny that way. Many of us have an almost superstitious devotion to routine. We think that we need to write—or at least write best—during a certain time of the day, at a certain place (whether clean, well-lighted or as messy as my workspace always was), under similar circumstances. We knew what worked, and we stuck to it.

Not that I'd generally been drinking while I was actually writing—although I knew some writers who did, and one who insisted that smoking dope as a deadline approached would accelerate his creative urgency. But for me, the drinking and doping were nevertheless an inherent part of the process, a process in which, as most writers will acknowledge, some of my best "writing" came to me when I wasn't sitting at the keyboard, and when I wasn't consciously thinking about the project at all.

Call it a habit or call it a crutch, but I had depended for decades on the down time that my drinking facilitated every evening for the inspiration I needed in the morning. I had slept well since stopping drinking, but there had been less at stake. Now that I had a big project at hand, would I be able to write anything worth reading without anticipating my self-medicating reward at the end of the day? Deprived of its sedative, would my brain hop onto that hamster wheel again?

With self-medication no longer my key to compartmentalizing, would I somehow be able to keep these two projects in mind at once—albeit at different stages—without the walls that alcohol built in my brain? And compounding that challenge, would I be able to write and research the Dwight book simultaneously—a necessity given deadlines and access—when it had always been my pattern to finish all of the research before starting any of the writing?

Just reading that paragraph above tangles my brain. If such worry reflects a mind prone to overthinking everything, and thus further complicating any challenge, well, now you know why I drank. Or at least one of the reasons. I drank for pleasure, but I also drank for work. The first step says that "our lives had become unmanageable" because of alcohol, but the paradox for me was that I'd used alcohol to manage my life. Through decades of drinking, I'd managed to ease the stress at the end of the working day. I'd managed to slow my brain and eventually stop it from whirring. I'd managed to fall asleep, or at least pass out. I'd managed to sustain a productive career over decades.

And now I was attempting to manage to do most of that without my old routine. To undo what had allowed me to do so much, so well and for so long. I now had a lot at stake, a lot to think about, and to worry about. I wasn't about to start drinking over it, but I wasn't sure how well I'd be able to write, if I were able to write at all.

Another "first" provided an even greater challenge, and a more immediate one. Maria and I had a decision to make about a Caribbean cruise that loomed imminently. We had booked it long before I had quit drinking, months before my CDA had been approved. We loved cruises, went on one every year or so, first with our two daughters when they were younger, now just the two of us—empty nesters. We'd paid for everything, including the flights to and from Fort Lauderdale, the port for so many Caribbean cruising itineraries.

After my alcohol-fueled meltdown, we had put all mention of the cruise aside. Hell, if her initial inclination had been to pack her bags and leave me, there was no way she'd agree to share the close quarters of a ship's cabin for a week. And maybe there was no way I should even be thinking about going, if I were serious about not drinking.

So, in the days after my embarrassing, alcohol-fueled flame-out, Maria and I hadn't initially discussed or even mentioned the cruise. It was the very expensive elephant in the room. Now that Maria had decided to stick around, play this out, the question was whether the cruise was a wise idea for someone so freshly sober. If we didn't go, we'd be eating the plane tickets and cruise fare. I wanted to test the sea legs of my sobriety; Maria initially resisted, but finally agreed. If she loved cruising and still loved me, might as well give it a chance.

We both loved the feeling of being in the middle of the ocean, the glorious sunsets, the gentle rocking of the waves. And, cheapskate that I am, I hated the thought of kissing a few thousand non-refundable bucks goodbye. So maybe the timing wasn't right, but I was convinced that I could refrain from drinking, one day at a time, on a cruise ship just as well (if not quite as easily) as I'd been doing it at home.

So we committed to embark on my first cruise without drinking, less than a month after I'd quit. With many more years of sobriety under my belt, I'm pretty sure I wouldn't counsel someone whose wounds were as fresh as mine to proceed with a cruise, particularly if that were someone whose cruising pleasure was closely bound to the rituals of over-the-top drinking. But my routine onboard hadn't been that much different from my drinking at home. I didn't start until dinner, and I didn't stop until sleep. Since I didn't attempt to sneak my nightly marijuana onboard, I'd drink more onboard for the desired stupor, but otherwise I remained pretty regular in my habits.

Now that I seemed to be sleeping better without the alcohol and dope I'd thought for decades that I needed to fall asleep, the question was what the rest of the cruising experience would be like. What would we do with all those hours and dollars free that I had previously spent on alcohol? Because we'd be surrounded by hundreds of others who felt that alcohol was an essential lubricant to their cruising pleasure, who might start the day with Bloody Marys as the hair of the dog to counter the buckets of beer from the night before.

Where a cruise ship for so many meant freedom to drink as much as they wanted—with no place to drive, no sense of decorum to maintain—I had just started to discover freedom *from* drink. Because I had learned from meetings, and from past experience, that my real problem was that once I had the first one, I needed to keep going. I wasn't like Maria, who could have half a glass of wine at dinner, and leave the other half (for me to finish). Drinking made me drink more, like I had an unquenchable thirst, or a bottomless hole to fill. And, for the first time on a cruise, I'd be watching Maria drink, her pre-dinner martini and maybe a half-glass of wine, while I contented myself with water.

Fortunately for people like me, cruise lines know that it takes all kinds to fill a ship. Every daily schedule on pretty much every cruise has a "Friends of Bill W." meeting among its activities. I had seen this when I was still drinking, knew what it was, but had never paid it any more attention. (Most also have a "Friends of Dorothy" daily meeting on their schedule, a reference to Judy Garland, a place for gay people to get to know each other.)

This meeting would become my lifeline, there if I needed it. And whether I needed it or not, I was curious about how it would function with a group of strangers on a cruise ship. As it turned out, all the ship does is reserve a meeting space at a convenient time in an otherwise empty room—maybe one of the ones used for crafts or talks, maybe even a bar that doesn't open until later in the evening.

Then it's kind of the luck of the draw to see whoever shows up, or if anyone does. Some might show up the first day, see if the group dynamic is to their liking, and then attend daily, or sporadically, or not at all the rest of the week. Now that I've been on a few more cruises sober (and been to more than a few meetings), I know that some meetings might have as few as two or three (particularly on days when we're in port and people are returning from excursions) or as many as a dozen.

My first meeting on this cruise was in the lounge off the library, an hour before dinner, the perfect time for me. I was the second one there, joining a Black guy from New York, maybe late 30s or early 40s. Then came a Colorado couple, white and around the same age, whom we learned had met and gotten married in the program (which I discovered later is no rarity). That was it for the first night, though others would join as the week progressed, including a singer who was one of the featured evening acts in the theater, and a young woman who seemed to bond with him.

I was a curiosity throughout the week, the guy who had just gotten sober and was risking it on a cruise. Though I never really felt that I was. As they say in the program, "the obsession to drink had been lifted," unexpectedly and surprisingly easily (though I cautioned myself against proclaiming that). I had once been a guy who drank; now I was a guy who didn't. I felt comfortable in this skin.

In the middle of the ocean, or even just leaving a port, that hour meeting a day provided an anchor. It underscored the values of the program, the focus I'd need to maintain, the expansiveness that had spread the 12 Steps, through "attraction, not promotion" as the program insisted, to all parts of the country and corners of the globe. These were values you could build a life upon, a better life than the one you'd been pissing away with alcohol. No matter how good your life had been—and I'd had a wonderful one, with few regrets, and the pleasure I'd taken in alcohol not among them—you could find a life enriched beyond all anticipation through the "spiritual awakening" that was the direct result of working the steps.

Or so my cruise mates testified, as I'd already heard repeatedly at my meetings back home. These onboard meetings of kindred-spirit strangers would start with someone assuming the role of leader, and there was always some take-charge guy (always a guy) who quickly presented himself as the default choice if nobody else stepped up. The meetings would start with the moment of silence, a prayer (Lord's or Serenity) and a reading from whatever was at hand—at least the 12 Steps or even the full introduction, which some who had been in the program for a while could pretty much recite from memory.

Then there'd be a topic—"Shame" or "Amends" or "Resentments" or some other key word from the program—and we'd share whatever the topic sparked in us. Drinking was almost never the topic, though the program was ostensibly devoted to giving up drinking. To fill the hour, we might talk about what we'd been doing on the cruise, if anybody had taken any excursions, and what we'd seen, usually other folks acting embarrassingly strange while inebriated, talking too loud, slobbering all over themselves. We remembered when we had been like that, and we gave thanks that we no longer were. We reinforced our sense that how we were now living was better, or at least they did for me, since their sobriety, whether years or decades, was a whole lot more solid than my comparatively shaky start.

We ended with another prayer, or maybe the same one, while holding hands in a circle. Then we went back to our cabins or to dinner, restored for the rest of the night. Occasionally we'd see each other outside the meeting and offer a smile of recognition. Because of our program, because of our meetings, we felt like we were sharing a journey unlike that of anyone else on board. We were on the same lifeboat, shipwrecked survivors.

So, that was one hour out of every day. What about the rest? Despite the stereotype of pool games, tropical drink concoctions and party-till-you-drop-atmosphere, cruising can be the perfect way to get away from it all—whatever "it" is. If you're awake early and your mind is clear, each sunrise offers a blank slate. I lived for that sunrise, those first glimmers. As the day progressed, I felt like the sunny heat was baking the alcohol right out of me, and lifting some of the mental fog in the process. If I did nothing but sit and stare at the endless ocean, the repetition of waves as far as the eye could see in every direction, my meditative reflection was itself transformational. One day at a time became one breath at a time.

The variety of cruise experiences was what had attracted our family in the first place, more than a decade before I quit drinking, before our daughters had entered their teens. None of us were much for group activity or forced hilarity. But I'd always loved boats and water, and I really liked the fact that one price would cover everything, the cabin that would be your hotel, the ship that would be your transportation, the meals and snacks—everything but drinks and tips.

We had discovered on our first cruise that you could make your own kind of vacation, find plenty of quiet space if you wanted, participate in whatever interested you, leave the rest alone. And it was so economical for the four of us—the girls stayed much cheaper in our cabin, there was no extra charge for hotel, transportation, food, anything. Just a final settling for tips. And alcohol.

For me, alcohol had been a focus of these vacations, just in a different way than it had been during my land-bound life. The wines at dinner were reasonably priced, surprisingly, and if there was any left in the bottle, they would save it for you the next night. I would sneak aboard some cognac or brandy for my after-dinner drinking, and then buy plenty more to sneak aboard when we docked in various ports.

Until my first cruise after quitting drinking, I had never realized just how integral alcohol had been to my cruise experience, what a central obsession. Without American taxes and regulations, upscale bottles were steeply discounted from the price you would pay in the States. So among the lures for me was that I could drink better, and drink cheaper, than I could at home. Whether we were at sea or in port, there would be no place to drive, and no need to. And I would always bring plenty of duty-free liquor home as well. Along with smuggling back as many Cuban cigars as I thought I could hide safely.

Not only did every port carry the prospect of this sort of bargain hunting, but alcohol had skewed my whole sense of value and budget. I would rationalize spending a hundred dollars or more at a time on Cuban cigars, since I couldn't get them back home. And the liquor at these duty-free prices was such a bargain that you could hardly afford not to buy it. The more you bought, the more you saved. The only limit was how much you could carry back or smuggle in or consume before the cruise ended.

I had never once questioned expenditures that might approach a thousand bucks, money that would soon go up in smoke or be pissed away. Yet some of the port excursions seemed so expensive (especially multiplied by four, when we had taken the girls) that I kept a much tighter rein on the budget where those were concerned. It was funny the way I could justify spending on some things that were for me only, but dismiss other expenses for all of us as something we couldn't afford. I hadn't gotten to the point in the 12 Steps where we examined selfishness, but I was starting to get an inkling.

So, Maria would go to the spa, which I'd previously considered an extravagance we couldn't afford, while I spent more time onboard, alone, than I ever had, reclining in a deckchair, away from the clamor of the pools or the bars, sometimes reading, but often just watching the waves, soothed by the repetition. Reflecting, but not really focusing. More like letting my mind drift.

I knew by now that AA is built on repetition—meetings, rituals, those slogans that sounded like simplistic clichés but soon seemed deeper and richer in the simplicity of life they offered. "Take it easy." "Just let go." "Do the next right thing." For a program built on Christian faith, there's an awful lot in the Big Book that veers close to Eastern mysticism, in the need to live in the present and to let go of the clutching, grasping nature of desire. A cruise seemed like the perfect place to let go, to watch the waves, always moving, always different, always the same. Like thoughts. Just let go.

My life felt a whole lot lighter, physically as well as mentally. I'd previously had an "open bar" attitude toward cruise buffets, stuffing myself until I was ready to drop, making sure I had plenty of ballast to coat my stomach for the liquor to come. And maybe it was all that drinking that had stretched out my stomach, which then needed more food to fill it. Now that I was drinking no alcohol, I found myself picking rather than shoveling at those all-you-can eat meals.

I also found that I appreciated all the more the innocent indulgences that I now permitted myself. The coffee machines on cruise ships produce a notoriously foul brew, surprising when so much else onboard is first-rate. Instead of starting the day with cup after cup of bad coffee—the "open bar" approach—I bought us a couple of punch tickets to the premium coffee bar, where we'd drink lattes and cappuccinos, which I'd previously dismissed as another needless extravagance. Now the coffee drinks were something to savor, in smaller portions, rather than merely fuel for the day ahead.

I also bought a pass that allowed me all the non-alcoholic drinks I wanted, the ones not included in the price of the cruise. Though I'd never previously had a taste for sparkling water, I now got some sort of psychological kick from San Pellegrino and Perrier. Again it was a matter of drinking less and savoring, rather than gulping still water and feeling waterlogged.

Before, we'd never been tempted to try a recent refinement of the cruising experience—a smaller, more elegant dining room available for a nominal cover charge. After all, the regular dining room was fancy enough, and the food just fine, at least on the cruise lines we favored. But there was a sense of assembly-line dining, with fewer options and courses served like clockwork, as if we were in a very good banquet hall.

With some extra money and time on our hands, we paid the $15-$25 per person to dine at a time and pace of our choosing, in a more intimate setting. The menu had options typically reserved for the finest land-bound restaurants—lobster ravioli, veal chop, soft-shell crab, rack of lamb. These are the sort of meals that I'd previously felt I needed wine to enhance, but my sparkling water complemented the meal just fine. I was beginning to realize just how much food had previously been merely the complement for my wine, rather than vice versa. I had changed my habits in a way that I would have considered unthinkable just a month previously, and I was somehow doing just fine. One day at a time.

I'd resumed my after-dinner cigars after a week or so of experimenting without, and this was another savoring experience. I not only enjoyed them as much as I had when I was drinking, when a smoke enhanced the satiation of my wine, but I found that I appreciated it more. No longer was it just another in a series of toppling dominoes—dinner, wine, cigar, cognac, dope, sleep. It was my last remaining sin, and I reveled in it as such. Plus, one puff at a time was an almost meditative way of experiencing the present. Maybe this was a mistake; maybe one day I would rue continuing with a nightly cigar while quitting alcohol. (And, sure enough, one day I did.) But giving up one sin at a time seemed plenty.

Then I might end my evening with a virgin piña colada, which washed away the cigar residue like my cognac once had—even though I'd never had a taste for the alcohol version of the drink. I had once known who I was, what I liked and what I didn't, and now I was discovering anew all sorts of things that might please me, in a different way, if I'd give them a chance. One experience at a time, I was opening myself to a whole world of possibility from which I had previously isolated myself.

My quintessential cruise experience, as it was even before I stopped drinking, happened just before dawn on a day at sea. The cliché insists that "just before dawn" is when it's darkest, and maybe it is, but when a cloudless sky fills with stars, so many miles from any man-made light, you feel a sense of majesty, mystery and awe like no other. You feel so connected to something so much bigger than you, and so alone as well.

The decks are rarely emptier. You'll see some early morning runners, as obsessed with their routine as you have been with yours, taking their laps before others arise. You might see another early riser or two, maybe an insomniac, who has given up on sleep. Maybe he never feels fully rested.

If you had awakened an hour or two earlier, you would find some—louder, sloppier drunks—who had yet to go to bed, whose night was extending toward the approach of your day. And the closer we get to the actual minute of sunrise (as listed each night on the schedule of the next day's activities, distributed to each cabin), you'll see some shutterbugs with their expensive cameras, even tripods, determined to get the perfect shot (or twelve) so that they and others can see forever what you'll be able to see in a minute.

In the gradual transition from night to morning, you'll have to look for a sliver of light, closer to an aura, letting you know where the sun's rise will be at its most glorious. It will be just a little lighter there than the rest of the domed sky, the first crack in the night. And then the first curve of that yellow-orange orb will peek through that crack, emerging slowly, almost imperceptibly, until it is a more significant expanse of light, of the sun.

It will then seem to climb faster, a quarter-way visible, a half, and then soon enough a full sun, larger than you will see it when it's higher in the sky. All vestiges of night gone, for another day at least, until the sun makes its way across the sky (with no one paying much attention, certainly not observing it so intently, which the naked eye can't), until the process reverses itself, and the sun sinks into that endless ocean as gradually as it had risen, until one moment there's one last sliver of sunlight, and then the next there is not, just an aura of glow where that sun had disappeared.

At twilight, the deck would be more crowded, with more cameras out, and some people even applauding. It was beautiful in its own right, every bit as majestic as the sunrise, but it was also a sign for the revelry to begin, for activity to resume and intensify, for diners to continue dining, for drinkers to drink, for dancers to anticipate dancing well into the night. The casino would fill, as would the karaoke bar.

For me, this everyday miracle, at both the start and the end of daylight, had more deeply felt resonance than any of the activity in between. But it had long been an experience I associated with cruising in the middle of the ocean, or visiting other picturesque places. I didn't go out of my way to watch the sunset in my Des Moines suburban backyard. In fact, I was oblivious to it for most of the time, even when I had been outside, reading, aware that at some point the natural light of day was gone, and the porch's floodlight was illuminating my book.

Now that the program was beginning to seep its way into me, I was more conscious of everyday miracles, more aware that they weren't restricted to exotic locales. In some way I felt connected to the daily cycle of the sun, to the feeling that whatever was in its mysterious beauty was in me as well. I didn't have to call what I was feeling "God," or credit it with the creation of the universe. Just to know that there were forces and connections at work that I could see, that I could feel, but that I need not even try to explain—that was enough.

The 12 Steps promise that if you work them, which I was barely beginning to do, you would have "a spiritual awakening." And though I wasn't about to submit to conventional Christian notions of a creator, an afterlife, a heaven and hell, I did feel that something in me was being awakened, that I was channeling something that would remain in me wherever I was, whenever I worked or slept, when I needed to rely on what the 12 Steps called "a Power greater than ourselves."

This Power (or power, as I preferred) presented me with one of the first paradoxes of a program that is filled with them, one that I would ultimately realize was as resistant to rational logic as a series of Zen koans. In the popular Appendix II of the Big Book, the anonymous Bill Wilson addresses the varieties of "Spiritual Experience," assuring those who have never had (and perhaps never will have) the sort of flash-of-light, burning-bush experience that had changed his own life that they can accrue their own spiritual experience through "what the psychologist William James calls the 'educational variety,' because they develop over a period of time."

And here comes the tricky part: "With few exceptions our members find that they have tapped an unsuspected inner resource which they presently identify with a Power greater than themselves."

Huh?

What the program calls "a higher power" beyond ourselves can in fact be something within ourselves? It might take me a lifetime to figure that one out, but I definitely felt something within, a change of perspective, a connection to the rest of creation and to a realm that defies rational understanding.

There's another old saying in AA that says you only need to learn to accept two things: 1. There is a God. 2. It isn't you. I was feeling my way toward the second. I would leave that deck, and that ship, a changed man, committed and connected to something a whole lot bigger than just not drinking.

My load was lighter when we disembarked and headed home. Literally, spiritually and psychologically. We weren't hauling with us the usual bunch of oversized bottles, whatever the duty-free limit was for both Maria and me (all the bottles had long been mine, but half the limit hers). And I was no longer intent on smuggling a box or two of Cuban cigars into the country. I'd smoked mine on the cruise.

One of the things I was realizing as an alcoholic, if that's what I was, is that so many of us get an extra kick out of getting away with something. We sneak a little (or a lot) more to drink than others think is good for us. We test our ability to flout legal restrictions, and even plain common sense. We often drive faster than we should, and drunker. Many of us have indulged in illegal self-medication, coke, or weed or worse.

But now my conscience was free and our bags were lighter. Not drinking and not doping seemed like early progress toward simplifying my life, lightening my load. If I'd been halfhearted in my commitment to remaining sober before—one day at a time, at least until the heat was off—I now felt wholeheartedly that I was embarked on a path that offered a richer life than the one I had lived and enjoyed for decades. I hadn't quit drinking; I had stumbled into sobriety. And I would be truly losing something if I lost that. Or so I felt with the resolve of new-found clarity.

It was just a glimmer of a recognition, at that point, like the aura at the approach of sunrise, but it was enough to suggest there were richer revelations to come. I still felt like I was in the middle of the ocean, drifting, in my AA lifeboat of sobriety. I knew I still had a long way to go. But I was also beginning to realize that, in order to move forward, I would have to go all the way back.

What had I thought I was getting away with? What could I see now that I couldn't then? In order to understand the nature of my drinking and the progression of my disease, I would have to retrace my steps, from the beginning. The steps that would take me to those slippery porch steps I had been unable to climb, when I had experienced my last drunk. How the hell had I gotten here?

Part II:
Baby Steps

7. When Two Worlds Collide

In AA, they say that "you're only as sick as your secrets." In journalism, we know about "sunshine laws," which require transparency in processes that some would prefer to keep under wraps, behind closed doors. Without feeling like I'd been keeping any secrets, I know I'd been living a significant amount of my life—the drinking part, at least over the past decade—behind closed doors. It was time to open the doors, and the windows, let in some fresh air and sunshine. Time to clean house, to take stock, to get rid of what was no longer necessary.

In AA, they call telling your own story the "drunkalogue," and it is divided into three parts. Of course it is. The power of three seems to pervade the program. In order, those parts are: What we used to be like. What happened. What we are like now. So, I have kind of flip-flopped the first two here, spotlighting "what happened" first before indulging in the longer exploration of what I used to be like, as I was developing that drinking problem that I didn't acknowledge for decades.

In any case, I needed to know how I got here before I could move onward. Such self-examination—what AA calls "taking your own inventory"—is a never-ending process, just as staying sober is. And the longer I'm sober, the more I discover about how much I didn't know. Or didn't realize. There are extended stretches of my life that I hadn't thought about in decades, and some memories that seemed too painful to revisit. But I needed the hurt in order to heal. Here is some of what I think I know now, much of which would never have occurred to me when I stumbled into AA.

Though I had never suspected that either of my parents was an alcoholic before I committed myself to the program, I now think it's possible that they both were. Maybe years of meetings have brainwashed me. Am I seeing alcoholics in every closet? Under every bed? Or have I found a clarity and perspective after emerging from the fog of my own drinking? I'll admit it—I'm not sure. Maybe it's a little of both.

But if they were both alcoholics, I'm pretty sure that's the only thing they had in common. Other than us, their children, and their love for us. They say that opposites attract, but the attraction of opposites, if it doesn't combust early on, can generate tension for decades. And in my family, you picked sides, and paid for it. Or you tried to appease both, and you paid for it. Maybe you even switched sides, and paid for it, as I would, though the process of writing this has me reassessing everything about both of them. The older I get, the longer I'm sober, the less I understand my parents. The less I know about a lot of things.

When I was born in 1950, the frame of reference was just so much different for social behavior in general and drinking in particular. Everybody smoked cigarettes, at least everyone I knew. Today, I know almost no one, friend or family, who smokes cigarettes. I'm pretty sure my mother smoked them through each of her five pregnancies; she certainly did through her one with me, her first. And drank through it as well. There was no cultural clamor about the dangers of smoking and drinking, no Surgeon General's Report, no edicts for moms-to-be.

And there was no consciousness of alcoholism, except perhaps as a weakness or moral failing. Few in the 1950s would have considered my father an alcoholic. He was neither weak nor a man of moral failure. He only drank beer. He was exceedingly calm, rational, reserved and dedicated to both his work and his family. Perhaps in that order, as my mother suspected, but none of his children ever questioned or doubted his devotion. Alcoholics were comic figures in popular culture, slurring and stumbling, and my dad was no comic figure, no Dean Martin or Foster Brooks.

He was a mover and shaker in the advertising industry—mail advertising, which the rest of the country knew as "junk mail," but which our household referred to as "direct mail." He supervised what were then big accounts—*Reader's Digest, Look, Life, Better Homes & Gardens,* plenty of other periodicals that relied on subscription campaigns by mail. When his company was bought by a much larger corporation, a "key man" clause kept him with the new conglomerate and provided even more security for our family and our future. He invested prudently and wisely. He didn't squander his paycheck on drink, like an alcoholic would. He was what we could call a good provider, and a dependable man.

Alcoholism wasn't a term in common parlance back then, but it would have been associated with the bums on Skid Row. In Chicago, Skid Row was West Madison, just beyond the train station from the Loop. My dad worked in the Loop, as everyone's dad did. (No one's mom worked.) He was no candidate for Skid Row. West Madison and the whole of the West Loop are now prime gentrification territory, filled with chic restaurants and galleries. The bums are now the "homeless," and I'm not sure where they live.

I knew from my earliest consciousness just how different my father was from my mother, a difference that she in particular would emphasize. She considered him remote, though we never did. When he was available, he was available—to play catch, to answer questions, to coach any of our Little League teams or take us to speed skating meets. But he brought a lot of work home with him, and every evening would find him retreating to the basement with a 12-pack of beer and a briefcase of paperwork, to do whatever he did to support us. The next night, more work, the same basement, another 12-pack.

The common consensus at the time was that you couldn't have a drinking problem if you only drank beer. Beer was barely considered alcohol. He did manage his career very well, and he never got mean or violent around us when he was drinking. I didn't hear him slur his words. He went downstairs to work and drink alone, and didn't finish until after we were asleep. He never drank anything but beer.

And it was what we would now call bad beer, at least in this age of craft beers and boutique brewing. No one back then even drank imports. It was Bud or Schlitz or Hamm's ("From the land of sky blue waters...Hamm's the beer refreshing"). My dad was such a creature of habit that when we much later traveled as a family to Germany, where great beer reigns, he sought out places that served Budweiser. To Americans.

The only problems at home concerning his drinking involved my mother stewing upstairs, occasionally yelling something downstairs at him. He'd less occasionally respond. When he started to travel more, we learned that he was prone to sleepwalking, in his hotels, and that he once was locked out of his room in his underwear. (He never wore pajamas, though it's good he didn't sleep naked.) I don't know if the sleepwalking episodes had anything to do with drinking.

I don't know if he drank more than his friends or associates, and, from what I could tell, when I saw them drinking together, it seemed to affect him less. But he drank daily, regularly, habitually, and he drank a lot. Those were different times. Everybody drank a lot. At least everybody my parents seemed to know.

If you've seen *Mad Men*, you know what it was like. That series particularly hit home with me because the lead character's name was Don. Like my dad's. Like mine. If only Don Draper's wife on the show had been named Joan. Like my mother. But Joan was a different character on the program. Don and Joan are no longer very common names—in a couple decades of teaching, I've never had a student named either, and I've had plenty of students with names that you would never have heard in the 50s.

So trying to recreate the past is like conjuring a different world, a world in the newness of suburbia, in which the culture collectively was making up the rules as it went along. Just like on *Mad Men*, where the downtown office and the suburban home were like two different planets. Back then, there weren't even any expressways linking the Chicago suburbs where I was raised to the city itself. My dad took the commuter train, five days a week, and there were bar cars on there where you could smoke. And drink.

You could also smoke on airplanes then, and for most of my formative years, as if there were some illusion that the smoke from the back of the plane couldn't affect the air of the non-smokers toward the front. And you'd dress your best for airplane trips, a rare luxury, before deregulation, price wars and other gimmicks made them more like airborne bus trips. You could drink on planes then, and you can drink on planes now, but those bottles always seemed so tiny to me. Plane trips were more glamorous back then; smoking and drinking were more glamorous.

Our 50s suburban home was made of stucco. Perhaps homes still are, but I really have no idea what stucco is. Or Formica, a brand name for a countertop that was then as ubiquitous as Kleenex. It wasn't wood, or granite, though it could sometimes resemble one or the other. Plastic? It was some material as new and shiny as suburbia, a "laminate" that its manufacturer still promises is "as tough as it is beautiful, [it] shapes itself to virtually any design concept."

Once our family grew and became more prosperous, our countertops were as tough and shiny as you could imagine. Our threadbare rugs became wall-to-wall shag carpeting. Our record player became a hi-fi, a piece of furniture, and then a stereo. These suburbs and the things with which we filled them represented a brand new "lifestyle" after the horrors of the war (in which my dad did not serve; heart murmur) and the depression before it. And as far as I could remember, this new life had pretty much everyone drinking and smoking like there was no tomorrow, a paradox because the future looked so bright.

Even though my dad only drank beer, every house had the requisite liquor cabinet and bar, and so did ours. In there were the mixings of the drinks whose names I'd heard long before I'd had any idea what they were: Tom Collins, Gin and Tonic, Whiskey Sour, Screwdriver, Martini and Gimlet, Old Fashioned. I think the Harvey Wallbanger might have come a little later. And the Tequila Sunrise, which the Eagles' hit would popularize. I still don't know what's in most of these, nor have I ever had most of them. Even when I began to incorporate hard liquor into my drinking, I preferred it straight and simple, the most efficient delivery system.

I don't remember anyone drinking wine back then, even with dinner. (But, whatever they drank, everyone seemed to smoke even through dinner.) When I first learned to distinguish, white wine was Chablis, and red wine was Burgundy. By the time I started drinking, they were Chardonnay and Cabernet. Then Merlot, until everybody started making fun of that.

Like I say, this was a whole different world than the ones my children inhabit, the two daughters who are now older than my parents were then. Hard to wrap my head around then. Whatever the old normal had been—before my time—this was the new normal. So the fact that my father drank so regularly and so much never struck me as anything off-kilter. If I'd thought about it (which I didn't), I probably assumed that every other house had a father who retreated to the basement every evening with a 12-pack of beer. And perhaps they did.

My mother didn't drink like that. Maybe women in general didn't, for all I knew. Sure, she drank, but she was always a very different drinker from my father, and drinking seemed to affect her more. I mainly remember her drinking socially, and she was very social, much more so than my father.

She loved go out to dance, and he never would. Dance, that is. They would go out, and he would sit, while she danced with the husbands of her friends. They either held or were invited to some sort of party every weekend—bridge club, or some place there would be dancing, or just a group of friends, drinking. I sensed early on that she was more enthusiastic about being with other people, and that their friends were mainly her friends and their husbands.

When the parties were at our house, I couldn't avoid hearing them and their friends get louder and louder, laughing and arguing until there was no distinction between the two, someone occasionally stage-whispering that there were kids upstairs who might be woken up. Later and later, and still louder and louder. My mother often the loudest of all. We weren't asleep. We were hearing our parents differently than we did when they were alone with us, hearing the alcohol-fueled exuberance, the careening beyond control that seemed both exhilarating and a little frightening.

As if they didn't care. As if maybe I didn't know these people as well as I'd thought.

When the parties were at the homes of others, we heard stories about how my drunk mother had gotten out of the car driven by my drunk father, and she had started walking while he kept yelling at her to get back in the car. Or how he had embarrassed her by saying something to someone we couldn't imagine him saying. Like drinking had made him a different person, even different than he was at home when he was drinking. We always heard these things from our mother, generally while our father was still sleeping. Late into the morning. Perhaps past noon. Sleeping it off, we'd now call it.

The differences in their drinking just underscored and exaggerated how different they really were, in pretty all much ways you could mention. He was blond and light skinned, with an almost Nordic (which he wasn't) reserve; she was brunette and tan. He was a man of a few, well-chosen words; she would say anything that popped into her head, heedless of consequences. No filter, we'd now say. He was the rock you could always depend on, at least when he wasn't sleepwalking in his underwear or driving drunk. She was the wild card—moodier, flightier, unpredictable one, the one you had to watch out for.

He had been raised a well-heeled Republican; she was a blue-collar Democrat, the first in her family to attend college, the apple of her father's eye. His father was remote and withholding (at least according to our mother); her father was generous beyond limits, maybe even beyond his means, and effusively, boundlessly loving. (Her father was also definitely an alcoholic; everyone knew it; he would die from it.)

She would compare my father to her own father, never to my dad's advantage, though it is was part of the family lore that one of the main reasons she married my dad was because her dad was so impressed with him—with his maturity and sense of responsibility. He would be a good provider, a good husband and father, a man you could trust to do right and to do well. My father seemed to love his father-in-law as well, though this was another difference between them: I never heard him pass even the slightest negative judgment on her side of the family, while she was merciless in her judgment of his.

My dad was the oldest sibling, with three younger sisters who adored him, and two of whom thought my mother wasn't right for him, or good enough, or something (at least according to my mother). She bonded with his middle sister, and with his mother, both of whom were very warm and very funny, contrary to her objection to the rest of his family. My dad's mother died very young of a heart attack, in her late 40s, maybe, with no warning. It was the first time I ever saw my father weep, and maybe the last. After her death, we had even less to do with my father's family.

How did my mother and father get together? They were both very attractive people, and look like movie stars in their school photos. My mother had been named "Sweetheart of Sigma Chi," my father's fraternity at Northwestern University, where he majored in journalism at Medill. I have no idea why—journalism was still mainly a trade rather than a profession, particular at the newspaper level, with a deep distrust of college kids and their book learning. And my dad had come from a privileged, patrician household in the well-heeled Detroit suburb of Birmingham. My mother's father owned and ran a gas station, and played the ponies.

In order to get married and have a family, he'd need a bigger paycheck than journalism could then provide. And of course he would get married and have a family, one kid right after the other, as soon as he graduated from college. Because that's what people did then.

And they married whomever they'd been dating in college when they graduated. Because that's what you did—either you broke up or you got married.

(My mom had dated one of my father's fraternity brothers before my dad. If they'd stayed together, she would have married him.)

So, they both graduated from Northwestern one June, married the next June, and I was born the next June, in 1950. My parents had started their married life in the Detroit suburbs, returning to where my dad had been raised, and that's where I was born. But something happened, something to do with how much my mother missed her own parents in the western suburbs of Chicago, and within the year we'd moved back there.

In retrospect, with two children of my own, all of this makes better sense to me, and different sense from what I'd long been led to believe. She was away from everyone other than my father who might comfort and support her, and she needed more comfort and support than he could provide. My wife and I also relied heavily on family and friends when we made the transition to parenthood. But the family narrative has long been that this was the first sign (or at least an early one) of weakness and instability on the part of my mother. When she became a mommy, she needed her own daddy, couldn't stand to be even a couple of hundred miles away from him.

My mother was an extremely light sleeper, and she needed the radio on softly in order to drift off. My dad slept deeply, soundly and loudly—he snored, which kept my mother awake. The soundness and the snoring might well have been byproducts of the beer. They slept in twin beds and never went to bed at the same time, she upstairs in the bedroom, listening to the radio, he downstairs with his work and his beer. We did things together as a family on weekends, and they went to social gatherings together on weekend nights, but otherwise my parents seemed to be very different people living very different lives while sharing the same house.

My dad often slept on the couch, either napping or all night. Each of his four sons has become a great couch sleeper, often developing that habit while drinking but sustaining it after becoming sober (as three out of the four of us have now been for years). Each of us married a dark-haired woman, like our mother. I'm not sure if any one of us ever even dated a girl who was blonde or a redhead.

In some ways, perhaps, we have internalized the disparity between our parents. Back then, without anyone ever telling me I needed to (at least not that I remember), I knew that I had to pick sides. Not between my father and mother—I loved them both. But between his bloodline and hers. And my side was preordained: I was darker in hair and complexion, like my mother and grandfather. I intuitively knew that between the warmth of her family and the comparative coldness of his (underscored by her perspective), I preferred warmth. I'd root for the underdog, which made me a Democrat and also a lifelong, diehard Cubs fan (my dad rooted for the Tigers, and remained an American Leaguer by switching to the White Sox).

So, I was on her side, and became more so through my teens, as I eventually rebelled against everything my clean-cut, conservative, button-down father represented. Except for the beer, which fueled my teenage rebellion, and which I generally took from his stash. Give me the wild anarchy of my emotional mother. It wasn't until I became a husband and much later a father that I realized just how strongly I identified with my dad, though I would never consider myself, even now, as mature and rational and responsible as he was. But his emotional reserve and drinking habits became mine.

I really miss being able to talk with him. And having a beer with him. The two went hand in hand.

He died when he was 49, of an inoperable brain tumor. My mother than spent two decades idealizing a marriage that had rarely been ideal when he was alive.

There's a beautiful country ballad about what happens "When Two Worlds Collide." Jim Reeves sang it first and dozens have sung it since. Our family is what happened when two worlds collide. But the 1950s and the 21st century seem like two worlds, colliding in my memory, as I attempt to sort out what I haven't thought about since those early days.

And my decades of subsequent drinking followed by more than a decade of sobriety seem like different worlds as well, as if I remember things that I did or that happened to me, and they seem like the experience of a very different person. And maybe that's why I've been moved to write about all this, to see if I can find a way to make these worlds, these experiences, these memories, these people cohere.

To put the pieces of the puzzle together. To connect the dots.

8. Paradise Lost

THROUGHOUT MY TODDLERHOOD, I felt like the Sun King. Everything orbited around me. My smile made everyone else smile (even if they weren't sure if it was a smile or just gas). When I was fussy, for whatever reason, everyone wanted to make me happy, to make that sun shine again. I was the center—of attention, of love, of two generations of a family that I held together through my gravitational pull.

It was only decades later that I remembered that feeling, and could put into words what I couldn't then. But that feeling was undeniable, and, back then, it was all I knew. So, once it was gone I had a big hole to fill. I long tried to fill it with alcohol, but drinking just made that hole bigger, a bottomless pit. Having been born into paradise and exiled from it, I would spend the rest of my life feeling damned, incomplete.

Until I stopped drinking. And started filling that hole, one day at a time.

I now feel the glow of a similar radiance from Hailey, our first granddaughter, born two weeks ago as I type this. I've never seen a more adorable baby, at least since the births of her mother and aunt, our own two daughters. Our world orbits around her; just to hold her feels sacred, a way of stopping time and ensuring that all is right in the universe. Because that's the kind of baby she is.

And that's the kind of baby I was. Not that I have any memory of the time when I was as tiny as Hailey is now, but I do have the photographic evidence, the smiles on the faces of my parents and grandparents, just beaming with joy at my adorability. And I have strong memories of slightly later, indelible impressions left by the wonder that was me.

The first concerns my potty chair. While making my transition from diapers to the toilet, I had left the dinner table, gone to use the potty chair in the bathroom, and returned to inform my parents and grandparents about the miracle I had wrought. They all followed me back to the bathroom, and there it was. They each expressed delight, amid some laughter I didn't understand, at what they called my first BM outside a diaper.

Throughout the 50s, in my family at least, it was always a BM—a bowel movement—never the cutesy "poo-poo" or whatever, or the coarser "shit." (I don't think I ever heard that word until I was a teenager.) My family as a whole was incredibly private about bodily functions—I never so much as heard either of my parents fart, though I learned to stay out of the bathroom for at least an hour after my dad had been in there for a while.

So this was an overreaction of delight, at the BM I had produced, all on my own, without a diaper or parental supervision. I was so proud of myself, like I was the Picasso of poop. I guess I really had my shit together, for the first time, though it would be more than a decade before I learned that expression.

The other two indelible examples of my singular charm concern music, perhaps a sign of my developing obsession and future profession. When I was two years old—I had to Google all this—there was a big hit titled "Walkin' to Missouri (Poor Little Robin)" by Sammy Kaye, or "Swing and Sway with Sammy Kaye" as it was billed on the 45 ("vocal by Tony Russo and the Glee Club"). All I remember is the chorus—"Poor little robin, walkin' walkin' walkin' to Missouri"—and the fact that I could not get enough of it.

Anyway, we were at a diner-type restaurant, with my parents and grandparents (always my mother's parents, since they lived in the same suburb we did and our lives were inseparable), and there was a jukebox, which there was in every restaurant we frequented. And "Little Robin," as I remember it, was on that jukebox. The deal back then was a dime a play, three for a quarter, if memory serves. Grandpa Schock, who doted on me even more than everybody else did, put in a quarter, and I played "Little Robin."

Three times. And when that was done, he put in another quarter, and I played "Little Robin" three more times. It seems to me I might have played it 20 or so times in a row, but that can't be right, because surely I would have worn the patience of other diners and the owner before then. I remember someone from the restaurant coming over to my grandpa and asking him politely to knock this off. Even my mother suggested that this had run its course.

But always boisterous and occasionally belligerent, Grandpa Schock responded that this was his grandchild, and that I could play "Little Robin" as long as I damn well pleased, or at least until the quarters ran out. Maybe my grandpa already had a few drinks in him, but nobody ever pushed him around. And as long as he was there, nobody would ever push me around. Because I was the Sun King. If I wanted to repeat "Little Robin" for an hour, we'd do it.

Third and last example of how adorable I was, and how insufferable. A few years after I'd graduated from the potty chair to the big-boy toilet (and when my grandma had taught me to say "I have to go toidy," whenever I needed to use it), Perry Como became my biggest obsession, a fixture on pre-rock radio and a staple of our weekly TV viewing.

I loved everything about Perry—his soothing voice, his friendly manner, his cardigans. I loved him so much that I insisted that I *was* Perry, and I wouldn't respond to anyone in the household if I were addressed as anything other than "Perry." And I wore more cardigans than any other pre-schooler ever had.

At the time, everyone had called me "DeeGee"—D.G., for Donald George, since I couldn't be "Don" because my dad was. I wouldn't learn until I started school what an embarrassment of a name "DeeGee" was, but for this extended period—weeks? Months? A year? Who knows?—I would be nothing other than "Perry," and the rest of the family acceded to my wishes. As always.

(When I mentioned these two examples to Maria as signs of my early infatuation with music, she said they also showed how obsessive I was from the get-go, that I just didn't stop, maybe couldn't stop, where others would. It was the whole too-much-ain't-enough syndrome, from my very first memories. She was right, of course. Even as I think I'm gaining some clarity, she can still see me more clearly than I see myself.)

I'm sure the wonder that was me would have been knocked for a loop anyway, as I ventured farther beyond the household and encountered kids my age. They were perhaps wonders in their own households, and wouldn't be as impressed with me as my family was. But it was an inside job when I was knocked off the pedestal, without any idea how quickly and significantly and irrevocably my world would change.

I didn't know the words for any of this at the time, but my mother somehow became pregnant with another child, who would become my brother Dick (now Richard, after he suffered his way through the implications of a name worse than "DeeGee"). I loved my brother, and love him now, but his arrival introduced me to a world of ambivalence and ambiguity where previously I had only known wonder. And where I had been that wonder.

And now he was.

It was bad enough that some of the time and attention that had once been given to me was focused on him, along with all the smiling, all the beaming. But I was expected to join in, to join the chorus in serenading the new star attraction. And I learned quickly that whatever jealousy I was feeling was improper, forbidden, that if I wasn't eager to share my toys, or my time, with this interloper, I was a bad brother, a bad person.

So, as much as I enjoyed having some younger company, and even someone I would soon be able to boss around, I resented the hell out of the intrusion that had cast the Sun King out of Eden, and made me not only a supporting player, but a flawed one in the eyes of those critiquing the performance. I was still me, whatever that was, but I had gone from being the source of all that was good and loving in this universe to someone wrestling with deep-seated jealousy and spite. Almost overnight. Whatever I was, whatever I had become, I was wrong to feel the way I felt.

Our daughter, Kelly (Hailey's mom), went through something similar when her sister, Molly, was born, and I had a lot of sympathy for her. She had been the center of our universe for more than three years, and now had to share attention with her baby sister. And, of course, Molly received an inordinate share of attention.

So Kelly responded as best she could, knowing intuitively and instinctively how wrong it would be to seem resentful or jealous or anything but loving toward her sister. Instead, she went deaf. For a whole weekend. Whenever we said anything to her, she'd respond, "I can't hear you!"

She was as adamant about her deafness as I was about being addressed as Perry Como. Though not for nearly as long. And it returned some measure of attention to her, while letting us know that if we forgot about her, we'd lose her. Kelly and Molly are now each other's best friends, unquestionably, after a relationship marked by the twists of jealousy and rivalry that likely mark that of any siblings.

The other thing I most remember Kelly saying, over the course of many years, is "It's not fair!" I would like those to be my last words, on my deathbed, on my tombstone.

But at least we stopped at two children. If the shock of the new required a difficult adjustment for me, the shock of the newer was cataclysmic. And not only for me, but for the whole family. Dick had been born a little more than two years after me, and now Doug was born a little less than two years after him. We were starting to see a pattern, and that pattern wasn't boding well for any of us.

Did my parents plan to have three kids within four years? I have no idea. I know that each of the births was greeted happily, as a blessed event, but I don't know whether this was the result of a healthy, loving sexual relationship or the aberration our mother would later make it seem (with no filter, she shared frustrations with her children that were none of our business, making it seem that the only times she had sex with our dad resulted in these children). I still don't know whether they had any conception (sorry) of birth control or family planning.

What I do know is that having three very active, competitive preschool sons spaced two years apart proved devastating for our mother. I can't remember exactly when, but she took to bed for months on end after Doug was born, and was unavailable to any of us. We were told to let Mom sleep, while our Grandpa and Grandma Schock took care of us, and enlisted Martha, the older white-haired woman who had worked in their house and helped raise my mother, who was brought in to do the same with us. In my memory, it seems like she might have been a hundred years old.

Doug was, as they say, a "handful." Not in a bad or mean-spirited way. Not a bad seed. But more like a mischievous Dennis the Menace, always getting into everything, nonstop energy and activity, and thus getting into trouble. Where Dick and I would acknowledge parental authority, Doug was oblivious, like a force of nature. He was also as irresistible as he was irrepressible—obviously a darling as well as a demon.

So, where I'd been an only child past the age of two, I was now the oldest of three brothers when I was four, and the youngest would soon be sucking all the air out of the room. Whatever this meant for me personally—less adult attention, more sharing, two younger siblings to play with and push around—it also had a huge impact on our larger family dynamic. We moved into a much bigger house, a sign that my father was doing much better in his career. He must have been, to afford all those kids.

We also saw our dad a lot less, for apparently he had to work harder and travel more to pay for that house and these kids. He was pretty much traveling Sunday night or Monday morning through Thursday, dealing with the major accounts he serviced. There was *Better Homes & Gardens* and the other Meredith magazines in Des Moines, *Reader's Digest* somewhere in New York, *Look* magazine wherever it was based, and regular stops in Lincoln, Nebraska, which was the home town of his boss and thus a base of operations, even though my dad's home office was in Chicago, on Michigan Avenue, where so much of the city's advertising revenue consolidated.

The absence of my father put more pressure on my mother, when she was finally out of bed and up to the task. It also meant more tension when he was around, when he had a lot of stuff to do—with the yard, the kids, the work in the basement with his 12-packs—but little to do with her. To the contrary, it often seemed like he busied himself elsewhere to avoid her. She'd yell; he'd hide. Business as usual.

Like I've said, I've belatedly realized that such stress would have been a lot for anyone to handle, particularly for a woman with her own mood swings and emotional issues. In some ways, this was the life she had dreamed of, the one that everyone she knew wanted—the handsome husband, the suburban house, the kids. And it was a nightmare, one from which it was hard to see how she would ever awaken.

It had to be emotional whiplash for her own life to change so dramatically, from the belle of the ball at 21 to mother of three by her mid-20s, coupled with postpartum depression and my dad's absence (even when he was there). It was heroic, in its own 1950s sort of way. Hell, when our very capable daughters were in their mid-20s, even taking care of a puppy was a challenge.

There's no question that having such very different parents with very different temperaments had a lasting impact on their offspring, leaving a legacy of therapy, hospitalization, and, at least in my case, a pattern that would be self-perpetuating. Because when I was young I had both normalized and idealized my parents, and figured this was the way of the world.

Men were strong, reserved, stoic, and they drank at least in part to keep their feelings in check, and to build some sort of wall that kept their wives outside. Women were flighty, emotional, unbalanced and needy. The latter needed the former for stability and security. And the former needed the latter to liven up their stolid lives. Men loved women, but didn't take them all that seriously. At least back then, or that's the way it seemed.

So I stepped into a scripted pattern that led to a lifetime of repression and denial, a deepening hole, and a whole lot of drinking.

Initially I didn't know any better, and then I didn't know anything else. I will try to spare readers such excruciating detail in every stage of my development, but those formative years established patterns that I had never contemplated until after I stopped drinking. And then realized how big a hole I had been trying to fill with that drinking, and how strong were the walls I had been trying to build. The seeds of alcoholism were sown more than a decade before I had taken my first sip. I was a messed-up kid from a messed-up family, and I'd had little idea of this until I had become a messed-up adult.

AA insisted that I needed to knock down those walls and let the sun shine in.

9. Family Vacations

OUR WHOLE FAMILY SPENT THE most time together during our two annual summer vacations, the same ones every year. Not only would we travel as a family, we would visit family. No hotels, which apparently we couldn't afford yet. No airplane trips, because back then there weren't any of the discount fares we take for granted today. Air travel in the 1950s was more of a special-occasion luxury.

So we'd always drive, hundreds of miles. There were also no interstates back then, so the best we could do was four-lane highways with stoplights. And the windows open, because cars didn't routinely have air conditioning. We'd all pile into the family station wagon, filling every last inch with pillows and snacks and books or games or whatever might keep the three of us kids occupied for five minutes at a time.

Those drives were hell, invariably. We would wake early, before sunrise, to start our drives before traffic got heavier, and we would arrive late, after dark, hot and sweaty and exhausted and crabby. All of us. The squabbling that the three of us did on a regular basis intensified within the close confines of a packed station wagon. Less than half an hour into an all-day journey, one of us would ask, "How long until we get there?" Then we'd start fighting about who was on whose side of the seat and who was getting squished into the window. And my dad would swing his arm furiously but aimlessly toward the back and shout (this is a man who otherwise never raised his voice), "Do I have to stop this car and separate you?"

The answer was always an unspoken "no," and we'd ease up at the threat, though soon enough we'd be at it again, or needing to stop for a bathroom, or whining about how hungry we were. And it would seem like this trip was going to take forever, because it was. Our mother would tell our father to "do something." He would threaten to stop the car. Again.

She would also vent at him because of the flapping luggage rack, which did require us to stop. Frequently. There was no room in the station wagon for vacation luggage for a family of five, so my dad would strap the luggage to the rack on top. Because he wasn't the handiest guy in the world, those straps would start flapping as soon as we hit the open road. And since the noise itself was so annoying, he'd have to decide when to stop and try in vain to make the flapping stop, or to keep barreling through and hope that nothing had fallen off.

Since my father had a limited amount of vacation time, a couple of weeks, and we had all summer, there were times when he'd leave us after a couple days, drive back to Chicago, and return for a weekend a week or two later. It must have been tough on him doing all that driving, all by himself, though I never gave a thought to this at the time. But maybe it was easier as well, with no one arguing or whining or telling him to stop. Maybe this was his vacation from us.

Our closest trip felt like the longest, a drive to the Michigan cottage on Lake Huron that had been in my dad's family since he was a boy. It wasn't a bad drive from the Detroit suburbs, where he'd been raised and I was born, and his family had spent much of their summers at the cottage. But it was twice as long from the suburbs of Chicago, a drive that began and ended in darkness, and one that would require plenty of stops for meals and snacks and bathrooms and gas. The long final stretch was on a two-lane highway, and it made a couple hours seem like an eternity, a long day's journey into night.

The cottage itself was frozen in time, and always the same every summer we went. It was part of a private complex of a couple of dozen summer homes, scattered here and there between the woods and the beach. Located on Michigan's "tip of the thumb" (as the map makes the state look, like a mitten), it was as big as a real home, with six bedrooms and two and a half baths, but still rustic, with an old-fashioned icebox and only the fireplace for heat.

The private summer community, gated decades before the age of McMansions, had its own tennis courts and nine-hole golf course. We had a boat for fishing as well. Though lacking in pretense, the summer idyll suggested the sort of patrician wealth of our Grandpa Mac, as we called him, that never trickled down to us, as our mother always reminded us.

Where my father's family was concerned, I took my cues from my mother. I was on her side, genetically and temperamentally. She found Grandpa Mac cold in comparison to her own loving father, and so did I. Grandma Mac was warmer and funnier, and we both liked her a lot. My dad's sisters thought no woman was good enough for him, or so my mother thought, and said so, though she got along best with his middle sister. Her husband reminded me more of my other grandfather, the loving and garrulous one. Uncle John would start each day with pre-dawn Bloody Marys, as they were the two early risers. And early vacation drinkers, apparently, though our mother never drank like that at home.

The cottage at that point was open to everyone in my dad's family, but you had to schedule so that everyone didn't descend at once for an extended period of time. When we were there, my grandparents would come for a long weekend, and the married sister and her family, a little younger than ours, would plan their trip so there was some overlap with ours.

Away from the confines of our home and the isolation of our mother with her energetic sons, the family dynamic was totally different. There was no pressure, no tension, except whatever my mom felt around my dad's father. The kids ran free—to the beach, through the woods, along the streets. There was no perception of danger anywhere.

For adults, it was a place to socialize, which meant parties at many of the adjacent cottages, which meant a lot of drinking that got louder as the night got later. We weren't part of the social life of the surrounding Michiganders, but our own cottage got into the spirit in more of a family style.

So my mother and uncle greeted the morning with Bloody Marys. For my dad, it was always beer, and he always had a beer. Not at dawn, but early enough. We saw little difference in him whether he was drinking or not; he always seemed to have things under control. And everyone at the time knew that you couldn't have a drinking problem if you only drank beer. We never thought of anyone up there as having a drinking problem, no matter how much they drank. It was vacation, and it was mostly beer.

As families expanded and we grew older and my dad's other sisters got married and had kids, that normal of alcohol consumption encompassed pretty much everyone. Grandpa Mac didn't seem to drink much, but his kids sure did, and so did their kids, first sneaking them and then sharing them with their folks. Still mainly beer, so nothing to worry about. But it was case upon case, daily. A truly humongous amount of beer. Frat worthy on an *Animal House* scale.

I came to love all my dad's sisters, my aunts, and found them funny and warm, once I had relationships with them independent of my parents. Once my dad died, my mother had little to do with my father's family, and the trips to the cottage pretty much ended. But occasionally I'd visit one of the families. And every once in a while there would be a reunion at the cottage, now that some of us kids had kids of our own.

The drinking still started early in the day, and went well into the night. At least two of my aunts and two of my uncles were plainly over-reliant, drinking upon rising and continuing until they were very shaky and their voices slurred by the end of the day. They drank more than I ever would. One of my aunts never made it to a particular family wedding, because she somehow hit her head, drunk, on the floor of the hotel lobby, after falling or passing out, while checking in. Her husband went to the hospital with her and then came to the reception alone, where he drank himself into oblivion before the dancing even started. This was my Uncle John, my mom's Bloody Mary buddy, and by now it was plain that he was a terminal alcoholic.

One aunt and uncle (though not those two) preceded my entry into AA, though my aunt insisted that she was no alcoholic and had gone in support of her husband. I couldn't say how rampant alcoholism might be on my dad's side of the family, and whether that drinking issue was genetic or the ingrained habit of family tradition. All I know is that whenever we were together we all drank a lot, maybe more than most of us did when we weren't together. Certainly more than I did. Which is how I'd long figured I didn't have a drinking problem, by measuring my consumption and its consequences against theirs. It was as if we were fish and beer was water.

At one of our reunions, one of our aunts was backing out of the long driveway, to drive the block or two to the cottage where she was staying, when she hit a tree. She just left the car there, bumper crumbled, and started to weave and stagger her way home. Earlier that evening, her drunken husband had happened upon some of my drunken siblings who were amusing themselves by setting gliders on fire and aiming them off the cliff toward the big lake.

He yelled at them, "Are you drunk or are you just stupid?!" This became a family catchphrase. As if it were an either/or question.

Our other family vacation every summer was to Hendersonville, North Carolina, where my mom's parents had moved, for reasons I later discovered had something to do with my grandfather's drinking. The drive took twice as long as the one to Michigan's "Thumb," but it was more interesting and leisurely, extended over two and a half days, circling through mountains in a whole different part of the country. Where only the town names had provided much interest in Michigan, once we got past Detroit—there was Bad Axe, the county seat, and tiny Kinde, "the bean capital of the world"—both the topography and the pace of life were very different after we had headed south.

My mother's parents had moved to North Carolina just a few years after we had moved to Glen Ellyn to be near them. My grandfather was still young, early 50s at the most, so this semi-retirement from the gas station he had owned had to be health related, and the health problems he had—the ones that would kill him a decade later—were drinking related.

The gas station itself wasn't good for him, as I would learn when I went to work there in my early teens, and when he returned because the business had experienced a downturn without him (amid suspicion that the guy he had left in charge was skimming). It was called Schock's Super Service, and though he sold off brands of gas—first Phillips 66 and then Skelly—what a gas station really sold back then was service.

It was a business built on customer loyalty, and customers remained loyal if they liked you, and you took good care of their cars. There was no self-service, or pay at the pump back then. When you came for gas, we'd wash your windshield, check your oil and your tire pressure, schedule maintenance if you needed it. On weekends we'd have a full schedule of cars to be hand washed.

This full service extended to my grandfather's office in the back of the station, where some of his regulars would have a drink with him while we were servicing his car. Maybe one shot of whiskey for a customer, but that made for many for my grandpa over the course of a long day.

There were rumors that he made book on betting events in that back room as well. And he always seemed to have some good Cub tickets—given to him by good customers (including Clarence "Pants" Rowland, a front-office exec for the team, and, no, I have no idea why he was called "Pants") and given to good customers. Except on opening day, when my grandpa always took me, and my dad if he could get away. And other games that would allow me to skip school under some pretext or another.

My grandpa's station functioned as kind of a semi-private club, where men could get away with things. There was no other place in this suburban downtown where you could get a drink or place a bet. No place where there was a condom machine except his men's room (news that would spread among my teenage cohort, who much preferred the privacy of the machine to asking a pharmacist).

No other place where I could steal cigarettes as easily as in his back cupboard, first packs, then cartons, which certainly he must have known from inventory though I smuggled them out without being caught. I started smoking regularly and drinking when I could when I was working at his station at age 14, when the thrill of the illicit was a big attraction and this place seemed to have it all.

But his life and health had required a Southern retreat, a convalescence. North Carolina had none of that, and my descent into delinquency wouldn't occur until he and my grandma returned north and the family vacations in North Carolina ended. While they lasted, they were even more idyllic than the ones in Michigan. Because there were fewer of us, our family and our grandparents, and there was more focus on us, the kids. In Michigan, it could seem like the kids and the adults were on separate vacations, meeting for meals or for fishing on a boat.

Here, everything revolved around my mother and her three young sons. This meant my mother had more help, an extra set of parents, and experienced less tension, less pressure. She wasn't in this alone, as she often felt with our father. And our father had none of the resentment toward my mother's family that my mother felt toward my father's. He loved my grandparents, and they loved him. One big happy family.

My Grandpa Schock drank whiskey rather than beer, and he played cards with his friends. For money, I suppose. Grandma Schock played cards as well, but those were games she taught us, first Go Fish, then Gin Rummy. She didn't drink, but she didn't seem to mind that he did. And everything seemed so relaxed in North Carolina, even the drinking.

It was obvious to my grandparents that our youngest brother Doug was a handful, and that my mother could not handle him. So there was one long summer when we returned home and he stayed down there, the whole summer. We didn't envy him the undivided attention he received; to the contrary, we were a little scared by the message this sent—that if you didn't act right, you too could be cast out until you shaped up.

I later learned about the concept of "unconditional love," but I already knew about conditional—how you were loved if you acted the right way, and yelled at if you didn't. You were a "bad boy." Doug had been a bad boy, though an irrepressible one, always smiling.

Our summer trips to North Carolina ended after five years or so, when our grandparents returned north, and my grandpa went back to running the station. His drinking got worse, and he lived less than a decade after his return, dying of alcoholism in his early 60s, liver failure. We continued to go to the cottage every summer, for a dozen or so years, until I decided I wouldn't go anymore.

I didn't feel as much a part of this expanding family. I didn't want to leave my friends. When our family left, and I had our house all to myself, I could do what I wanted. I was starting to lead a very different life.

10. Kick Out the Jams!

EVERYTHING IN THE 1950S HAD BEEN so different from now—the attitude toward drinking, the smoking (even on airplanes and pretty much everywhere else), the family driving vacations, before interstate highways or budget airfares or hotel/motel chains.

When we flash forward to the 60s, the world becomes more recognizable as the one in which we live. Those of us who turned 16 in the mid-1960s (Bruce Springsteen, Tom Petty, me) were the perfect age for rock and roll, and for the cultural tsunami of its wake. Nothing has more profoundly influenced my life, my values, my career, my rebellions, my excesses—pretty much everything I hold dear and everything I've had to overcome—than rock and roll.

It made things pretty simple, at least at the start. During a period that prized disruption and was perfectly in discord with my raging hormones, everything either was rock and roll or it wasn't. Cool or not. Drinking, drugs, smoking, premarital sex, leather, skipping school, petty shoplifting and vandalism, dressing as if you didn't care how you looked (when you so desperately did)—all of that was rock and roll. And therefore cool.

Parental values, caution, haircuts, behaving rationally and responsibly, working a straight job, buckling down before "the man" or "the establishment"—none of that was rock and roll. And therefore to be avoided or challenged at every opportunity. Sounds simplistic, and it was, but it felt right at 16, and some of it has stayed with me to this day. For better and worse. I never wanted to have to put on a suit and tie to go to work like my dad did, and I never have. I never wanted to make money and materialism a primary focus, and I haven't. As I tell my students, I've had two careers—rock journalism and academics—and no one goes into either to get rich. Or, really, to grow up.

One of the things they insist in AA is that, if you're an alcoholic, your maturity stalled around the time you started drinking for real. For me, that was 13 or 14, and that sounds about right. I still have the kneejerk response to challenge any authority, even when common sense dictates otherwise, and to say things I know will get me into trouble. And do things that will get me into trouble. As I've tried to make baby steps toward maturity, I avoid giving into those impulses as much as I can. But I still have them. Even in my early 70s, I still feel too much like I did at 17.

The paradox for those of us who began drinking heavily early on—and smoking cigarettes, because, back then, the two went hand in hand—is that we did so because it seemed grown-up. Our parents did those things, and even though we were rejecting the values of our parents, and the future they augured, we wanted the freedom we thought they had to make our own rules. So we acted being cool by emulating the behavior of our uncool parents? Drinking to rebel against their drinking? It gets a little twisted here.

At some point as I continued to drink more and more heavily, into my 30s and 40s, drinking did a 180 and became a way to recapture the impetuosity of lost youth. Most of my friends had come to terms with their adulthood, and few of them continued to drink as hard as they had through college (or to smoke dope the way they had then). By the end, I was drinking mainly alone, an antisocial drinker.

I was a case of arrested development, and the series of jobs I had both encouraged this and enabled it. Record store owner. Rock critic. Even university professor, perennially surrounded by those in their late teens and early 20s. When the students never get any older, you can try to fool yourself that you aren't aging either. Maybe you'll even meet them at a bar at the end of a semester, because you still drink like they do. Or more than they do, but mostly alone.

I never once thought about what daily drinking was doing to me, and what it would be like to give it up. Why would I? I liked to drink. That's why I drank so much. Just like I still loved rock and roll. And still do, even stone cold sober.

Dating back to my Perry Como, pre-school days, I had loved music long before I discovered rock and roll. But I was indiscriminate, with no taste, no idea what the good stuff was or why it was good. Though rock and roll and I pretty much came of age together, I'd been too young to hear Chuck Berry, Little Richard and all the other seminal figures the first time through, belatedly experiencing that music either as oldies or through the Beatles and the Stones.

I was aware of Elvis Presley, but he was the guy our teenage babysitter worshiped, so I dismissed him as silly, girl's stuff. (I would initially do the same with the Beatles a few years later, when I briefly considered myself a studious teenage folkie, god knows why.)

Though I'd earlier bought "Wake Up Little Susie" by the Everly Brothers, who I'd later learn were certified great (and whose music I still love), the year of my musical awakening was 1960, when I was nine, and then 10, and when the record I remember playing over and over again, as much as I'd once played "Little Robin," was "Poetry in Motion" by Johnny Tillotson. I later learned it was dreck, and I have no idea why this particular song hit me so hard, or even what it meant, but I was hooked.

I don't remember hearing or caring to hear anything else by Johnny Tillotson (or the Everly Brothers, for a long while). The first artist I embraced as a young person's artist was the immortal Bobby

Rydell. I was so hooked on "Wild One" ("I'm a-gonna tame you down") and "Swingin' School" ("Chicks! Kicks! Cats! Cool!") that I embraced Bobby like I had no other singer since Perry Como. In fact, Bobby might as well have been the Perry Como of rock, despite the tidal wave hair. Innocuous, non-threatening.

And ultimately disposable, quickly to be discarded for more serious and significant musical passions, once I learned that those existed and what they were. The point is that this was my music, these were my artists, not something I had inherited from my parents. I had somehow discovered this stuff on my own, from radio stations my parents never listened to. And the more I heard, the more I wanted to discover.

Pretty soon, I was studying the Top 40 with an intensity I had never devoted to schoolwork. And I was spending all my money on books (the Chip Hilton sports series) and music. As I would continue to spend so much of it for the next half century, and beyond. I was obsessive from the get-go, and I would remain so. The objects of the obsession might change (some did, some didn't), but the obsessive nature never would. Or at least never has. There was a big hole inside of me, and I was obsessed with filling it. Well before I tried filling it with booze.

When I was 10, such Top 40 music didn't speak to the deepest part of me. There was no deepest part of me. There was only surface, and that surface was smooth, until it got rocky. Despite the disruptions wreaked by my two sibling intruders on our home life, I still felt kind of like the Sun King through grade school. I was a good athlete, better than the others, and a good student, smarter than the others. At least in my eyes. Teachers liked me, and I basked in that approval, as I had with that of my parents.

But just as they had inside the home, things changed quickly and significantly. I'd never heard of the "awkward years," but my early adolescence was devastatingly awkward. In short order, I got glasses, braces, pimples. The good-looking kid (at least in his own mirror) had become an ugly duckling of an adolescent. I grew tall and gangly, tripping over my own limbs.

I went to a bigger school for sixth grade, the year that I turned 12, and bigger ones yet for junior high and high school. I had so recently seen myself as a very big fish, but as the pond got bigger, I was barely a minnow. Others were better athletes, better looking, probably even smarter, though nobody really cared much about that. My coordination couldn't keep pace with the gawky growth of my skin-and-bones frame. My voice cracked, making me hesitant to talk. How had everything gone to hell so quickly? And so thoroughly?

If I could no longer excel at the things the good kids did—the popular ones, the jocks, the cheerleaders—I would soon become very good at being bad. Not bad like the greasers, the hoodlums in training, with their black leather and threatening manner. I could never pull that off. But bad like a misfit, someone who just didn't care—about school, about parents, about what the other kids thought. Suburban bad. Rock and roll bad.

And it was here that rock provided my life with a soundtrack, a spirit and an incomparable shaping force. *Hail! Hail! Rock and roll! Deliver me from the days of old.*

By the time I was 16, rock was definitely speaking my language, or I was borrowing its. The music was in tune with my raging frustration, not merely in popular anthems such as the Rolling Stones' "Satisfaction," the Animals' "We Gotta Get Out of This Place," and the Who's "My Generation," but all of the rawer, garage-band uprisings that emulated whatever from the British Invasion that was crudest and easiest to copy.

"Pushin' Too Hard," "Psychotic Reaction," "Talk Talk." Sense a pattern? Then there was "Leave Me Alone," a Chicago cult hit by the Knaves that hadn't re-entered my consciousness for decades until I started writing this, but now seems to perfectly encapsulate my feelings back then:

"Why don't you choke yourself and leave me alone!" On the same Dunwich label as the Shadows of Knights, whose "Gloria" had reverberated far beyond the local Chicago airwaves. Both bands had names that sounded sort of British and sort of disreputable. These guys weren't rock royalty—they were just like us. Maybe a couple years older, a little more talented, or a little more driven. Longer hair. But not that big of a leap.

I could live in their world, and I could make it mine. This music was a revolt against the very same suburbs in which I lived, the same dynamic that would ignite punk rock a decade later. There was a direct line between this and that—an embrace of aggressive amateurism, attitude, noise; a rejection of refinement and maturity. As someone who turned 16 in 1966, I had found the roadmap for my life in this music.

Back then, if you were a real rock fan, someone who bought records regularly and sought them out, rather than just turned on the radio, you were part of a marginal cult rather than the mainstream. You were living by different values in a different world, certainly a world far different than the white-bread Republican suburbs that were the only other world I knew, and would give me so much to rebel against.

You couldn't learn about what was cool from school, or even from friends. You would need to read the emerging "rock press," first the mimeographed *Crawdaddy* and later *Rolling Stone*, with its emphasis on San Francisco as the center of cool. (Did San Francisco have suburbs?) You would need to spend as much time as you could in Chicago, at Rose Records in the Loop, and the smaller, hippie boutiques in Old Town. Your world was expanding in a way that made you feel even more isolated in conservative western suburbia.

Other than music, pretty much everything that I thought defined me was illegal or risky or both. I was too young to smoke or drink legally, but I was exceeding a pack a day ("He can't be a man 'cause he doesn't smoke the same cigarettes as me!") and drinking as much beer as I could whenever I could. My dad had plenty; he wouldn't miss it. I was soon having sex, at 16, monogamously (I've been a serial monogamist throughout my life) but recklessly in regard to contraception. *Que sera sera.*

And just as rock was discovering marijuana, so was I. Talk about right age at the right time—my high school class of 1968 was the first in our conservative suburb to smoke dope before college. Older siblings of friends had started "experimenting," and they not only brought their stashes back from campus, they shared them. It was like an initiation ritual, turning someone on for the first time, and we were the beneficiaries, the acolytes.

So, there were still two major groups in school, the "socialites" (preppies and jocks) and the "greasers" (black leather, greased-back hair, blue-collar families in a white-collar school district). Those of us on the misfit fringes weren't big or obvious enough to be identified as a third alternative, but we were the incipient "stoners," the ones with a big secret.

Marijuana was seriously illegal at the time, and getting caught could conceivably screw up your life. Big deal. Everything I was doing could screw up my life—drinking and driving drunk, screwing without regard to pregnancy, skipping class so often I had gone from an honor roll student in my underclass years to one getting C's and D's as a junior. I would have to make a valiant recovery my senior year to get into any college, let alone a good one.

But except for the college deferment that would keep me out of the draft, and thus out of Vietnam, I just didn't care. About any of it. The goals and boundaries of the so-called "straight" world weren't for guys like me, or the ones who made the music I obsessed over. No, for me, the real charge was getting away with something, living on the edge, refusing to play by their rules and either making my own or living without any.

I was no longer living with my family. I mean, I was sleeping in their house and checking in for the occasional meal, but most of my living was done well away from home, with friends who were also distancing themselves from their families. In some ways, that's how I picked them, or how we found each other. I seemed to gravitate toward those raised by single parents or parents who both worked and thus had little supervision, or even an empty house or apartment.

I had one friend who was at the other end of the economic scale, from a family so wealthy that they had an indoor swimming pool, a sauna, a bar with beer on tap, from which we could drink freely. Maybe after steaming in the sauna and rolling naked in the snow. It didn't really matter if his parents were home—I never met them. The house was so big that you wouldn't run into them, and they weren't the type to play nursemaid.

I never felt that my own parents didn't love me, and they were always there when they (or I) thought that I needed them. But they didn't really understand what was going on with me, nor did I, and they had enough other stuff to keep them occupied. The only real battleground with my parents was over the length of my hair, the visible influence (and the defiant attitude accompanying it) that might contaminate my younger siblings.

After having three sons in four years, at an interval of two years between them, they took four years off. And then resumed, or were surprised, by the birth of their fourth son. The addition of David gave Doug someone younger to pick on, as Dick and I had unloaded on him. Resuming the two-year schedule, Katie came next and last, and my father was delighted beyond all measure. A girl after all these boys, and a name other than one that began with "D."

I now feel as close to David and Katie as I do to Richard (no longer Dick) and Doug, and David and Katie are definitely the two siblings who have remained most closely in touch, their families all but intertwined. But they then seemed like add-ons to the essential family dynamic, the chaotic core of the Three Stooges. Katie was a full decade younger than me, so by the time she started kindergarten, I had already entered my teenage beer-drinking, cigarette-smoking estrangement.

My parents had encouraged my initial interest in rock records, and I will be forever grateful. They took us to see the Beach Boys, drove us to see the Stones, and let my brother Dick and I take the train and then the el to the south side of Chicago to see the Beatles at Comiskey Park. (A couple decades later, such permission for a couple of suburban boys, 14 and 12, would have been far less likely.) They grumbled a little about all the money I spent on records, but nothing serious. I had a job; it was my money. And they pretty much paid for everything else.

The rest of my family had a summer life that centered around a club that had a swimming pool and tennis courts. Our mother was a tanning fanatic, and she would spend every day there, all day, on a deck chair. My brothers were tennis players, as my dad had been, as

I once had been, occasionally, until it became plain that first Dick, then Doug, was better than me. The natural order of ability had been upended. I couldn't tolerate this. If I could not win, I would not play.

I no longer had any interest in our family vacations—even to places that I now wish I'd visited, beyond the annual trips to the Michigan family cottage—and my parents barely paid lip service in asking me. When they were gone, I had the house all to myself, and there was nothing I could have done on a trip to compare with what I could get away with back home. I later learned that, long after my family moved to Lincoln, Nebraska, and I had left the family home for good, David and Katie elevated the "open house" tradition to notorious levels of high-school debauchery. There must be something in our genes, or our role models, or both.

Once I had my driver's license, the family that had long defined my life now seemed even less a part of it. I had a job for spending money, spending most of it on records, some of it on beer and, eventually, dope. I had friends whose lives were also pretty fluid and aimless, and none of us had to do much checking in or deal with checking up. Years before it became army policy, "don't ask, don't tell" became the policy not only in my family but in others that had adolescents living on the fringes.

"Your sons and your daughters are beyond your command," sang Bob Dylan to parents who weren't listening, though their kids had gotten the message.

My brother Dick was getting that message as well, as a teenager balanced between two worlds. He was still playing tennis and enjoying the family vacations. He was always kinder and more thoughtful than I was, a friend to the neighborhood children whose existence I barely acknowledged. But he became immersed in a relationship with his first serious girlfriend, growing his hair longer, starting to become more interested in Beat literature and radical politics. And music.

We had long shared a bedroom, and maybe I influenced him some, but I think it was more a matter of mutual influence and finding ourselves taking different paths to a similar destination. The more rebellious strains of rock meant more to me, while the literature and politics that to me were part of the fashion statement went deeper with him. The term in vogue then was "counterculture," and when I was feeling my way toward it, Dick was thinking his way into it.

Feels funny typing this, because it has been more than 40 years since anyone has been introduced to my brother as anything other than "Richard." But he was always "Dick" back then, a different person. And he was increasingly interested in going with me to hear any band that crossed our radar, experience any scene with a promise of radical adventure. At 14 or 15, he had to be one of the most culturally aware kids his age in the western suburbs. We both spent a lot of time in the city, where we increasingly felt more at home.

Did I have a drinking problem at that time? Didn't think so then, not sure now. Studies suggest that the earlier you start drinking heavily, the more damage the alcohol can cause, and the more likely you are to become (or be) an alcoholic. But drinking just seemed to be one manifestation of an all-encompassing condition, one of the threads that if you pulled any one of them, the whole thing might unravel.

I knew at the time that I had maladjustment issues, and I was proud of them. The term that was popular among our band of midwestern misfits wasn't "hippies," which seemed like a media label, but "freaks." Because we didn't seem to have much in common with or want anything to do with whatever was considered normal, conventional, responsible, straight. Didn't have a clue to what we did want or to what the future might hold, just knew that it couldn't be found in the confines of white-bread suburbia.

Yet it was within these confines that I encountered my first absolutely real, raving, no-doubt-about-it alcoholic, a man whose existence was far freakier than anything my friends and I could conjure. Yeah, my dad drank a lot of beer, and my grandfather had died from drinking too much, but this guy, the father of my first real girlfriend, lived only to drink.

He resided in a small downtown apartment near the railroad tracks, above the small stores. His drinking had cost him his marriage, and his job (whatever that had been), though not his rights to have his daughter visit him. We benefited from his lack of responsibility, and we laughed at his delusions, illusions and DTs. He was a generally nice man who had only the most tenuous grip on reality. One minute having a friendly conversation with him, and the next screaming about something, even trembling. We'd get out of his reach or out of the apartment, and return after he'd settled down.

I suppose one of the reasons my girlfriend was my girlfriend was because she had been shaped or warped by a situation like this. I tended toward people who needed fixing or wanted leading. I always wanted to be in control, the lead guy, like I had been in childhood and no longer was, unless the situation was under my command.

I was a loyal friend, but otherwise a lousy one. It was all about how you could boost my ego, reinforce my identity. If you were to be my friend, I would call the shots, decide what we were doing, where we were going, what risks we would take with you as my accomplices. If you were my girlfriend, you would underscore my value, and you would look to me as someone who could initiate you into this life that had its own music, its own values. You would make me the envy of other guys, guys who didn't have a girlfriend as cute as you, or as adoring, or as sexually willing.

In contemporary parlance, this was "toxic masculinity," though to me what seemed toxic was adolescence. And I'm not sure I began to leave that adolescence behind until I stopped drinking, on the cusp of 60. Even now, I have those whiplash instincts to resist authority, to make my own rules and to break those when I feel like it.

My other experience with alcoholism around this time was staggering. My grandfather died when I was 17, his liver shot, his skin a sickly yellow. It was the first death that truly devastated me, but I didn't see any cautionary lesson in it, nothing that made me concerned about my dad's drinking. Or mine. I thought it was kind of romantic that he'd played hard, lived hard, died hard. I'd had a special relationship with my grandpa, not only through the gas station, but as the first grandchild. The night that he died, he deliriously and a little tearfully asked me to help him break out of that hospital. As if it were a prison. He wasn't in his right mind, as we would have said back then.

The shock of it rocked my whole family, though neither his death nor its aftereffects should have come as much of a surprise. Losing her rock sent my mother into a deeper spiral of depression. She was such a light sleeper, and he was such an early riser; they had started every day with a pre-dawn phone conversation that could last for more than an hour.

My dad stepped up in truly heroic fashion. Not that he could take the place my grandpa held with my mom, but he did everything else he possibly could to help us navigate through grandpa's death. Still traveling for work during the week, he spent every weekend at my grandfather's gas station, early in the morning (when he was not an early-morning guy), pumping gas, washing cars, trying to get a handle on the business.

There had been discord between my grandfather and his manager, a very popular presence at the station, and their relationship suffered as business did. My grandparents suspected that one of the reasons for their smiling employee's popularity was that he had been giving away the store (which wasn't his to give) during their stint in North Carolina. The manager maintained that he was doing his best to hold things together for a crazy, irresponsible drunk, who was drinking away the business and drinking more as the business faltered.

My dad not only took responsibility for the business, but for my grandmother, who had barely so much as written a check during her husband's life, and who was totally unprepared for his death. She not only moved in with us, but my dad built a whole addition to our house so she would have a sense of her own privacy.

Her presence added tension to our already tense household, since our mother had been far closer to her father than to her own mother. My grandmother had resented the closeness of that relationship, though my dad never did. My grandmother was as judgmental as my mother, and the two were often judging each other, even silently. Before my father suggested another option, moving her into her own apartment and paying for everything, my grandmother threatened whatever delicate balance the rest of the family had achieved.

As the fissures in our family foundation continued to widen, my father retreated into the basement, as always, with his twelve pack. I spent as much time away from home as I possibly could, doing little more than sleep there, spending almost all of my waking hours at school (or skipping it), at work, with whatever friends had pretty much the same latitude as I did. I found most of what passed for my stability outside the house, and I found most of my identity in my music and my vices, smoking and drinking and indulging with drugs that had escalated beyond pot, cheap speed and potent LSD.

Hell, everything was escalating during my junior year of 1967, the year my grandfather died, and into 1968, when I would graduate from high school. My truancy initially did, until that sense of purpose escalated to overpower it, the recognition that there would be a day of reckoning with the draft board if I didn't turn my grades around and find some college that would take me.

The music I favored became more adventurous, with rock challenging all sorts of boundaries and taboos. Hit singles gave way to conceptually audacious albums, Top 40 AM to the FM "underground" and "acid rock" inevitably led to LSD, at least for me and my friends. Some claimed to seek spiritual enlightenment, but I knew that I just really liked to get fucked up, and the more fucked up, the better (at least unless things got scary).

Despite the short-lived media hype over a "Summer of Love" out west, the drug derangement that we in the Midwest sought had a harder edge. The music that we favored offered less of the bliss of "be-ins" or "love-ins" and more of the soundtrack for mass protests and clashes with the cops. Those were truly tumultuous times—musically, politically, pharmaceutically, culturally—and that tumult seemed wildly exciting to a kid on the verge of college.

Just as there was never a better time to turn 16 than 1966, there was no wilder place to be in 1968 than Chicago, where the summer after my high school graduation would see the city in flames with rock and roll (or an unreasonable facsimile). I would not only get my first taste of tear gas when the Democratic National Convention brought the circus to town, but I would get a new sense of rock's chromosome-rearranging possibilities, when an unknown band called the MC5—unknown in Chicago, the Motor City 5 were already notorious along the Detroit/Ann Arbor axis—were the only band out of dozens promised to brave the police state that Chicago had become. (I would later write my first book about that band and that experience, and that book would help secure my tenure as a journalism professor.) Their "Kick Out the Jams" became a rallying anthem, a call to storm the Bastille.

I thought the music's crazed anarchy made it the funniest band I had ever seen, only belatedly deciding that it was also the most incendiary rock I had ever experienced (and ever would). It set my life on a course that wouldn't become apparent for a few years, for at the time my life had no course, really no goal at all except to start a brand new chapter. I really had no idea what college had in store for me, but I knew my life would be transformed, that it would start fresh. And I was ready to leave everything behind—family, friends, girlfriend—for whatever excitement lay ahead.

There were a few reasons I had selected the University of Wisconsin in Madison, less than three hours from home, for my college adventure. It was supposed to be a good school, according to recent magazine rankings. It was a hotbed of radical politics and protest—the Berkeley of the Midwest—and likely the drugs and sexual promise that swirled around such foment.

Mainly, though, I went there because in Wisconsin you could drink beer legally at 18. Free at last! Free at last!

11. The College Castaway

WITH THE BENEFITS OF ALMOST FIVE decades' hindsight, I can appreciate how much my students savor their college experience—how so many of them feel (even fear) that these will be the best years of their lives. They are establishing friendships that might last well beyond campus, generating memories that will lift them when the burdens of job, mortgage and family weigh them down. This is their last gasp of youthful freedom as well as their passageway to adulthood.

Their experience is not what mine was. Mine was miserable, way worse than high school, when at least my misery had company (and getting drunk, getting high, getting laid and going to concerts represented something that passed for a social life). Among everyone I know—my students, our daughters, my siblings, my friends that I have somehow made since college—my collegiate experience was singularly dismal, isolated, disconnected. No one else I know spent his first three years at three different colleges, and just couldn't wait for this whole ordeal to be done.

Madison should have been the promised land I'd envisioned. Could have been. A beautiful, hilly campus on a lake, with both the student union and my first (and last) college dorm situated on its picturesque shore. A legal drinking age of 18, and a whole stretch of downtown dominated by and catering to the student demographic. In an era of "don't trust anyone over 30," you didn't need to see or encounter or submit to those old folks, the straight folks. If you wanted to trip away your weekend on LSD, or join a fraternity, or take over the armory to drive ROTC from campus, or simply stumble your drunken way home after the bars closed, the choice was yours. Nobody stopping you from doing anything. And nobody making you do anything, even go to class.

Yet the sort of freedom for which I had long hungered somehow made me feel oppressed, unexpectedly so. And self-conscious about it. Why was I so disconnected, so out of the loop? How was everyone else able to talk to people they hadn't known and make plans and even friendships, while I seemed stuck in my isolation booth? (I would later learn that a whole lot of alcoholics feel similarly disconnected, not that I thought of myself as an alcoholic at the time.) Maybe there was something I could or should have done, but what? The very thought of approaching people unless I was sure they would accept me seemed so uncomfortable I just retreated into my shell. Before fall turned to winter, well before Thanksgiving break, I had already given up on campus life, on fitting in, on making a successful transition to living away from home. I just couldn't wait for this to be over.

And so it went. I never made one friend in college, at any of them. I never joined anything. I never went to a college party with fellow students. I never went to a sporting event, at a couple of big football schools. I barely went to class, especially those large survey courses, where a student in a lecture hall of hundreds would hardly be missed. I only lived in a dorm for one year, because it was mandatory. I hated college, and college towns. So, naturally, I have subsequently spent half of my supposedly adult life in two of them—Austin and Iowa City—and have found my latter-day career path as a university professor. Go figure.

It has taken me more than a decade of sobriety to realize this, but what so many others consider the best years of their lives were the worst of mine. I had anticipated this period as some sort of bridge between adolescence and adulthood, between who I had been and who I would become. And I never crossed that bridge, at least not at that time. I fell off. Or I retreated to the bank where I had been more comfortable, the teenage years and suburban culture that I had been so eager to escape.

This is where I should have known just how seriously, even singularly messed up I was. In AA, you often hear jokes about not getting the instruction manual that everyone else had, and that's how I felt. Everyone else seemed to know how to talk to fellow students they hadn't previously met, to make what I dismissed as "small talk" or "chit chat." Everyone else knew how to make that transition from high school, and to welcome it. Everyone else knew we were all in this big boat together. Except me. I was outside the boat. Thrashing. Drowning.

Again, why me? I'm still not sure. Other people are shy. I teach some of them, and even they seem to make friends, sometimes with other shy people. I simply did not, or could not. If high school had been a bigger pond, the University of Wisconsin campus in Madison seemed like an ocean. Some of my entry-level classes had 400 or more students in them. Some of those students must have talked to each other, gotten to know each other. I didn't. And I seemed to radiate those rays of the invisible protective shield—which it sometimes still feels I do—so that nobody approached me as they might someone more normal.

People I have known—then and now—have traveled to Europe with a couple bucks and a knapsack, having adventures, making friends. They bond with those in similar circumstances, even with those who speak a different language, as they explore lands foreign to all of them. I couldn't even navigate the establishment of one lasting friendship among college students, on a campus of thousands of them, just a couple hours' drive from my suburban home. Somehow, everyone else knew what to do. And I didn't.

Not that I was totally isolated in Madison, at least at the start of the freshman fall semester. I was assigned a roommate from Lacrosse, Wisconsin, and I met his friends, and we went out drinking. I didn't have much to say to them—they were preppier and I was hippier—and they eventually made other friends. As their circle widened, I fell outside it. Same with the one guy I knew from high school who had come to Madison. He was gregarious, making friends easily. I was not, did not. We saw each other a few times early that fall, and then we did not.

I'd been so much looking forward to this new campus life, and there was none. I mean, it was new, but there was no life to which I was connected, barely even my own. It seemed that the only life I had was back home, the one I previously couldn't wait to leave, but now one I grasped like a lifeline. As the semester progressed, I was increasingly calling my high-school girlfriend, the one who I was sure I would outgrow and leave behind, now that I was a college guy.

Pretty soon, I was taking bus trips home (freshmen couldn't have cars on campus), as often as I could deem it reasonable. Every month, then a couple times a month, then practically every weekend. We had classes five days a week, but I'd typically leave on Thursday and not return until Monday night. Nobody knew how much class I was missing, and nobody cared. I really felt like I didn't exist in Madison, like I wasn't registering, that it was only back home that I had a full-blooded identity. In Madison, I was a ghost. It was like I'd all but given up on campus life within the first few weeks and wanted to circle back to the life I'd known, the one where I felt more comfortable.

It was my fault, of course, or at least it was because of who I was. And still am. Just a year or so ago, I went to a weekend conference of journalism educators in Lincoln, Nebraska, and I felt pretty much the same as I had a half-century ago on campus. As if I were the lone outsider in a hall full of strangers—the one who was alone, not talking with anyone, not joining with others to eat lunch, sticking to myself. Barely leaving an imprint.

To do otherwise would require me to get out of my comfort zone. As a college initiate, drinking a lot of beer also made me feel a little more comfortable, or at least less uptight. Maybe just oblivious to my own discomfort. Not that I would make conversation with strangers, but I would feel less strange being alone, less concerned with what others might think. I pretty much quit taking my meals in the dorm, the ones we had paid for, because it was too uncomfortable to put my tray on a table and join people I didn't know at some random table. It was just easier to be alone at a bar, with pizza or bratwurst and a few beers.

The money I didn't spend on brats and beer went to records, where I was going wider and deeper into my pursuit than ever, into jazz and blues and anything else that connected with my all-consuming passion for rock. I bought my first Miles Davis and Muddy Waters albums in Madison. I knew nobody who could match my record collection, and it was my one source of pride, and perhaps my identity. I was known, if known at all, as the guy who had all the records that he wouldn't let anyone else borrow. I didn't want fingerprints on them, or dust from albums left out of their sleeves. I was pretty particular about my possessions, a control freak before I ever knew the term.

Occasionally, some friends from high school would come visit, maybe with my brother Dick or even my girlfriend with them. I think this happened twice. They would think that Mad City lived up to its reputation, and we would have a great time, getting drunker than hell, closing the bars, weaving down the streets to find whatever car we had misplaced. This seemed more like the college experience I had been missing, but I could only have it with those who already knew me and I knew accepted me.

At least one of these boisterous visits culminated in my passing out in the hallway of my dorm. Someone had brought a gallon of very cheap wine, and we had started guzzling it. We knew better than to mix beer and wine, but sometimes what we knew went out the window when high spirits trumped common sense. And after the first glass or two, it tasted just like grape juice, and went down as easily.

And up even easier. There I was, on the floor of the hallway, face up, vomiting a geyser of red spew back onto my face. There would soon be a spate of rock-star deaths, and in at least a couple of cases the cause was rumored to be choking on their own vomit. Far better, we would joke, than choking on someone else's vomit.

So, is this when I discovered I had a drinking problem? Fat chance. If anything, I had a drinking solution to a much bigger problem, which was my abject misery and inability to live with that discomfort. That problem was me, though I hardly realized it at the time. Because my problem had always been everybody else—the kids my age who couldn't appreciate just how cool I was. The conservative suburbia in which I was raised within such a conventional family. The corporate future that looked like such a dead end. There was, as the Sex Pistols would later sing, "No future."

"Twenty years of schooling and they put you on the day shift"—Bob Dylan, "Subterranean Homesick Blues."

"Tradin' your hours for a handful of dimes," Jim Morrison, The Doors, "Five to One."

It wasn't me. It was the world that was fucked. And I couldn't wait to break free from whatever I could, to leave home for that radical state university to the north, where beer and free love would be flowing through the streets of Madison, Wisconsin, and I would be caught up in that current and swept away. Instead, I was standing on the sidelines.

A half-century later, I'm still a little amazed when college students find their way to AA, when they realize that something is seriously wrong with their drinking. I've always figured that students drank, and some of us drank a lot. Big deal. On the scale of what were considered serious problems with serious consequences for students when I was in school, drinking beer or even cheap jug wine barely registered on the scale. Society might soon be urging us to "Say No to Drugs," but nobody ever said say no to beer. You couldn't be an alcoholic unless you drank hard liquor, or so we'd thought.

Even marijuana was considered far more dangerous for societal consequences than beer, or booze in general. And the marijuana back in the hippie days was pretty weak compared with the designer strains to come. It sometimes took two or three joints to get much of a buzz. But if you were busted, you might be throwing away your life, or so we'd been warned.

What the hell. I was throwing my life away anyway. Going to college at the time meant nothing to me, other than a draft deferment. I was uncomfortable around people I didn't know. (I still am.). And all those people seemed to be comfortable around each other, or at least willing to make the effort. I didn't know how, or didn't care to make the effort. So I guess I convinced myself that this made me somehow superior, this refusal to make small talk with strangers, as if to do so were phony.

"Hiding in my room, safe within my tomb, I touch no one and no one touches me," Paul Simon, "I Am a Rock."

How precious! The Simon and Garfunkel anthem of maladjustment goes on, "I have my books, and my poetry to protect me." I had my books (yes, Beat poetry among them) and my record albums to protect me. I dove deeper into my musical obsession, opening new doors of aural exploration. I was insatiable for musical discovery, and I had a lot of time to explore. Time when other college kids were doing other college things—becoming friends, going to parties, getting drunk or stoned in a social setting, maybe even going to class.

In AA, you also learn of an illusion called "the geographical cure," the belief that if you just move somewhere else you will leave your problems behind. You won't, not if your problem is a drinking problem. Or, in my case, a living problem, an adjustment problem, an "inside job." Perhaps drinking was a surface symptom. The problem with the geographical cure is that you are always taking yourself with you, and if the problem is you, you aren't leaving it behind.

By the end of that freshman year, I was as eager to leave Madison behind forever as I had been to arrive just nine months earlier. The problem was I had nowhere to go. My girlfriend back home had finally broken up with me, tired of having a part-time, drop-in boyfriend who was away at college at least some of the time. And my parents had moved the family to Lincoln, Nebraska, where my dad's boss lived and had consolidated most of the company's activities. My mom went reluctantly (though she came to love Lincoln) and her widowed mother accompanied them, even more reluctantly. My brother Dick likely had it the toughest, since he would be transferring before his senior year in high school, leaving a serious relationship with his girlfriend behind.

And me? There was no way I'd return to Madison. There was nothing waiting for me back home in suburban Chicago—no girlfriend, no job, not even the family. To return there would have meant dropping out of college, losing my deferment and likely getting shipped to Vietnam. So my dad made me an offer I couldn't refuse. It seems that Nebraska had a very liberal policy for qualifying for in-state tuition, which he had researched. If I would transfer from Wisconsin to the University of Nebraska at Lincoln, and would live at home (rent-free), he would let me pocket the difference.

Because Wisconsin had been exorbitantly expensive for out-of-state tuition, that difference would be a few grand a semester—more than enough to convince me to leave radical, boozy Madison and become a halfhearted Nebraska Cornhusker. And it would give my parents the opportunity to monitor me, to make sure I was going to class and doing my homework. I would be more under their supervision than I had been since I'd first gotten my driver's license.

It would only be for a year, a year that would ensure that I once again felt disconnected from campus life. I would be living at home and just driving over for classes. I was biding my time, extending my limbo, not knowing what might come next and not really caring. Surprisingly, I enjoyed my year in Lincoln more than I had the one in Madison. I had my routine and my family and didn't feel so alone. Every afternoon, after class, I'd watch a rerun of *Perry Mason* before dinner and fall asleep in the big La-Z-Boy recliner (which is still in the front room where I type this, for sentimental reasons).

My parents were easy on me, knowing I'd been on my own and mainly concerned that I paid due diligence to my schoolwork. And my brothers became more interesting to me. Dick and I were similarly alone and isolated, biding our time until we could move back to Chicago (where he would return after college and still lives). Doug was the antithesis of me, outgoing and naturally popular, the mischief that he'd made when he was young now transformed into energy, vitality and the most natural athletic ability of the three of us—or, now, the five of us. David and Katie just made themselves at home in Lincoln, where Katie met her future husband as a schoolgirl and where they still live.

On the weekends, I'd go to the drive-in movies with a 12-pack of beer, with one of my siblings with me. Doug became willingly corrupted. Dick and I often ventured farther, often to Omaha, the closest place I could find anything approaching the record selection I'd known in Madison. Once we drove to Denver to see the Jefferson Airplane, who were much different and much better live than they were on album. We stayed at the Y, on the cheap.

Dick was still an exceptional tennis player, so he had those connections, but otherwise we continued exploring the music, books and politics we had brought from Chicago (and seemed to be in short supply in Lincoln). Doug had a lot more of a life—instantly popular with his fellow students, both boys and girls, involved with every sport and a standout. That he wanted to spend some time with me made me grateful. I didn't have much going on, though I didn't feel as bad about it as I had in Madison, where I was surrounded by others who seemed to have so much going on, and where I had felt invisible. Now, even within my immediate family, all of my siblings seemed to be living lives and making connections that were beyond me.

It was in Lincoln that made some sort of half-hearted decision to major in English, after flirting with psychology and sociology in Wisconsin. Why? Because Nebraska was supposed to be pretty good in English, at least in comparison with other disciplines. And I was pretty good at writing, always had been, and increasingly fond of reading—with no social life to distract me beyond the family household. This seemed like the easiest way forward toward a degree, the path of least resistance. And then I'd have to hope that the war was over, or the draft was. I wasn't thinking any farther into the future than that.

So, two years, two state schools, and I knew I'd be heading home for my third year. Home being the Chicago area, not only for me but for Dick, who would graduate from high school in spring and had also decided to go to college in Wisconsin (Beloit, a well-respected liberal arts school, where he would meet his future wife and friends with whom he's still in touch, and from which he would graduate, just like you're supposed to.) Home was where I still knew some people and knew my way around. There was simply no reason to start somewhere fresh, again, and feel the isolation that had afflicted me throughout my first two years of college. It was time to get on with my life, whatever life I'd had.

It was time to start fresh. Again. I had yet to hear the definition of insanity that I would learn in AA—doing the same thing over and over again and expecting a different result—but I had taken some of it to heart. No more college towns. No more campus culture. I would somehow make college fit into the kind of life I knew and where I felt comfortable rather than try again to insert myself into the conventional campus life.

12. Into the Great Wide Open

THROUGHOUT MY DRINKING LIFE AND well into my sobriety, I'd thought of this period as I entered my 20s as the big leap into adulthood. After spinning my wheels at two big universities over two years, as if in perpetual limbo, I was now lurching forward. Soon after returning to Chicago's western suburbs, I had my first apartment lease, a new college, a new job and, much sooner than you'd expect, a new wife. And then my first mortgage for a house in the suburbs. I would soon have my college degree and my master's degree. I would have my own business, which would lead me to the career that has since supported me for decades. I had new drugs—cocaine (like everybody else in the 70s) and amphetamines, which let me drink more. I was smoking between two and three packs of cigarettes a day, typically making my way through half a pack before finishing my obligatory morning coffee. I recognized even then that I had what I called an "addictive personality," that I was a person of compulsive routine and habit, and that some of those habits weren't necessarily healthy.

There's a lot here to, uh, "unpack," as we say in academic circles. And I have to admit that I barely recognize that guy, let alone connect his life with mine. Because by the end of that decade, by the time I turned 30, I had no wife, no business of my own, no steady job, and no clue what was next. Just as I had been at 20, but I was getting kind of old for this. Wasn't I?

From this distance, the line blurs between the first chapter of my adulthood and the last chapter of my adolescence. Getting married at 21, to a girl who was 18, seemed like an adult thing to do at the time, but it might have been the ultimate in youthful follies—borne of an innocent romanticism and the hope that something so impulsive could last forever. And my life through my 20s, drinking beer and smoking dope and listening to music obsessively, going to clubs and concerts and even making my living by doing so, seemed like an extension of how I had lived since high school. Even the record store we opened was like a teenage clubhouse, with beer in cups and bongs for sale. No adults allowed! You could live this life in perpetual adolescence, like Peter Pan in an acid flashback.

I didn't know then what has become increasingly obvious to me in retrospect, that my protracted adolescence wouldn't end until I was in my early 30s. And even then, even now, I can feel the fears, the insecurities, the irrational impulses of a teenager. There are parts of my rock-and-roll self that I have never outgrown, and, for better and worse, likely never will.

"Relieve me of the bondage of self," asks one AA prayer, and it has rung true with me since the first time I heard it. I can still feel the bondage of self as a palpable presence, a vice-like tension on my skull. I used to feel it much more often, and knew just how to ease it—with a few drinks and a joint. And with those two to three packs of cigarettes a day. But those were temporary salves for an existential wound. When you're incarcerated within the bondage of self, it can feel like a life sentence, with no parole.

Another problem, at least as AA insists, is that you stunt your emotional growth when you start relying on alcohol. I had started drinking at 13. When I returned to the Chicago suburbs at the age of 20, I was more than ready to leave my teens, but I was hardly prepared for what might happen next. I knew I couldn't stay in college forever. (Thank God.) I had no interest in adulthood as embodied by my parents—the commuting, the careerism, the lawn mowing, the wearing of Bermuda shorts and socks. So, here I was, a rebel without a clue (as the Replacements' Paul Westerberg sang and Tom Petty borrowed)—13 going on 23.

But at least I had some sense of purpose. Or at least a sense that I was moving forward, toward some next phase. Finding and renting my own apartment seemed like a semi-adult thing to do. Finding and enrolling in a small liberal-arts college (rather than the education factory of a state university, like the one where I now love teaching) seemed like another step forward. And getting a job doing something that I wanted to do—clerking in the record department of a big department store in another western suburb, reinforced that I was somehow forging my own life. After a series of random jobs—pumping gas, cooking burgers, delivering mail—this was a job where I was surrounded by music and would devote myself to selling it. It seemed like a higher calling. I'd spent the previous two years not working, except for summer jobs. My generous parents had wanted me to focus on school, not that I considered it much of a focus.

I was recently reading *Beatlebones*, by Kevin Barry, where I serendipitously stumbled upon this passage: "In the maelstrom rush of your twenties, in the campaign to selfhood and determination—in finding out who you are..." Exactly. That's where I was and what I was doing. Maybe everyone goes through this, but my maelstrom would generate tidal waves of tumultuous change, with aftershocks that would reverberate for decades. When I headed back to Chicago, I couldn't envision that the fresh-start decade would soon find me dropping out of college and then graduating not only from college but from grad school.

That it would soon find me getting married, buying a house, opening the record store, exchanging and developing a new identity based on coordinates that hadn't been part of that identity when the decade began. And that by the end of the decade, all of that would be lost again. I feel dizzy and shell-shocked just remembering it. But I had no idea at the time that this zigzag pattern would continue to mark my life, that every decade would find me ending on a note I couldn't have anticipated at the beginning—starting a new adventure in the process, one that would put me someplace by the end of the decade that I had couldn't have imagined at the start. There's absolutely no reason why new chapters in a life should align so well with new decades, but in my life they did. Nothing premeditated about any of it; only in retrospect did it seem to fit a pattern, a pattern befitting a guy born in 1950, smack dab in the middle of a century. Whether or not this is what life is like, it's what *my* life was like.

So, my 20s:. As long as there was a war and a draft, I would need to be in school, and North Central College in Chicago's western suburbia was as good a refuge as any. I had never seen it or heard of it, but I learned it was known mainly for cross-country running (of little interest with my smoking) and that it was decent academically. I registered as an English major, because that is what I'd become in Nebraska. I liked to read, and I knew how to write, though writing had yet to bring me any pleasure or deeper commitment. I still didn't talk in class or make friends—I was a commuter student to a campus where most other students lived—but I somehow fell under the wing of a professor who thought I had some critical chops and an effective writing style. Her support would prove crucial as I continued my college education and tried to figure out just who I was and where I fit. She taught me how to enrich my life through novels, not merely pass the time.

But school was then of far less concern to me than whatever was happening in my personal life, my real life, away from campus. When I had returned to the Chicago area, the holy grail was finding a girlfriend. I needed one, to complete myself. And I had learned how difficult if was to sustain a long-term relationship when I was at college. After my high-school girlfriend had dumped me while I was in Madison, I'd had a couple of other flings, girls I'd known in the western suburbs, and had found sustaining anything long-term while I was in exile in Nebraska to be futile.

Now, I was somehow full of hope. I would be home, and staying home. I figured that as soon as I settled in, I would be able to settle down with someone. Though I had long cast myself as the brooding loner, living on the edge, I always needed an ally in this us-against-the-world scenario. I needed someone who saw the value in me that I'm not sure I always saw in myself, and whom I could present to the outside world as intrinsic evidence of that validation.

Without someone else, I had always felt incomplete, hollow inside. Which was okay during that thoroughly hollow year in Lincoln, when I never really connected with anyone outside my family anyway. It was just assumed, or at least I assumed, that this was a transitional year, and that after I'd waited it out I could resume something that approximated real life. I read my way through it, drank my way through it, napped my way through it. Listened to a whole lot of music, and went to the rare concert that came to Lincoln or Omaha. I was just doing time.

So now it was time to fill that hole in the center of my identity, where a girlfriend would complete me. Whoever she was, she would provide evidence to the outside world that someone more attractive than I thought myself to be had somehow been attracted by me, however surly and inscrutable I was. That someone else recognized something in me that I wasn't sure I recognized in myself, an insecurity that extended to sexual validation. And this would inevitably be someone younger than me, with that inherent imbalance of power, because why would someone my age want to be with someone as needy as me? And as controlling.

Plainly, this was all about me. Always had been. Any girl who submitted to this serial monogamist found that the role had been written as supporting actress, or sidekick, to someone who demanded top billing. If she were with me, my friends (few as they were) would be our friends. My music would be our music. My priorities would be our priorities. We would do what I wanted to do, go where I wanted to go.

I got my way by demanding it. Not vocally, for that would be immature. But by showing through silence and body language how I felt when I was displeased. I would pout, silently. And this not only happened when someone close to me did something I didn't like; it was even more pronounced when she hadn't read my mind to discover what would please me. Like a soul mate would. I was pretty demanding, without vocally demanding much.

In some ways, this was even more insidious. Or I was. I wanted someone who could anticipate what I wanted even when I didn't know. And when I didn't get it, I would become silent and isolated, wait for her to ask me what was wrong, as if I could tell her. At parties, I would disappear into another room, wait for her to realize I was missing and to come find me, coax me back. All of this was twisted somewhere inside me, and my soul mate would have to be able to untangle it. Whoever she was.

How easy would it be to find someone to submit to this? Easier than you might think, at least in the early 70s, when there was more pressure to pair up than there seems to be now. To a high school girl with her own insecurities, a college guy, even one like me, could be a catch. Here is what I had that I could trade for all that I needed: I was a couple years older, more experienced. I was smart, and clever enough to convince them that I was smarter than they were, even if I wasn't. I was plugged into popular culture, and popular music in particular, and I was politically very aware. I could show a suburban girl a whole new world in the city, or what little I knew of it. And I was monogamously faithful, even suffocatingly so, until my oppressive presence would simply wear some poor girl out.

So I needed to find my next target, or victim. With brother Dick joining me on the move back to the Chicago area, mainly because he still had a girlfriend there, I had my first connection. His girlfriend had a friend who was very attractive, bright and outgoing. One of the popular girls, a former cheerleader. And she seemed very interested in meeting me. She also had a boyfriend, but that was her issue, and she soon dealt with it.

Within a couple weeks, she and I were inseparable, joined at the hip, while still getting to know each other. Within a month, she was an integral part of my identity. Two years later, she was my wife, a precocious high school graduate who seemed wiser than her years while I seemed emotionally stunted in mine. And very needy. All I know is that I was as clueless about my destiny as I was determined to have one. And this was the next chapter.

Partly, I blame literature. Once I made my commitment to the holy grail of a lit major, I was immersed in the Russians, *The Brothers Karamazov* in particular, a novel that seemed to demand that youngish men make huge decisions that would forge their fate irrevocably. Character is destiny. And, God knows, I was a character. Or determined to become one.

As my soon-to-be teenage bride was nearing her high-school graduation, her father accepted a transfer and would be moving their family to Florida. She was somehow still unclear about college, especially the financial aspects, despite sterling grades. With her family leaving, I suppose she could have officially moved into my apartment, where she was spending so much of her time anyway. She could have gone to Florida and plotted her next move from there.

But neither of us could bear the thought of that separation, and her devoutly Catholic family wouldn't have been able to accept her "living in sin." Sure, things could have worked themselves out. She could have gotten a job, an apartment, a roommate or two. But the Brothers K had convinced me that this was the turning point, the time to throw caution to the wind. It was time for the grand gesture, of the heart, not the head.

We would marry—me right after turning 21, she at 18.

You can probably see where this is going. I couldn't, at least not then. As Chuck Berry once sang, "It was a teenage wedding, and the old folks wished them well." The old folks likely knew better, or should have, but they hoped for the best. And I had the first sign of my new, mature identity to present to the world—married man. For better or worse. Till death do us part.

I'm trying to remember whether our wedding was the first I'd ever attended. None of my friends had gotten married, and we married before her older brother had. He was an amateur photographer with artistic aspirations, and was entrusted with shooting the wedding and aftermath. None of the photos turned out. The reception was in her parents' back yard, to save money. The only present I remember was a sheet of blotter acid from a long-haired, spaced-out friend, for some honeymoon tripping. I also remember that my dad's youngest sister was wearing a dress that scandalized the other adults, everything hanging out, as if she were more of a free spirit than the kids who were my friends. My mom never let my dad forget that.

None of us had any idea what we were doing.

I don't want to minimize my starter marriage, but neither do I want to open old wounds, excavate old grudges, point any fingers, except at myself. I had invested a whole lot in the sexual attraction that had brought us together, and what it represented. Sex and alcohol were both forbidden fruit to a guy my age, and certainly hers, so there was the thrill of getting away with something. We'd had sex whenever we could, knowing that so much of the time we couldn't.

Now, we were married, and legal, and we could, all the time. So who cared? The sex that had been such a rebellious act had become a sign of domesticity, even an obligation. I really liked her a lot, and liked the way she represented us to the world, but I was unprepared for being around someone else all the time. Yeah, we'd been inseparable, but that was still part of the chase. Now we were together, forever. And I was feeling claustrophobic.

Now what do I do? Have another beer.

Any attempt I made to distance myself made her attempt to close that distance, as a good wife should. (Or so she thought, or we both did.) The quieter I was, the more vocal she became, and the needier she seemed, at least to me. It was like my mom and dad all over again, the only marriage model I had, the relentlessly expressive and emotional wife and the increasingly reserved husband. So I built the wall the way my dad had—drank beer every night, fell asleep on the couch.

But if every day were the same, my wife would be trapped in a sexless marriage, and I couldn't have that. So there was the special-occasion recreation, the LSD that would dissolve that bondage of self, at least for a long night, and bring me closer to her and whoever else was tripping with us. This could be unpredictable, an adventure, but the adventure typically involved my letting down my sexual guard and melting into my wife.

There was also speed, increasingly on weekends, cheap tablets of white cross, gobbled by the handful. And relentlessly reliable. Amphetamines made me mindlessly horny, as turned on as my natural state was turned off. So, throw the various pharmaceuticals into the mix, and there was enough sex that it could almost pass for a normal relationship, whatever that was. And reinforce my assumption that my body was a chemistry experiment, and that however I wanted to feel, there was a pill, a puff, a swallow, that would make me feel it.

If I was a prisoner to the bondage of self, self-medication was my temporary escape. There was nicotine to relax, a couple packs of Marlboros a day. Two cokes in the morning, after a few cups of coffee, to get me started. And then the beer at night. Every day the same, like Groundhog Day. These habits, these rituals, were who I was.

Meanwhile, I was starting to extend that identity, one that I could present to the outside world, something more substantial than the inner hollowness I felt. I was a husband. I was a student, a much better one since my conversion to the gospel of literature. I was a record store clerk, a really good one, one who knew more about the music we sold than just about anyone else could. Music was my obsession; my life was music and literature. And marriage. And getting stoned at concerts, and drinking beer at the end of every day.

Nobody at the time would have said I had a drinking problem. Others drank more, and drank to get drunk. I didn't. Except on weekends. Otherwise, I drank daily but responsibly, maybe a couple beers with dinner and a couple after. According to the conventional wisdom of the era, alcoholics drank pint bottles in paper bags. Not beer.

The drugs were considered more problematic, illegal as well as dangerous. Prison was a major threat, and might have been a deterrent to a person without such a stake in his rebel image. Smoking dope was a much bigger deal at the time than, say, driving drunk. But as a guy who fancied himself living on the edge, I wasn't really worried about drug laws. Or drinking and driving. Or, now, even pregnancy, which had previously been more of a concern, with a monthly reprieve.

As a married man, I was still piecing together the identity I would assume, the life I could envision. After graduating from college as an English major, a degree that led nowhere financially, at least as far as I could see, I added two more major pieces to the puzzle. Since I was now pretty much managing a record store—doing all the ordering and stocking, handling everything but the finances—I decided it was time to open my own. My young wife supported the decision. She always did. My dad made the initial investment (and never pushed to get it repaid).

Why open our own store? It was time to grow up. I felt under-appreciated and undervalued where I worked, and saw no way for that situation to improve. I couldn't have a career clerking for somebody else. I wanted all the perks that came with running my own store. I wanted to get my records earlier than everyone else, and free. I wanted the concert tickets that record labels would provide, better ones than I could buy. As with the rest of my life, I wanted to be running the whole show. And if I never anticipated doing this for the rest of my life, this seemed like a feasible step toward some workable version of adulthood. Whatever that might be.

If there are intimacy issues in a marriage, working together as well as living together isn't the best strategy for resolving them. But my wife would be a great asset at the store—far more outgoing than

I was. We turned it into a sort of clubhouse, a place where music lovers and hangers on could linger and listen. Kind of like a coffee shop, but with beer, from the refrigerator in the back room, and then poured into red cups. Johnny B. Goode Records & Stuff—the stuff was drug paraphernalia, rolling papers and bongs and the like.

I would later learn that I had no instinct for being an entrepreneur—no business sense, no stomach for working without a safety net. We did fine with the store, because the 1970s were a boom time in the music business, and I knew enough about music to offset everything I didn't know about running a business. But those days when there were few customers and little money, as happened with any suburban downtown business, seemed to deepen the hole in my soul. Which I then tried to fill with more beer, to stop my mind from whirring and doubting. And which reinforced the wall between husband and wife.

God knows, she did everything in her power to make me feel loved, to let me know how much she appreciated me. Birthdays in particular were an occasion for the grand, over-the-top gesture. For one birthday, she hired a blues piano player, a recording artist, and she and my brother Dick facilitated this great surprise party, bringing in the blind piano player and a piano, for a celebration I could never forget.

For another, she directed me to look in the garage, where there was a gleaming new motorcycle. I had always wanted one—it fit the rebel image. I had never ridden one. Now I had my own. I was floored, dumbstruck by the extravagance. How could I thank her enough? I couldn't, but she didn't seem to care. Seeing me happy, however briefly, without reservation, was its own reward.

And though I recognized that I had some insecurities to face, some inner demons to conquer, my life had come to feel more rewarding than not. With my emerging identity as the music guy, the guy with the record store, I started feeling connected to a lot more people than I ever had before. Many of the best friends I made during that period started as customers, people who wanted my recommendations on music and then deepened the bond over months to go to concerts together, go to each other's houses and listen to music and get stoned together. We even joined a mixed bowling league with a couple I'd met in the store—get drunk while bowling and then stoned afterward. After spending my first two college years practically in an isolation booth, I now had friends and customers and connections all over the place. I was no longer the campus ghost; I was the very visible record store guy.

The store forged an alliance of sorts with a nearby arts gallery started by an informal community of painters and photographers. One of their members designed the Johnny B. Goode logo for our store; others became good friends and customers. One became one of my best drinking buddies, a former Marine turned photographer who still slept with a pistol under his pillow and joked about hippies and all that "free love shit" he'd missed out on when he was in Vietnam. (I'd missed out too, but less dramatically.) He looked for fights on weekends when we hit the working men's bars, what hipsters now call "dive bars." I thought he might be an alcoholic, but he had a depth of experience that was different from mine. If there was a toxicity within such friendships, at least I had friends.

When the record store closed on weekend nights, the gathering would sometimes shift to the gallery, where lively discussion and debate, for the sport of it, would last well into the early morning. I loved the friendly arguing, for the hell of it, the sense of being smart it reinforced in me, the engagement with ideas that I had missed since graduating (though I had so rarely engaged with others in college). I found I missed school, which I had resisted before I became enraptured with the formal study of literature. These people at the gallery were kindred spirits, as passionate about art as I was about rock and literature, and as we all were about politics.

I wanted academic validation, proof that I could hold my own at a higher level than the no-name school that had given me my degree. So I applied at the venerable University of Chicago, and I was accepted. It was close enough so I could commute, it offered a master's program in literature that took only a year to complete, and it would give me an academic merit badge.

I did fine, though again I don't remember ever talking in class, and I would make much more of the opportunity now than I did then. I hadn't realized that taking a course on James Joyce from visiting professor Richard Ellman was akin to studying Elvis with Peter Guralnick. But I made it through *Ulysses* with more understanding than I would have attained on my own, and reinforced a lifelong love for *Dubliners*.

My first day in class, there was a shock of recognition when I heard a name called that I remembered from high school, and was surprised when I turned to see that it was she. She had been another one of the pretty, popular ones, whose path rarely crossed mine once I had decided that it was easier to excel as an outcast. But now we were in the same program, and both still living in the same western suburbs, so it wasn't long before we were car pooling.

We had a lot of time to talk on those drives, and I was surprised to learn that she had found high school as painful as I had, that she had never felt she really fit. Rather than attempt to navigate Chicago's notorious rush hour (actually hours, from 3-7 on the drive home), we'd typically kill a couple hours at the bar near campus favored by English majors. By the time we left, I wasn't in a condition that I would now consider safe to drive. But drive I did, convinced then that I was actually more careful after I'd been drinking, so as not to get pulled over. And I learned a lesson from her that I would later hear articulated in AA: "Don't judge your insides by somebody else's outsides"—that is, don't assume a pretty, popular girl had it any better than you did.

Once I had completed my graduate degree and had steeped myself in lit crit, I wasn't quite ready to return full-time to the record store in suburbia. I had higher aspirations, inflamed by higher education. I had some writing muscles that I wanted to continue flexing. Something to keep my mind busy. Something in addition to the record store, not instead of, though I'd figured the record store wasn't my lifelong destiny and retirement package. All I knew was that I had proved to myself that I was a pretty smart guy and a pretty good writer. If I found something to write about, maybe I could find somebody to publish me. I would have much preferred to have written the Great American Novel. But I didn't have it in me. I still wasn't sure just what I had in me.

13. Forging New Identities

IF THERE'S ONE THING I'VE learned in this life, it's that often you don't really know where you're going until you find yourself there. And wonder how you got there. All I know is that there was no master plan (never has been, never will be) and that one thing led to another. All I know is that I was determined to show that I was exceptional, which was mainly why I applied to a grad school that only took exceptional students. I was determined to show the world. To show myself. But who was this "I"? And exceptional *how*? Exceptionally *what*? Without a clue, I muddled ahead.

Yes, I had shown myself to be someone who would test limits and push toward the extremes. Through my teens, I had distinguished myself by smoking cigarettes and dope, drinking beer, becoming more deeply obsessive about cultish rock and roll, becoming more sexually active, fancying myself some sort of political radical and otherwise not giving a fuck. Yet I really wasn't much different from so many others who found their identities forged by and reflected in the rock and radical '60s.

You probably knew somebody like me, or many somebodies. If you were of the same age at the same time, maybe you were the same guy. (Or girl, though I considered girls a whole different species back then. And most of them weren't much interested in what I was. Or interested in me.)

Through my first two years of college, I had gone off the rails. I had become truly exceptional in ways that nobody would ever want to be. Exceptionally isolated and disconnected, alone and anonymous on a campus of thousands. Either I had gone haywire, or haywire had finally caught up with me.

As soon as I had the chance, I had started over, changed course, had come home and begun to assemble the pieces of the identity that would represent me, at least for a while. I had gotten married, younger than anyone I knew who didn't have a baby on the way. I had become passionate about reading, rather than continuing as the guy who had just done well enough in school to stay out of the draft.

And I had opened my own record store. Bet you don't know anybody who did that. Though, at the time, such counterculture entrepreneurism was becoming more common, as a way to avoid succumbing to the slow death of corporate life. Or what we still called "straight life." Within blocks of my store, one guy my age had a small bookshop, another a head shop, yet another a hip clothing boutique. None of those businesses lasted as long as mine.

I then earned a graduate degree at a top university, a very selective one. This was exceptional since, back then, most folks stopped with their BAs. So I was distinguishing myself in different ways, with an adult diploma, an adult marriage, an adult business. It was time to put away childish things.

And maybe my family in Lincoln was among them. Still the oldest of five kids, I was now a young adult—a married man—no longer under my parents' control or supervision. I think they were relieved at that, since we had survived my "don't ask, don't tell" adolescence, and they hadn't really wanted to know more than they needed to. Now we could talk to each other, relate to each other, like grownups would. I appreciated that, particularly with my dad, whom I accepted as the voice of reason in the way I never was, truly an adult in the ways I would never be. He was then thirty years younger than I am now. The mind boggles.

The move to Lincoln had lifted the family into a higher-income bracket, particularly after his company was sold and he was retained through a "key man" option. Early retirement was on the horizon. Maybe by 50 or shortly after. He and Mom were already talking about the places they would go, the cruises they would take. They had mentioned San Diego for some reason as the place they would go in retirement. For now, though, they still had three kids at home, our siblings who were growing up as Lincolnites (Lincolnians?). For them, there was more privilege, less want than there had been for Dick and me. Not that we'd wanted all that much, but now there was a boat on the lake, and water skis. There were more cars in the driveway, better ones. The house would become party central whenever my parents dared to leave Doug on his own, a tradition that he would pass along to David and Katie. Most of my family took to Lincoln, and made it their home, a central part of who they were. Unlike Dick and me, who would be forever Chicagoans.

My dad, who remains my model of mature adulthood, had always been responsibly prudent with money. But now he had enough of a cushion that he started to loosen up. The seed money for my record store seemed more like a gift than a loan. He was paying for all of Dick's college, as he had for me and would for the others. When my car gave out, he gave me another. And then he decided to take everyone on what would be a truly extravagant vacation—certainly in comparison with those summer family visits I had outgrown. He would fly all of us to Europe and pay for everything, the first experience across the Atlantic for any of us.

I had excused myself from family vacations since I was old enough to drive, preferring the house to myself (and whoever wanted to party with me) to traveling with the family. My wife was of course included in this generous invitation, and she would not only certify my adulthood as someone who would have more freedom than parental supervision on the trip, she would serve as refuge and ally, for retreat into our own room whenever tensions arose, sometimes among siblings but mainly between our parents. She sometimes seemed to fit in better with my family than I did, as she did in most social situations. It's a cliché to refer to your wife as "my better half," but now that we were considered a unit, she plainly was, in social settings at least. It was easy to like her; with me, you had to work at it.

Whatever my dad had envisioned, the trip seemed like a disaster at the start, when our mom seemed as committed to disruption as my dad was determined to have the time of our lives. A few hours after our frazzled flight and arrival, doing our best to resemble one big happy family, she tearfully announced that she wanted to go home. *Now.* She said my dad had never cared about how depressed she felt, and that he refused to allow her to get therapy because it would reflect badly on the family.

He replied, soft-spoken as always in response to her higher decibels, that this wasn't true. He made it seem like this was all in her head, which was partly what she had implied at the start. Somehow, peace was restored, or at least a temporary cease-fire, and she stayed rather than leaving as threatened, and we proceeded on one of those whirlwind bus tours without the subject being broached again.

I'm not sure whether things had gotten worse between them, whether leaving her home in Chicago suburbia for Lincoln had intensified my mother's instability, or if I was just unaccustomed to being around them so much. But being married made me awfully grateful that my own stability didn't depend on theirs. The rest of my siblings just seemed to accept this as business as usual between my parents. Something would set Mom off. Dad would provide the calming presence. Repeat. At night, we'd all drink, at least those of us who were old enough, and some of us who weren't.

I remember David as being particularly precocious on that trip, going out drinking with us while our parents were elsewhere, downing more beer than he could handle, slipping the amused waitress a slip of paper with our hotel and his room number on it. And then vomiting in the street as we staggered home. He may have been 14, not old enough to drive legally back home, let alone drink. I loved being in Europe, soaking up the culture and food and the beer, and vowed to return soon. Though by the time I did, more than a decade later, I seemed like a whole different person, living a whole different life.

In the meantime, I felt like my life was better than it had been. Look at me! A wife that everyone liked and some envied. A good business selling music that I loved. Our record company reps who came to the store to take orders seemed to really like us, a couple of kids who were so obviously excited to be on the periphery of the music business. They showered us with promo records (freebies to play in the store), posters, concert tickets and invites to the artist parties that were so frequent when the industry was flush.

In addition to the feeling of privilege that such a meet-and-greet or listening reception entailed, I took full advantage of the expansive buffet and open bar. What was snack food to others became dinner to us (plate after plate of those riblets, cheese cubes and bacon-wrapped thingies), while I drank all the Heineken I could manage but otherwise could not afford. More than seeing how the other half lived, I learned to drink how the other half drank, in quality as well as quantity. I packed it away like there was no tomorrow, though tomorrow there might well be another party, or at least next week.

It was an intoxicating experience, on a number of levels. I no longer felt so much like I was on the outside looking in, a perspective I'd had all my life. Now I was becoming something of an insider. I wanted more.

"Rock critic" had hardly seemed like a career path a few years earlier, when it was mainly restricted to semi-underground rags like *Crawdaddy* and *Rolling Stone*, which I read avidly to discover music I couldn't hear on the radio. By the mid-70s, however, most newspapers at decent-sized cities deemed it necessary to cover rock, and often to have someone assigned to that specific beat.

Rock had gotten so big post-Woodstock—big impact, big business. It could no longer be dismissed as a passing fad, or treated as a freak-show novelty. What had once been kids' stuff had become mainstream culture. Its concert audiences would soon fill baseball and football stadiums, and its record sales would reach previously unimagined levels of mega-platinum. We were on the verge of *Frampton Comes Alive,* Fleetwood Mac's *Rumours, Saturday Night Fever.*

Much of the rock coverage in the daily newspapers wasn't much good. Somebody who actually knew something about the music would really stand out, because more often it seemed as if the youngest person in the features department (though I didn't know it was called that then) had just been handed that job. Like later when we would assume that anyone younger just had to know more about the Internet and social media, that's how it seemed with rock journalism back then.

In Chicago, I read and envied John Milward, who had been distinguishing himself at the alternative-weekly *Reader* as an ambitiously literate writer who was both passionate and knowledgeable about the music. When the *Chicago Daily News*, the best of the dailies, decided to launch a weekly section aimed at youth culture, it hired

Milward as its rock guy. Such a move not only showed that there was a path of upward mobility in rock writing, it left a void at the *Reader*.

I kept monitoring the situation, reading all four dailies as I had for years (first for the sports coverage, now for the pop culture as well) and also seeing who the *Reader* would find to take Milward's place. Nobody regular stepped in, and often the weekly had nothing about music at all. There was opportunity here.

I had spent my lifetime preparing for this opportunity without even knowing it, developing an encyclopedic knowledge of the music that obsessed me, honing my critical skills through listening and reading (and maybe even taking lit crit courses at UC), finding some sort of voice as a writer. There was nothing premeditated about any of this—you would never submerge yourself this deeply if it were simply job prep. This was my life, and now it appeared that there might be a way to get paid for it.

Before I could (or at least did) act on this impulse, we received news from out of the blue that would shatter my life. My dad had gone to the doctor with recurring headaches, which seemed like a minor affliction for a guy who had never been sick a day in his life. It turned out that he had a brain tumor, a large one, the severity of which they wouldn't know until they operated. But it didn't sound good, didn't look good.

And it wasn't. When they got in there, they said this was terminal, that he had six months to live. Some close friends urged him to explore experimental drugs in Mexico, but he wasn't the type to seek desperate measures. To the contrary, he seemed calmer and more accepting through the whole ordeal than any of the rest of us. It was a lesson of death, and of life's preparation for it, that has stayed with me ever since. We really have no idea what is going to happen. And whatever it is, you accept it with grace.

And not merely with grace, he decided we would all take another extravagant vacation together, in the months he had left, this time to Hawaii. And we really did have a ball, despite the shroud of mortality, the inevitability we were facing.

Now that I have fathered two daughters who will forever be my baby girls, and whose emancipation has also generated occasional tension, I have a different perspective on the struggles of the early 20s. And as I consider where we all were—at least the three brothers who were the oldest of five—I realize that what I considered my particularly rocky road on the way toward a provisional identity simply goes with the territory.

Here's what Dick experienced in the years after graduating from college: Became a high school English teacher, went to work for a Chicago blues label, enrolled in law school at the University of Chicago. Became engaged to a woman whom he'd known at Beloit but hadn't dated until both returned home to Chicago suburbia. Married that January, following our dad's diagnosis. Also Dick became Richard, having changed from Dick the name by which he has been known from his 20s on. He's the first in our family who decided he had a drinking problem, that he had become too reliant. He quit, decades ago, though I didn't think at the time that his drinking had been a problem. He drank way less than I did. And he's never gone the 12-step, AA route, which he seems to consider kind of glib in its self-help spirituality.

Doug married at around the same age I had, before Richard did. He dropped out of college, as I had, but never went back. He had a lousy experience with a lawn-care operation in which our dad had invested, until he quit that and went back to working in bars. Like me with the record store, he went from working in a bar to owning one, and then two. He blazed a trail of his own and has achieved a level of financial security I envy. He's also one of only two of the five of us who still drinks, but not like he (or I) used to.

So each of the three of us had so many balls in the air, as far as identity and destiny were concerned, into our twenties. And then we each found ourselves on some career path from which we have not wavered—Richard's still a lawyer, Doug still owns bars, I am plainly still writing—before turning 30. After our dad died, when it was time that we ourselves had to become adults. Our dad's death was equally profound and pivotal, and painful, for David and Katie, and they grew up faster as well, but they still had their teens to navigate.

Now there was only one parent left, and she could not be the one to guide us, take care of us. We would need to take care of her—more or less, some of us more (thanks, Katie!), some less. But the way our dad had faced death, with a trip to Honolulu that was a celebration of our life as a family, with a stoicism and good humor and not much real suffering (that he shared, at least) until the last few days, he became even more of an example to all of us of how to deal with the things that really mattered, and how to put everything else in perspective.

As I struggled with his death, I became a different person (again). I quit smoking cigarettes, a habit that had approached three packs a day. Not because cigarettes had caused his cancer, though he had once smoked heavily himself before switching to a pipe because of the Surgeon General. No, this was an existential decision, an extension of my literary self. Life was short, and I didn't want to spend any more of it enslaved to this particular habit. I only really enjoyed a handful of cigarettes a day, after meals or the occasional sex, with my coffee, a few others. The rest were just addiction. Just like I would later recognize with my drinking, I was an all or nothing guy, a heavy smoker or not a smoker at all. A drinker or not a drinker.

The new guy who didn't smoke would need new habits to reinforce this decision. I quit going to bars, even to hear music for awhile, because bars were where I smoked more and everyone else did. I saved the money I would have spent on cigarettes, a couple cartons a week, to treat myself to something I couldn't afford otherwise. I ate ice cream. And I started running, jogging, something of a national craze at the time, in order to clear my lungs and make me feel all the better about breathing through them. Running for a half-hour or so each morning, around three miles, became a kind of meditation for me, before I had ever experimented with meditation. I would find my mind clearing and I would be thinking about nothing at all, not even about running, on the prairie path that ran through the woods near my home and away from any traffic.

One thing leads to another. It was the running that led to my writing, just as the quitting smoking had led to my running, just as my dad's death led to my quitting smoking. It all connected in retrospect, though none of this had been premeditated. But I found that a half-hour was about the right span for three or four paragraphs to compose themselves in my head, and that once I got done running, I could type them out—not writing so much as transcribing.

The next morning, I could reread what I had written the previous day, revise and then run again and add another three or four graphs. At the end of three or four days, I would have a finished piece, ready to submit. And this was how I became a writer for the *Chicago Reader*, and soon its de facto rock critic.

The first piece I wrote this way that the *Reader* published was a review of Graham Parker's third album. My dad had died that spring, just two weeks shy of his 50th birthday. My *Reader* debut occurred that fall. I had written a short note of introduction, put a stamp on the envelope and sent it to them. Without any communication, they published it within a couple weeks and then sent me a check. Seventy-five bucks, if memory serves. The most exciting freelance check I would ever receive, and more than you're likely to get for a freelance album review 40 years later, if you can find anyone to pay you anything. Digital technology has returned us full circle, back to a time when it's hard to imagine sustaining a career by writing about music. (Why should anyone pay the cow when they can get the milk for free?)

But getting paid and published for that first piece was easy, so I sent them another one, a somewhat longer review of Cheap Trick's second album. And waited, for weeks, and then months. When nothing appeared, I figured my fledgling freelance association with the *Reader* was over. It turned out that I had been very lucky, because the *Reader*'s editors really liked Graham Parker. And they were indifferent toward Rockford's Cheap Trick, who had yet to break big nationally and were still more of a powerhouse in the suburbs and along the Illinois-Wisconsin bar circuit than they were in the city.

I'd pretty much forgotten about the submission when one week the *Reader* surprised me by running it as a feature, with a bunch of photos, rather than a review with a stamp-sized album cover. And subsequently paid me double what I'd gotten the first time. From then on, I would frame what I'd write as features or columns—what newspapers would call "think pieces" or "thumbsuckers" when they didn't include interviewing—and from then on pretty much everything I wrote for the *Reader* was published pretty much the week I submitted it, which was pretty much once a week, for the next three years.

This routine became the focus of my life, its rhythms my rhythms. I soon learned that anything the *Reader* had by Tuesday could be printed and on the street that Thursday. So I started driving my typewritten stories to the city rather than trusting the mails, earning myself a couple days' leeway in the process. I would go hear some music on Thursday or Friday, even Saturday, and then do my writing over three or four days, three or four or more paragraphs a day after my habitual morning run, then finish Tuesday morning, drive it to the *Reader* Tuesday afternoon. Repeat. The day after finishing and submitting one I would be thinking about the next. Even back then, I have always been a creature of extreme habit, of ritual and repetition.

I was still working and living in the suburbs, but my real life was in the city, where the *Reader* was, where most of the music I wrote about for the *Reader* was and where the larger circle of connections was that I began to develop through the *Reader*—club bookers and publicists, bands, fellow writers, fellow music fans who were *Reader* readers and with whom I became friends. All of this was a whole new world to me.

I also began drinking more, at least partly because I was out in public more. Cigarettes had been my nervous tic, something to do with my hands when I was uncomfortable around people, doing something, smoking, when I was otherwise doing nothing. Drinking became the replacement, so I always had a bottle or glass of beer in my hand rather than that cigarette, swallowing rather than inhaling, one after the other when I was around people and uncomfortable.

Nervous habit. My wife would often argue that I was drunk, and that I should let her drive home. Sometimes I did.

14. Spinning Wheel

My wife and I still had our record store together in the suburbs. We still had a house together in the suburbs, our second, both bought during an era when houses were comparatively cheap (though double-digit interest was the rule), when the record business was booming and when we weren't all that picky. And she was still very much a part of my social life and persona—still my better half, the one who could easily make conversation with those she didn't know and charm most of those with whom she came in contact. But she was also developing a life of her own, in the suburbs, after she received her BA (from the same college I had) and started teaching high school near the college which was near our home.

Truth be told, much of my life by then was spent living in my head, very much alone, focused obsessively on what I was writing, what I would be writing next, what might be coming along to write about after that. The writing itself—which included the morning revision of previous graphs, then the running in which new ones formed, then the typing to transcribe what had been written in my head while running—never took more than an hour or two. But the process of writing filled my head all day. It still does.

The *Reader* people had become more curious about me, about us, and we became a part of that social circle, at least on the periphery. Turns out the film critic had been in one of my classes at the University of Chicago, a course on the detective novel (which I had known little about, going in), where he had been the star pupil, practically considered an equal by the professor, and I had been such a nonentity that I was surprised he remembered me.

I also met Lloyd Sachs, who became my lifelong friend. He had a master's degree in journalism from Medill, and he wrote about everything that interested me—movies, books, music, the media. He had freelanced some for the *Sun-Times* and for *Rolling Stone*, as well as the *Reader*. We were both big sports fans and baseball fans in particular (he as obsessed with the Giants as I was with the Cubs). He had been friends with Milward, the *Reader*'s previous rock guy, and now became friends with me. And still is, for which I am grateful.

The *Reader* validated me in a whole different way than my marriage had, and it gave me a professional identity I could adopt as my own. At the time, journalism in Chicago was known both for its drinking and its spirited competition. My brother Richard promised me that when I landed my first *Reader* cover story, he would take me on an evening's tour of all the well-known journalist bars—Riccardo's, the Billy Goat, O' Rourke's and last call at the Old Town Ale House, the places made legendary by such raucous drunks as Mike Royko (who got meaner when he drank) and Roger Ebert (who just got louder). It was a rite of passage—I now belonged. In my mind at least—those guys wouldn't have known me from Adam.

I didn't know then that the *Reader*, where so many were single and creatively free-spirited, was also a Peyton Place of romantic entanglements, past and present, and that it would take some time to figure out who had slept with whom and when. I also had no idea how much my wife had charmed one of the four college classmates who had started the alternative weekly and still worked there and owned it. She had also long sought some validation, felt some insecurity, and as my life turned more and more inward, the habits and obsessions of writing that didn't include her, she radiated outward. Married to a shell of a man like me, who wouldn't?

Her secret boyfriend (and maybe not the first) was unmarried, but very much part of a couple with another woman who worked at the *Reader*. She apparently became suspicious long before I did, because I was pretty oblivious. It wasn't until I was on a trip through Texas and Louisiana—my first visit to Austin and the Broken Spoke, my first time at a crawfish boil in Cajun country—that she told me tentatively on the phone that she didn't feel like she wanted to be married to me any longer.

I was stunned, flabbergasted. Everything had been going so well, at least on the surface. We had coexisted better than my mother and father had, and they had stayed together. I flew home as quickly as I could book a flight that night from Baton Rouge, determined to do whatever it might take to save my marriage. When she picked me up at the airport, it was if we were both experiencing this unexpected mishap together. No other person was mentioned; she had just come to feel like she could not be married anymore. Not married to me.

She agreed to marriage counseling, which seemed like a positive step, until we went. The marriage counselor quickly assumed what I had never suspected—that there was another man involved. And, moreover, that it was all my fault, that I had closed myself off to my wife and she had reacted the way a woman would in that situation. At least that was what I heard, and it made me very defensive. I was moralistically, rigidly, in the right. Whatever I had done, she had done wrong, had broken her vows.

It was an untenable position, wanting her back, yet deep down unable to forgive her, knowing I would be throwing it in her face, wanting to hurt her as badly as she had hurt me. But with words, not cheating on her, because my sexual wires were still crossed. I quit going to marriage counseling, but she kept going to that counselor. I started going to another therapist, a very reserved man who reminded me of my father, and I would continue to see him long after that marriage was dead and buried.

I'd thought the end of my marriage was the worst thing that could have happened to me. Turned out to be the best. I would subsequently feel the same about my last night of drinking, that embarrassing debacle that turned my life around (again). Sometimes you just don't know what is best for you, and things happen for a reason that you couldn't know at the time. Fate, happenstance, serendipity—I have come to believe that my life has worked out better on its own accord than anything I could have possibly planned. The same was surely true for my ex-wife. She would subsequently earn her PhD., become a mover and shaker within the Chicago non-profit community and part of the MacArthur Foundation, the folks who administer the so-called "genius grants." (I never got that call.) She would have become none of that if she had stayed with me, second billed as supporting actress within my internal drama.

Though I can now take a higher road than I did then, I can't say that I was surprised or sorry when things didn't turn out well between her and the guy she left me for. I just don't dwell on it.

Meanwhile, I drank more, not to feel better, but to feel numb. And I did a lot of drugs, increasingly cocaine, which mainly made me feel like I wanted to do more cocaine. I was staying out, drinking and snorting, because there was just this void, the abyss, waiting for me alone at home.

Inevitably I started dating, or tried to, because now more than ever I really needed someone else to validate me, because the woman who had supposedly known me best had rejected me. These prospects, or victims, were mainly people with whom my rock-critic calling card would prove beneficial, who would have some impression of me or my byline that preceded me. One worked for a concert promoter, another was in a band, another was at a radio station, a couple more were journalists.

I might have wanted to want to have sex with some of them, and with a couple I did (drug stimulated), but with most I didn't even bother. Mainly, I think, I wanted to want to have sex with them. I very much felt I needed to be part of a couple again, but such coupling required an intimacy that made me uncomfortable, and not merely or mainly the physical intimacy.

Meanwhile, my work proceeded as if nothing had happened, because, in my work, nothing had. I saw myself as a master of compartmentalization, and just because something had collapsed in the marriage compartment, or the dating compartment, the writing compartment and the rock compartment remained fully operational, flourishing even, and perhaps even more crucial to my identity and some semblance of well-being than previously.

I reached another fork when the *Sun-Times* made kind of an informal, backdoor approach, based on the quality and consistency of my *Reader* work. Rather the newspaper's well-liked Rick Kogan did, inviting me to meet him at a hotel bar off Michigan Avenue for the obligatory drinks. He had become the de facto rock critic at the daily, by virtue of being young and a very good writer on just about anything. But he didn't really know or care that much about rock, certainly wasn't obsessive about it like I was. He really liked Styx; I really didn't.

After we talked and conspired over a couple of beers, he set up a meeting with his editors, to whom he'd praised me as one of the greatest emerging rock critics in the country, or at least Chicago, or at least good enough to fill the slot at the *Sun-Times* that would allow him to write and range more freely over a variety of projects.

They offered me freelance work, but plenty of it, maybe three or four reviews a week, featured profiles in the Sunday paper and higher visibility with a larger readership than I'd ever reached. The *Sun-Times* would have its rock critic, without paying a rock critic's salary and benefits, and I would be making a lot more money from a lot more writing than I ever had at the *Reader*.

And I would still be appearing weekly in the *Reader* as well as often in the daily *Sun-Times*, effectively serving both, at least in my mind. But my agreement with the *Reader* had by then evolved into what they termed a half-staff position, with some regularity of salary and minor benefits, as well as an annual bonus. I had pushed for this, more for the validation of being listed in the staff box each week than for any real financial boost.

After six months or so of my serving double duty for the *Reader* and the *Sun-Times*, my *Reader* editor suggested that it no longer made sense for me to have a staff position there when I was becoming so closely associated with the daily, who were also kind of a competitor. He didn't bar me from the weekly's pages, but simply put me back into the pool of freelancers, paid by the piece. I continued writing for the *Reader*, but not as much, and I half-joked that the weekly had fired me in the nicest way possible. I suppose I somehow blamed my estranged wife.

Ultimately, there was no doubt that my future lay with the *Sun-Times*, if I had to choose between one and the other. It was a no-brainer. My wife (neither of us had hurried to rush into a divorce) was still with her *Reader* boyfriend, though most of the others at the paper thought he was a jerk and sided with me. But there were no such entanglements at the *Sun-Times*, where the path was wide open and I would get all the chance I needed to compile all the clips

I could. I figured they would have to hire me eventually, and that if they didn't, another paper surely would.

Meanwhile, my routine at the *Sun-Times* required plenty of self-medicating, or so I thought, as I turned to coffee, beer and marijuana to manage my increasingly compartmentalized life. My old *Reader* routine of morning running and writing no longer applied, for now I was writing reviews on evening deadline, seeing a concert that I'd have to leave by 10:30 in order to drive to the newsroom to file before 11:30. I was not a person who felt all that coherent, let alone creative, after dinner, but I had to become one in order to do the job that now defined me.

So I'd jolt myself with caffeine after dinner, before the show, and start feeling that adrenaline rush that I typically associated with morning. During the concert itself, I would be taking copious notes, sometimes writing full sentences, even whole paragraphs, more than enough to fit in the 15" space (about 500 words) allotted for my review in the next morning's paper.

I'd still be feeling that surge when it was time to drive and then write (in the ATEX days before internet access and portable, personal computers). Or, rather, type, like I had after running, because most of the review was already fully formed in my head, and there wouldn't be time to pause for inspiration. I began to compare this to a jazz pianist, who would start a solo and then have to keep going, with no chance to return and revise. After a half hour or so I'd be done, the review finished and filed, and I'd feel even more elated because I'd pulled it off. Or, occasionally, down and deflated because I felt like what I'd filed was a mess.

My emotional arc on such nights of reviewing, which were most nights, was totally out of whack with my internal clock, my circadian rhythms, whatever. I was someone who felt most creative clarity in the morning (and still do, as I type this, in the morning) and who was typically pretty spent by the end of the day. Now the end of the day demanded that I be at my creative peak.

And so it was no longer the end of the day. In the immortal words of Blood Sweat & Tears, "What goes up/Must come down." But just as I'd had to compress what had previously been four mornings of creative adrenalin into four hours or so, now I had to hit the brakes, hard, in order to get some sleep, in order to do it all over again the next night. So I'd head right from the newsroom to a bar, down three or four quick beers, and then drive home to suburbia, to finish the night off with a joint, usually smoking while I was driving so I could collapse when I got to my house. It's a good thing there were so few cars on the road at that hour.

Do this for a few years and you understand why so many musicians have such substance issues. Not that I'd compare my sedentary work, largely unheralded, with the exertions that elicited such adulation, but they also would be hitting their peak around the time normal people went to bed, and it was the high point of their day. And then how do you fill those hours of emptiness when you're still so keyed up—either to extend that great feeling or come down from it.

So partying into the night and then sleeping all day before the next show would become the nocturnal norm for them. Not that I could ever adopt that. I still woke early in the morning, no matter what time I went to sleep. Making it all the more important that I get to sleep quickly, at least as quickly as I could after taking that hour for the beers and dope without which sleep would be impossible. Or so I'd thought.

That routine became my life, or essential to it, particularly after my strategy worked and the *Sun-Times* hired me, full-time, my first grown-up job working for somebody else. And it only took me until

I was 30 to get it! Vacation, benefits, a decent starting salary. Yet it also prolonged my Peter Pan adolescence. My job was to listen to rock, go to concerts, hang around bars, just what I'd been doing for fun for so long. And then write about it. What others paid to do for their entertainment, I got paid to do.

Because newspaper work isn't always a matter of routine, there were times when my habits got the best of me. Like the Monday night when I had settled in to watch football, after a few beers and a joint or two. My work day was done, and I wasn't planning on going anywhere. Until I heard the news the way so many Americans did, from Howard Cosell, that John Lennon had been shot and killed.

Soon after, my phone started ringing, and I didn't answer, because I knew it would be the newspaper. And I was in no shape to drive the 50 minutes into the city, let alone write when I got there. And I really wasn't in much shape to think all this through. I still wasn't a staffer at the paper at the time; I was hired by the assignment, paid by the piece. And this was an assignment they had yet to give me, because they couldn't reach me.

But this was my beat, and it was a huge story. I had some sort of obligation, or it likely wouldn't be my beat for long. So after an hour or so and a few cups of coffee, I called the paper, said I'd been out and asked what they wanted me to do. They wanted me in there, asap, to contribute to a memorial section they were putting together for the next morning's paper. There was supposed to be a big centerpiece story coming on the wire, but that fell through, and I ended up writing pretty much the whole section, multiple stories, on tight deadline. I remain very proud of the work I eventually did through that all-nighter.

I mainly worked nights, though not as late as this. So I wasn't in the newsroom as much as the others during the daytime. And when

I was, I didn't wear a sports coat or tie. I was often stopping there on the afternoon of a show, and my "work clothes" were what others wore to a concert, usually jeans, maybe a T-shirt. My hair was longer than anyone else's in the newsroom, the guys at least. I thought of myself as a rock fanatic who happened to work at a newspaper, rather than a newspaper guy who happened to cover rock.

So even though this was my first grown-up job, I didn't feel like much of a grownup. I was out listening to rock, drinking beers, getting paid for what we pretended was work. Many of the journalists who were a little older than me, and some a little younger, dressed more like adults, and acted like them. They seemed more like my parents' generation than like how I saw myself.

The lubrication of liquor, however, provided a common denominator. Those were different times in the newsroom, when many writers smoked and felt they couldn't write without a cigarette burning in the ashtray on their desk. And lots of them had a bottle in their bottom drawer. To end the week, when I had nothing to cover on a Friday night, I would join some colleagues at Riccardo's, a nearby restaurant with a bar favored by journos. Kogan had the prime booth, a curved one, sometimes occupied by three or four of us but capable of holding more when we squeezed in.

I'd plan to have a couple beers before dinner, but almost invariably I found myself drinking dinner. This was a competitive drinking crowd, and you were expected to keep up, to buy rounds when it was your turn and keep pace when the others bought. The talk got louder, the jokes funnier, and the voices slurrier as the evening progressed. I usually made it for three or four hours before driving home. And, somehow, I usually made it home, as if my car was on autopilot. Once I didn't: a road forked, as the sign indicated, and I awakened while driving to found I had crashed into that sign in the middle rather than taking either of the roads. (Maybe this was a metaphor.)

How many times did I drive drunk? Every damn time, at least on the way home. To think that I never hurt anyone, or killed anyone, or even got charged with drunken driving, seems like a miracle to me.

There were other occasions when I just wouldn't let the night end, at least not right then. Cocaine was generally involved. Because when cocaine was made available, I would be eager to indulge, never mind the company or the hour or the circumstances. There were nights in a club when I didn't have to review, too late for deadlines, when I'd be invited into the back office for a few lines. The guy who invited me was a friend, though our relationship blurred the distinction between the personal and the professional. Maybe he was my friend because I could do him some good. I didn't care. I didn't have many friends, and he had cocaine.

At such times, I had no concern about when I'd make it home to go to sleep. Or if. These things would resolve themselves, after the coke ran out. And the beers to help wash it down. I could feel pretty exhilarated until I crashed. Then it would be time to scrape myself together and go home, usually before the sun rose, but occasionally not.

My friend the club manager remained my friend after he left the club business. And left Chicago, to return to his parents' home near Philadelphia. He was getting clean, not just from the cocaine that he had shared with me, but from a heroin addiction which had pretty much consumed his life. The last time I saw him, I took him to see the Rolling Stones, who were opening their tour in Philly, and I stayed with his folks. He seemed healthy, happy, full of good humor.

Just months later, I heard that he had OD'd on a visit to D.C. It hadn't taken much, an amount of heroin that he might once have taken in stride, but provided a fatal jolt to a body that had gotten clean before this relapse. He was still so young, and it was such a waste. He wasn't the only one from that club circuit who would die so soon, so young, from a variety of excesses and mishaps. There but for fortune…

My friend Lloyd provided an oasis of stability and sanity (a notion that he would find preposterous) amid the chaos surrounding me. As much as we shared in terms of pop culture interests and taste, his indulgences almost never extended beyond a beer or two, and he had no inclination toward drugs. And he was a thorough professional when it came to his work.

Spending time with him proved a moderating experience for me, a retreat from the abyss. Another common denominator I had with Lloyd was that his serious romantic relationship had also hit the *Reader* rocks. He and his girlfriend had split around the same time my wife had decided she no longer wanted to be married to me, and his ex was now with the *Reader* movie critic who had formerly been his best friend. So he had that slot open as well, and I filled it.

In practical terms, in the lingo of the entertainment industry, I became his "plus one," and he became mine, as both of us made the circuit, either reviewing or looking for something to do, some alternative to an empty home. Our tickets were "comped," provided complimentary. In other words, free. And since a comped ticket typically came with a plus-one, we'd go together. Only losers went by themselves when they had a free ticket to what was for most a social situation.

Lloyd was no loser. He was the funniest guy I knew, and know. He could charm people in a way that I couldn't—making friends of co-workers, asking waitresses on dates (and they'd accept, because he was so warm and clever and disarming). There was a darker, depressive side to him, a side that switched off when he wasn't on, when he wasn't performing for someone's entertainment.

With me, it seemed like there was still this invisible protective shield, maybe a body language that said not to get too close, don't sit here; maybe something in my eyes that betrayed how guarded I was. How uncomfortable, both with others and inside my own skin.

Outside, in my professional life, my vistas had opened up, opportunity had arisen and I had taken advantage. I had a good job, and I was doing a good job. Inside, it seemed that things hadn't changed, that they couldn't. And I had no idea how to make them change. For better and worse, I was who I was.

Part III:
Stepping Out

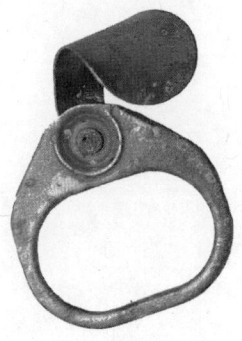

15. Maria, I just met a girl

MY LIFE STARTS HERE, THE ONE that I recognize as a continuous narrative thread, with an identity that no longer feels provisional. All that earlier stuff happened, as best as I can remember it, but it seems like it happened to someone else, to someone I remember but don't necessarily recognize as myself.

There have been roughly two halves of my life, before and after, and the turning point is when I looked across Park West, from the stairs above the main floor, and saw a young woman with long, dark hair and a white, frilly blouse. And I said to myself, and then maybe even to Lloyd, "You know, if I had a girlfriend like that, I think I could be really happy."

I'll try to spare you the sappy stuff, because it's even harder to engage others in your love-at-first-sight story than it is in your vacation photos. Because they weren't there; they can't feel it, can't feel what you felt, and couldn't understand it if they could. Because you can't really understand it, almost 40 years and two daughters later, a life that seems so coherent and cohesive after those earlier decades had felt so scattered.

There is a saying variously attributed in Eastern mysticism that "When the pupil is ready, the teacher will appear." A guy I know in AA was fond of saying, "When the alcoholic is ready to receive it, even a monkey can carry the message." What I'm trying to say is that rational explanation suggests that not only was I in the right place at the right time to fall for the right person, but that I had somehow become the right person as well. Or had started to.

I was no longer looking for a life's partner, someone to complete me, someone who could be everything for me and for whom I could be everything. I was still licking my wounds from a last, tempestuous relationship, and I had become all the more determined not to repeat the mistake (as I saw it then) of my first marriage. I had never imagined getting divorced; to get divorced twice would be unthinkable.

So that musing about the woman across the room and the happiness that such a girlfriend might bring me was like the early evening version of idle daydreaming. I would have never considered approaching her, because I had never considered myself the type to approach a woman I had never met to try to spark something, or even start a conversation.

But I kept my eye on her, as she moved around the intimate concert club with her girlfriend, and it seemed unlikely she was there with any guy. And then she and the other girl, toward the end of the night's music, when it was time to leave, started talking with a group of people, people I knew. They worked at or wrote for the Illinois Entertainer, a suburban music monthly for which I had also written some, and I knew them well enough that it wouldn't be awkward to insinuate myself within that group and find out what I could. This was starting to feel a little like fate.

So Lloyd and I went over to talk with them. And then Lloyd left, and I was mainly talking with her. She looked younger up close than she had across the room, and I'd figured this was a deal breaker, but it turned out she was in her mid-20s. Old enough for me to be talking with. Someone suggested we keep talking at a nearby bar, a place I'd never gone before or since. But she was going, so I was going. And we kept talking there. And by the time we left she suggested that I come to the Illinois Entertainer holiday party.

Which I did, focused only on her, not realizing that she had some kind of date to that occasion. But we were still talking, still getting to know each other. And it wouldn't be long before she was going out with me, at least occasionally, and then exclusively.

What was it about this girl? When I'd thought that a girlfriend like that might make me happy, I'd meant happy in a drama-free sort of way, after all that upheaval I'd experienced in my personal life. To say she seemed "nice" feels like damning with faint praise, but nice sounded awfully good to me right then. So did uncomplicated, in the sense of easy to get along with, not being scared to push the wrong buttons because there were no wrong buttons to push with her. Or, so, in my innocence, I felt at the time. Maria may well be the most complicated woman I've ever known, but that's also because I never had the time or inclination to know someone for as long as we've now known each other. The more you've been with someone, the more you've been *through* with someone, the more depth there is to discover. Especially once you've gotten old enough to be more interested in such depths beyond the surface attraction.

And once you get past thirty years, you've gone a whole lot deeper than first impressions. But my first impression had also been on the mark. She is essentially a nice person, a good person, in ways that I'm not. Or wasn't. Being with her all these years has made me a better person, certainly a different person. Easily a happier person, way more comfortable in my own skin. She is the primary reason why that darker, moodier, reckless guy that I've earlier been prone to romanticize (or ridicule) now seems like someone else. He was. Someone Before Maria.

As we were inching our way toward being together, she already had New Year's Eve plans, to see Todd Rundgren (one of her favorites) with a date. I spent the evening first having a nice dinner at the home of a couple I knew, married and in a band together, and then getting coked to the gills with them. I proceeded to a club to see the Cramps, a great band often mislabeled as "psychobilly," but whose performance could be both shambolic and transcendent, shedding some light on rock's dark underbelly. Pushing past the extremes.

My good friend the club manager (the same one who would die of a heroin overdose) took a look at my condition, and befitting the occasion, invited me to run the lights for the band, another first and last time. The whole evening was insane, the music, the lights, the drugs, the crowd, the occasion. It would be the last night like that I ever spent without Maria.

We proceeded slowly, by my memory, though Maria has always said she found me too aggressive. (Which I guess goes to show how determined and deluded I was, since "aggressive" isn't a term I would ever apply to myself in male-female relations.) She comes from a traditional Italian family, with three older brothers, and she was still living at home with her mother at age 27. And so was one of her brothers.

The whole family was very Catholic, but her mother warmed to me, despite the fact that I was nominally Protestant and legally divorced. I made small talk with her when I picked up Maria. Unlike others, I actually came to the door rather than honking for her. And her mother once said I was a "snappy dresser," which is about as far removed from my self-image as "aggressive." But we got along fine, and I liked the fact that Maria seemed to be something of an old-fashioned girl who lived in the old fashion with her mother.

She wasn't in much contact with her father, didn't even know where he lived, though he continued to work in an appliance store some 15 minutes away. He had left her mother over some combination of his infidelity and her crazed response, haranguing him at work, making life at home hell, more than a decade earlier. Their marriage had a similar tension to that of my parents, except my dad hadn't left. (And hadn't cheated, as far as I know.) He had just zoned out and then died way too young. Maria's mom and dad had split up, but they had never gotten divorced—the Catholic thing—and he still paid the bills on the house.

Maria's mother had emotional problems that went deeper than her marital issues, though it was hard to separate the two. She had been hospitalized and received electroshock treatment, like my mother. She had once changed her name and seemingly her identity. She no longer could drive. She was very soft-spoken and docile, but she would occasionally fly into rages, flashing the anger that Maria remembered from when she was a teenager and her mother was physically abusive toward her. Otherwise, she seemed a bit removed from reality, otherworldly.

Maria had also had a long-term boyfriend who had been physically abusive. And I'm sure my relative refinement was part of the attraction for her. I was just that much older, and I knew the city, where her life had pretty much centered on the suburbs. Red Lobster was the special occasion restaurant she'd known. With a dad who had left her and a boyfriend who had hit her, she just wasn't used to someone who would treat her decently. She was always waiting for the other shoe to drop.

In some ways, her family was very much like mine—the string of brothers and then the youngest sister, the disturbed mother, the removed father. But where my sister Katie was very much the princess of our family, Maria was anything but that in hers. Her brothers had all gone to college, but she had received no encouragement to do so, and few of her friends did. When her dad left, she developed abandonment issues that would persist for decades. She had always seemed like the afterthought in her family.

Once we started sleeping together, we were pretty much a couple, both of us monogamously inclined. I loved the fact that she would occasionally take the initiative, like surprising me with tickets to *Death of a Salesman* (with Dustin Hoffman and John Malkovich) for our first Valentine's Day, and taking me out to dinner. She wasn't a diva or a prima donna; there was no sense of entitlement about her. She didn't even seem to realize just how attractive she was, which made her all the more attractive to me.

I didn't know where this was going, or if it was going anywhere, but where it was right then was just fine with me. I enjoyed being with her, found it easier to be close to her than anyone else I had ever met. We traveled well together, seemed to enjoy the same things at the same pace. The biggest difference between us showed me that it didn't make much difference at all. I had gone to grad school; she hadn't gone to college—no interest, and she had long been told she had no aptitude. By her schools and then her parents. Which now seems insane to me, because Maria is one of the more innately perceptive people I've ever met—intuitive, with a terrific bullshit detector.

Whatever Maria lacked in "book larnin'" she has more than offset with common sense. She has long shown that she has more of it than I do. And she's a shrewd, incisive judge of character. She also refused to be intimidated in the slightest by my critical credentials. We went to a whole lot of music together, and she liked some that I liked, didn't like others, and very much had her own taste, her own opinions. And why not? But my earlier experiences in couplehood were that my taste became our taste, from glam rock to punk rock.

The one area where Maria very much knew her own mind, and which caused the tension to grow between us, is that she knew how she saw her future, including her immediate future. She wanted to be a wife and mother, to live in a nice house and be at home with the kids. Like her mother and my mother had, but unlike the nightmare bizarre twists their lives had taken. She still had the storybook fantasy; she thought it could work, with the right guy.

Only the guy she was with was in no hurry to move from where we were to where she wanted to be. Like I said, I thought things were fine, and I figured we could coast along until they weren't. So there was this undercurrent, and it came to the surface particularly after we attended a wedding, which seemed to be in season for us around then. When I first got married, nobody else was. Now it seemed like everybody was getting married.

A wedding would make her think "Why not me?" or that it was her turn. And then things wouldn't be going as fine for us, because she was unhappy. I thought I had a good reason for not rushing into remarriage—I wanted to be absolutely sure that this was forever, and that I would never go through another divorce. And I had those niggling reservations that turned out to be nothing—that she was younger than me (six and a half years, but who's counting?) and that she hadn't gone to college.

After one seemingly irresolvable argument, we broke up. She thought it was because I was interested in someone else, that she wasn't good enough, whatever. But it was mainly because we just weren't getting along, because she wanted her life to proceed in a definite way, and I just wasn't ready to follow her lead. I wasn't even ready to tell her when I might be ready. I just knew deep down that feeling pressured into marriage wasn't the way to a happy one.

So, we took a break. Both of us went out with other people, but our hearts weren't in it (at least mine wasn't). Being away from Maria took the pressure off, and without the pressure I could think things through on my own. And at the simplest and purest level, being with Maria had made me happy, when things were going well. And being without her made me feel empty, like I was sleepwalking through this part of my life, going nowhere, in order to prove some kind of point that I didn't really understand.

In retrospect, much of this anticipated the lessons I would learn in AA. Don't overthink or try to control everything. Let things work out the way they will. Follow your heart rather than your head. As any 12-stepper will tell an overthinking drunk, "Your best thinking is what got you here."

We got back together. Or maybe I crawled back. And knew without either of us having to say it that this meant that we would be proceeding along the course that made Maria happy. And that made me happy, because it had been in some way my decision. I had made enough of a mess of my life by following my own best instincts. Now I'd follow her blueprint, the one that I might have once dismissed as too bourgeois and conventional to build a life on. But I was so much younger then. I'm older than that now. (With apologies to Bob Dylan.)

16. Family Values

I HAD NEVER EXPERIENCED A better wedding, and couldn't have imagined one. We booked the reception at FitzGerald's, a roadhouse-style club in nearby Berwyn that was then and remains our favorite. We found a church nearby where the minister would officiate (a Catholic ceremony was prohibited because I was divorced). The bride was the most beautiful ever, and the groom was beaming. I have photographic evidence.

Maria's dad stepped up to the plate to give his only daughter the wedding she deserved. It was my second, but it was her first, and only, and it felt like my first and last as well. Open bar for five hours, a full buffet, great music from a band who had two members that would be in a bigger band (then, Spooner; now, Garbage). There was plenty of family, friends we'd had for ages, relatives of hers that I had never met, colleagues with whom one or both of us worked, musicians we knew. A gala affair that truly felt like a rite of passage, a turning point into some sort of adulthood.

After all, at the tender age of 35, perhaps it was time for me to leave childish things behind. Not the music, of course, which remained my passion and had become my paycheck, a pretty good one. But all those romantic notions of living on the edge, dangerously, rebelliously, like there was no tomorrow. That was kid's stuff. No one was slipping us blotter acid as a wedding present for my second marriage, as they had at the first. I knew there would be plenty of tomorrows, and that one of them would bring a baby. At least one. I had responsibilities to face and more in the future.

There was a big change in my drinking during our courtship—not in quantity, necessarily, but in quality. I had always been a beer drinker, pretty much exclusively, just like my dad. But Maria's oldest brother was something of a wine connoisseur, and he had started her drinking it, and she started me drinking it. Before long, I was almost never drinking beer, and had switched pretty much exclusively to wine—and not in a box or with a twist-off, but with a cork. Just like a grownup.

Did Maria move me away from that edge, save me from myself? Maybe. She was certainly an influence, though she had sown her share of wild oats before we'd met. But though she was younger than me, 28 when we married, she had already seen herself pass through that phase, and she was ready to settle down. In the literal sense, not just as a euphemism for getting married.

So, yeah, I was six years and change older than her, but she was the mature one, the one who saw the future in adult terms. Time to put my big boy pants on. We went on a real honeymoon, all over Switzerland, with side trips to Milan and Paris. By now I was pretty much drinking wine exclusively, and, because we were on this celebratory trip, for lunch and dinner both. As with the wedding, it couldn't have been better.

And as with the way it was before we married, I liked things fine, and would have been fine extending this period. But Maria heard the clock ticking, and, again, I was glad she did. Before our first anniversary, she was pregnant, and our marriage moved into a state of heightened anticipation and responsibility.

A year and a half after the wedding, I sobbed when Kelly was born, couldn't help myself when calling family and friends to share the news. Part of it was the drama—there had been some complications and an emergency C-section, on a morning when we had been led to believe this was a false alarm, and that we could be going home again with no baby. But part of it was just overwhelming joy and boundless love for this defenseless being we had brought into our lives, and who would now be our top priority. It felt like a life-changer, in a really great way.

And I vowed to be a father worthy of her. I consciously resolved that this would be the end—not of drinking, because drinking wasn't a problem I felt I had, but of recreational drugs, because they were illegal. I would need to hide such usage from my daughter, and I just didn't want to be that kind of dad, sneaking off, selfish. Incapable of handling things if she got sick or something and I was stoned. Time to grow up.

I suspect my resolve lasted a month or so, certainly not much longer. Having a daughter added a whole new dimension to our marriage, and to my life, and Kelly allowed me to discover a reservoir of patience I had never previously tapped. I loved (and love) her unconditionally, and if this meant rocking her in a chair well after midnight, even driving around so that she would fall asleep, that is what I would do. And couldn't do if I were drunk or high.

But our baby eventually settled into a routine, which permitted me to resume my own routine, which meant it was back to business as usual. Business was good, though I wanted better, more. Now that I was a father as well as a husband, I had more reason to think about my career as a career. There's a condition I later learned with which most alcoholics identify, of "egomaniac with an insecurity complex," like two sides of the same coin.

And that was me, in spades. On the one hand, the egomania had gotten me into this rock critic racket, the feeling that I knew more and cared more about rock than just about anyone else, and that I could write about it better as well. My work at the *Reader* had served as a springboard to the beat at the *Sun-Times*, which would then be the springboard...

To what? If I were as good as I thought I was, why was I writing for the second newspaper in Chicago, whose local readers were the only ones my work was reaching. And I thought I was doing great work and that it should take me nationwide, or at least to a larger newspaper. A better one. In the days before the internet, you were pretty much limited to your city, and to the wire services that made your stories available to newspapers in other markets, pretty much a hit-and-miss affair.

I had first-rate access, interviews with the Rolling Stones, U2, Bob Dylan, Madonna and pretty much everyone else among the reigning luminaries at the time. Sometimes I would parlay that access into an assignment for *Creem*, where my story on The Who ran on the cover.

I had started getting a taste of the great beyond, which had whetted my appetite. Brent Staples had been at the University of Chicago at the same time I was, and had written for the *Reader* as well, though I didn't know him except by name until we had adjacent desks at the Chicago *Sun-Times*. When he was recruited by the *New York Times* to become an editor within its book review (he has since distinguished himself on the editorial board, winning the Pulitzer), he started throwing prime assignments my way.

One of them was a rock history commissioned by *Rolling Stone*, and mine was the lead review on that Sunday. It wasn't a particularly positive review, but it impressed some editors in New York, reinforcing my impression that all the good work I had been doing in Chicago meant nothing compared to one piece in the *New York Times Book Review*. Rolling Stone's Anthony DeCurtis had liked the piece enough that he made it a point to get together with me on his next visit to Chicago, and soon I was writing regularly for *Rolling Stone* while working at the *Sun-Times*. I had planned none of this, but things seemed to be working out better than anything I could have planned.

So, my rock-crit validation went up another notch or two. At the *Sun-Times*, I'd already changed my identity somewhat, from the guy who thought about rock and wrote about it in the *Reader*, to someone who actually met, talked with and interviewed the people whose music I'd long loved. The Rolling Stones and Keith Richards in particular were among the most prominent feathers in my cap (Keith once sent us a Christmas card), with Bob Dylan my most thrilling encounter (and the weakest handshake).

U2, Al Green, Ornette Coleman, even Chicago laureate Saul Bellow, since the *Sun-Times* allowed me to stretch myself and take occasional advantage of the UC graduate degree. It was weird how a guy as shy as I was could make a living talking with famous strangers, but I always thought of it as doing a job, as if these newsworthy subjects weren't really talking with me but through me, talking to the half-million or whatever readers of the *Sun-Times*. Always nervous before the interview, I quickly felt at ease once I'd asked the first question. This was a job as well as a privilege, and I was good at my job.

Yet such celebrity access as well as the national magazine clips made others feel differently about me, or so I suspected, and made me feel different about myself. More than once I was introduced as someone who "writes for the *Rolling Stone*," and "has partied with the Rolling Stones." And I hadn't, though the first time I met the band was in a small rehearsal hall the size of a living room, with a large pile of cocaine on the piano.

"You won't write about this," said the publicist who had arranged the meeting of the cocaine. And I didn't. I also generally avoided backstage, unless an assignment took me there, or socializing beyond the professional bounds of an interview. I was there to get a story, not to make famous friends whose names I could drop.

Three years into my tenure there, the newspaper took a hit from which it has never fully recovered, and would render the validation I received from my career suspect. I had joined a paper that thought of itself as the best, or at least one of the best, writers' papers in country, with columnists including Mike Royko and Roger Simon, and Roger Ebert as the first movie critic to win the Pulitzer. Our former colleague Ron Powers had been the first television critic to win it. No rock critic had ever won it, and I saw no reason why I shouldn't follow suit. (To date, no rock critic—or popular music critic—has ever won it, and perhaps none ever will.) I took pride that I was in the midst of such talent and such tradition.

Then came Rupert. Chicago in general and the staffers in particular were blindsided when Rupert Murdoch bought the *Sun-Times* in 1983. It seems that silent partner Ted Fields, whose half-brother Marshall Field V had long been the beneficent face of ownership, wanted cash to advance his Hollywood aspirations, and he had forced the sale of the family newspaper so he could fund *Revenge of the Nerds*. (Which seems like karma in retrospect.)

The buyout offered by the new employers in the wake of the sale was attractive to many of the veterans and some of the best-known bylines, who could walk away with many months' salary while seeking new employment. They didn't have to look far, since the *Chicago Tribune* across the street had long had its sights set on Royko, and would welcome plenty of the other top talent that vowed never to work for Murdoch, the notorious media slumlord.

But the Trib had recently hired a very good rock critic, Greg Kot (who would enjoy a long career there). And I'd only been at the

Sun-Times for three years, so the severance based on years of service would have been chump change. Most of us who stayed didn't see much of a choice, except for Ebert, who was champion of the underdog and couldn't imagine joining what we saw as the elitist Trib. Hell, Royko himself was never the same after he made that move to Tribune Tower.

Though the *Sun-Times* maintained much of its newsroom staff, mostly those of us who couldn't afford to leave, a change in ownership meant a change in editors, which changed the whole culture of the operation. The *Sun-Times* was a tabloid in format, but had never fit the stereotype of flashy and fleshy photos and screaming headlines. Murdoch had already embodied that sort of journalism in New York and Great Britain, and he imported editors from Canada and London to make it work in Chicago.

Which it couldn't, of course. Because Chicago beyond all else is deeply Chicagoan, proudly provincial, and the very idea of outsiders who didn't know us daring to package the news they thought we wanted was met with resistance from the get-go, fueled by the public resentment of *Sun-Times* alums who had fled with denunciations of Murdoch. From Mike Royko: "No self-respecting fish would want to be wrapped in a Murdoch paper." Murdoch was also famously conservative, so the *Sun-Times* as the liberal alternative to the conservative Trib was no more. We were now the more conservative paper in town.

Though Chicago journalism already had a fabled tradition of alcohol intake, the newsroom had never seen anything like the Murdoch editorial braintrust. The powers that be would convene after their afternoon meeting to drink dinner and then return, loudly and boisterously, to tear up the front page and maybe the first few after them, all carefully designed, often by them, just a sober couple of hours early. This was journalism on the fly, emphasizing big pictures of celebrities or lesser-known women with fewer clothes, and it confused the staff and readership alike. Chicago had never seen anything like it. Yet many of these were very likable men, who didn't take themselves or their craft too seriously, and could be more fun than the sober-minded editors who had preceded them.

One of Murdoch's men, Charlie Wilson, became my benefactor, making it worth my while to stay even though I really had nowhere else to go. It seems that Charlie was something of a jazz buff, as some Brits of a certain age tend to be, and we ran into each other at an alcohol-fueled bash that the Chicago jazz community held in a downtown hotel during the dead of winter. In the midst of rooms of music, panel discussions, rare jazz films and lots of fans, he invited me to sit down and talk with him about the paper and my work there.

This gave me the opportunity to air my financial grievance, that though I had been serving as the paper's de facto popular music critic since my freelance days, doing all the reviews and profiles and think pieces and beat coverage that any critic would, the paper had belatedly hired me not as a critic, but as a reporter. Hell, I didn't care what they called me, but at a union paper, critics and columnists were on a higher pay scale than reporters. Drunken Charlie agreed with my drunken logic that I should be paid at the proper rate for the work I was doing, so he told me he would bump me up, raising my salary by almost 40%.

And in the sober light of morning, he made good on it, the first time I had ever received such a windfall in salary. There would be a second, with a similar jump, at another newspaper, also negotiated in a bar. I loved journalism.

But the money wasn't enough to satisfy me; it was more like a way of keeping score. As I've come to suspect, drinking (and drugging) was a symptom of a larger issue, the fact that I just couldn't feel good about myself without something outside myself. In this particular case, I still felt I needed a bigger readership and a better publication to validate me, confirm the worth of which I was overtly cocky but inwardly plagued by doubt. Just like I'd needed to go to a good grad school to show others (and myself?) that I was smart. (Or pretty girlfriends to show that I was attractive.)

I also saw the writing on the wall of so many markets with two (or more) newspapers where only one survived. I saw the *Sun-Times* as a sinking ship and I didn't want to be in the last lifeboat. I never thought it would survive as long as it has, as unprofitable political megaphone for other foreign conservative tycoons, but if I had stayed there, I know I would have lost my job by now. Just as pretty much everyone else I worked with there has, through a series of downsizings and buyouts.

So, I'd been feeling as if I'd had one foot out the door, and the baby following the marriage intensified the urgency. The question was, one foot out the door toward where? The two dream jobs for me would have been the *New York Times* and the *Los Angeles Times*, with the most prestige, the best access (as the strongholds of the bicoastal music industry) and the broadest readership. But those who held those positions were secure in them, as if they were tenured.

Other moves seemed more like lateral ones to me, though still attractive. I might move to a slightly smaller city, but one where the newspaper, perhaps the sole surviving one, had a better reputation and even a larger circulation. And where I would escape the stigma of Murdoch. Though, as it turned out, it wasn't that stigma that would impede my escape, but the higher salary I had negotiated.

On the horizon were two prospects, neither perfect, but both attractive employment opportunities. The first was the *Philadelphia*

Inquirer, the crown jewel of the respected *Knight-Ridder* chain, which had just lost its veteran rock critic, Ken Tucker, to the start-up *Entertainment Weekly*. It would be an honor and a challenge to become Ken's successor, and to work for Gene Roberts, one of the profession's top editors and one who had taken the paper to new glories.

The other was the *Atlanta Journal-Constitution*, in the midst of a revival led by another of the nation's top editors, Bill Kovach, who, like Roberts, had come from the *New York Times* and had brought others with him. Atlanta was widely perceived as the Athens of the New South, and its editor was transforming the paper to make it a worthy reflection of not only the city but the region.

The problem was that neither was Chicago, the city I loved (and love), but I couldn't leave the *Sun-Times* without either leaving the city or leaving newspapers. And newspapers were themselves a thriving industry at the time, though opportunities were narrow on my particular beat. There were only two dailies and each of them had one rock critic. And I was one of them, one who had to find another city if I were to continue doing what I loved doing.

I had no real affinity for Philadelphia, except its proximity to Manhattan, where I would be able to see shows and interview subjects in person with a quick trip. I mean, I liked Philly Soul and Hall & Oates just fine, but neither captured my soul the way the music from Chicago had.

The Atlanta paper had yet to attain the stature of the one in Philadelphia, but the mid-south climate was more attractive to me, and the region offered all sorts of exploratory possibilities—the Macon of Otis Redding and Little Richard, the Athens of R.E.M., the whole Southern rock thing launched by Georgia's Allman Brothers. And this was the gateway to the South and the Mississippi delta which was responsible for all American music, at least all of the American music that I loved. Give me some freedom and a travel budget, and I could do some great work down there, at least as soon as I figured out how to navigate my way through a city where every street seemed to be named Peachtree.

So, I made discrete inquiries through back channels and received invitations to fly to both cities, for rigorous rounds of interviews. Then came the big challenge—giving up dope, at least temporarily. As everyone learned in the early days when hiring often involved a drug test, marijuana remains detectable long after a more potent drug like cocaine. Depending on the kind of test (urine, hair, whatever), you can still fail a test for marijuana a month or more after last using.

I had no idea whether either newspaper required a drug test, and I certainly wasn't going to ask. So I quit, cold turkey, no longer using my nightly joint as a sleeping aid. I figured that by doing so this early in the process, I'd be fine by the time interviews might lead to a job offer and final screening. And I figured I'd revisit whether this was a habit I wished to resume once I was secure in my new position.

In retrospect, all of this should have served as some kind of warning sign—that I would be so obsessed over my marijuana routine that I would risk limiting my employment opportunities for the sake of the habit. That I would calculate just how long I needed to abstain and how soon I could return to my illegal habit. That I was so obsessed. And that the main thing that distinguished my self-medicating with marijuana and my alcohol consumption is that the former was illegal.

In the meantime, I kept my nighttime routine legal. While I'd occasionally indulged in a nightcap of brandy or cognac, particularly in winter, one (or more) now became integral to the getting-to-sleep routine. As did a post-prandial cigar, a smoke but no inhaling. I was now convinced I needed both of these, where I'd needed neither before, to fall asleep now that I was deprived of my nightly joint. I would need to drink a little more to compensate. At least until the interviews were over and the new position secured. (And no, I never reverted to drinking a little less once I added the marijuana back into the ritual. Why would I?)

The routine worked fine. They always did. As long as I had a routine, one I would adhere to obsessively. And my first round of interviews in Philadelphia went better than fine, so smooth that it seemed only the formality of discussing money remained. They liked me, they really liked me. For a shy guy in my personal life, riddled with insecurities, I can be pretty good at selling myself professionally. One of the higher editors mentioned that my salary was higher than *Knight-Ridder* scale, but we didn't take it any farther.

When the features editor bought me dinner at the Four Seasons, I tasted crème brûlée for the first time, and discovered a new favorite dessert. This seemed like a courtship, and I felt like the one being courted. I felt like we were 90% of the way there, and that somehow I would learn to adjust to cheesesteak rather than pizza. (Though I could never forsake the Cubs for the Phillies.)

When I returned home, I told Maria I could very much see us living there, or at least me working there, but we discussed how we'd both have to go before making a final decision. I remained in touch with Philly, awaiting the arrangements to fly both of us back, but first there was the visit to Atlanta, scheduled for just a couple weeks later.

And Atlanta complicated everything. It was warmer than Philadelphia, and cleaner, and newer, with a downtown gleam. The pace was slower and the people were friendlier—not the newspaper people, just people in general. I ate some terrific barbeque. I drove around to look at neighborhoods where I could see us living.

I didn't necessarily leave feeling as close to a job offer as I had in Philadelphia, but I felt both good and confident about the process so far. This was more about me selling myself, creating a need for a first-rate rock critic rather than filling a posted opening. I thought I had done a good job and had established rapport with those who had interviewed me. I had presented ideas for regional coverage, and the credentials I had brought with me—Chicago, *Rolling Stone*, clips from the *New York Times Book Review*—suggested that I'd be a good hire for a paper in the midst of an overhaul.

As in Philadelphia, I learned that I was making more money than those similarly slotted, but I figured that since luring the editors and others from the *New York Times* had presented similar challenges, that this shouldn't be an issue. I returned home conflicted, now hoping to slow the process in Philadelphia to give Atlanta time to catch up, not wanting to decide between the two until I had heard from both.

Timing almost never works that neatly. Within a couple of weeks, in early December, I received the call from Philadelphia, asking to make arrangements for Maria and me to fly there. There was no dollar figure attached, but this seemed to be a done deal, from their end at least. So I let Atlanta know that time was of the essence, as we made plans for the flight to Philly, figuring that if the offer was great I'd take it on the spot, and if it was less I would stall for as much time I could take for Atlanta to make an offer as well.

The morning we were to fly to Philadelphia, there was a huge snowstorm in Chicago, one that closed O'Hare and canceled all flights. When I called the Philadelphia paper, they didn't seem too concerned, and said to wait until all this blows over and we'd re-schedule. So I waited, not hearing anything new from Philly, still not hearing from Atlanta. Finally, curiosity got the best of me, and I forced the issue with the Philadelphia features editor who had been so enthusiastic about having me there. He said sheepishly that those above him had decided to reopen the search, that they couldn't make me the offer he had planned to make. I suspected the Murdoch stigma, but he later told me this was purely dollars-and-cents. They felt they couldn't afford me, and they couldn't afford to have a critic who resented having to settle for so much less than he had been making.

Atlanta never made an offer. Sure that I'd be deciding between two options, both of which I had some mixed feelings about, I now had none. As it turned out, the choice I never had the chance to make was the best one I could have made. Both editors left their papers not long after, with Kovach in Atlanta forced out after it was deemed that his remake was a little too radical, not the sort of playing nice the powers that be in the Atlanta metro were accustomed to receiving. Philadelphia promoted the rock critic from one of its other papers, who was already on the *Knight-Ridder* pay scale and who would do a great job for them.

Meanwhile, I was stuck in Chicago. But not for long. If I've learned anything in AA, it's that my best-laid plans are not necessarily what might be best for me, and that opportunities that seem to end in disappointment leave the door open for even better ones. If I could have micromanaged myself into a move to Philly or Atlanta, I wouldn't have made it to Austin.

17. Lost (and Found and Lost) in Austin

I STILL FELT STUCK IN MY POSITION, at the second newspaper in a city that might soon be able to support only one—but with no immediate prospects on the horizon, I resumed smoking dope. Every night. Why not? I enjoyed the feeling, the relaxation, the zoning out, the signal it sent to the rest of me that work time was over, thinking time was over, my overly busy brain could rest and rest would lead to sleep.

Yes, it was illegal, and thus not exactly the example I wanted to send to my young daughter once she was old enough to understand such behavior. So I would have to wait until I was sure she was asleep before getting stoned. And, once I did, I wanted as little interaction with others as possible, no phone calls, no visitors. Not even Maria, if all she was going to do was remark snidely on my being stoned. Again.

As I would learn in AA, it was a little strange that none of this struck me as even slightly strange. It was just strategy. I wanted to do what I wanted to do. Which was to get high and be by myself. Why? What fun was that? It was just what I wanted to do, and I was old enough to do what I wanted. My world was getting smaller and darker, just big enough for me and my obsession to nullify my consciousness. My sleep aids.

So, I added marijuana to my nightly routine, again, but I never subtracted anything, at least anything that had been working so well.

It was as if my existence had become something of a chemistry experiment, a complicated equation that now read: Dinner + wine + cigar + cognac + joint = sleep. Take away any of those elements, and the whole thing might fall apart. So I didn't.

But my professional restlessness didn't dissipate. I felt like I was on a treadmill of concert reviews of bands I had seen before, interviews with subjects I had interviewed before. I was good at my work, I still loved music, and I appreciated the freedom to travel and interact with famous folks whose names I could drop to make others jealous. It's just that I couldn't see spending the rest of my working life doing this, still at the *Sun-Times,* in the employ of the notorious Rupert Murdoch, writing about music aimed at those in their teens and 20s while I was ever growing older.

In the latter years of my 30s, I realized I was positioning myself for a midlife crisis, but not one that would find me acting out with a sporty red convertible and new trophy wife (Maria was already my trophy, but so much more). I started exploring with my *Sun-Times* editors, the pre-Murdoch holdovers, whether there might be ways to prepare me for more mature responsibilities, maybe a shift toward being editor of the book reviews (we had one, and he did a great job, but he was older than me) or taking more editorial responsibility in general. Such a shift wouldn't resolve the Murdoch issue, but might make me more widely employable and allow me to escape the prospect of an old man reviewing young people's music.

There are no secrets in a well-connected industry of communications, and whether because of my two interviews, which I had told only those closest to me about, or my discussions with my editors about shifting into some editing responsibilities, I received a feeler from the *Austin American-Statesman* about an opening it had for entertainment editor.

The editor there had cut her teeth in Chicago journalism at the *Sun-Times* (before I started there) and kept a pipeline open. She had previously hired a student of one of my former colleagues, who now taught at Northwestern University, and she tended to favor those who came with a similar recommendation. However she had heard about me, she flew me down, and I went through a similar process of interviewing (preceded by a similar abstinence from smoking dope) in Austin.

Every music critic in the country loved Austin, the site of the annual South by Southwest Music and Media Conference, popularly considered as "spring break for the music industry." SXSW (as it was generally known) in March and JazzFest in New Orleans a month later had been annual highlights of my spring calendar, since the iffy Chicago winter could last into late April. Austin was friendly, easy to navigate, with a storied musical tradition and great salsas, margaritas and barbeque. A smaller market than Chicago, and the newspaper wasn't highly regarded, but a great place to live. And if I truly wanted to leave the rock beat for a desk job, this would be an attractive option.

This time, I received an offer, almost immediately. Unfortunately, the offer was for considerably less than I was making in Chicago, little more than half, for a job that promised more work and responsibility and less fun. It would be a stepping stone—out of Chicago and into a different realm of the newspaper hierarchy—but I wasn't ready to make that step, at least for that money, with a family to support. Surely something better would come along, and, after all, I already had a really good job. But the folks in Austin understood that it had been a tough decision and why I had made it, and we stayed on good terms, promising to keep in touch.

As fate would have it, tragedy would reconnect us less than a year later. On August 27, 1990, Austin blues hero Stevie Ray Vaughan died in a helicopter crash after performing with Eric Clapton and others in an outdoor Wisconsin venue near Chicago. I was working this as a Chicago music story when I received a call out of the blue from the editor of the Austin paper. They were pulling out all the stops on this and asked me if I could feed them anything I had—quotes, details—that they couldn't get from a thousand miles away.

I said I would. I was able to get hold of Chicago blues mainstay Buddy Guy, who came to the phone sobbing. Stevie's death seemed so unfair, after he had cleaned up his life, kicked his addictions, became a 12-step devotee, and was setting an example for others to follow. One of them was his older brother Jimmie, another estimable blues guitarist who had just left the Fabulous Thunderbirds to record with Stevie as the Vaughan Brothers. Now the album they had finished would be Stevie's last musical word and testament. (Until all the inevitable posthumous from-the-vaults releases and reissues.)

When I was done reporting the story from a Chicago perspective I called Austin back, with a quote from Buddy and some other tidbits. As I was ringing off, I mentioned that I still loved Austin and wondered whether anything else had opened up. Funny you should bring that up, the editor replied. Their movie critic had recently left and their music critic wanted to shift positions. Would I be interested in becoming the new music critic?

Would I? Hell, yes. I didn't even need to think this through, weigh any pros and cons. This was the time, and this was the place. I had turned 40 just a couple months earlier, and we had found out that Maria was pregnant with our second just a few months before that. New job, new baby, new city, new life—it was now or never.

This time through, the Austin paper knew what I made, and I knew what they could pay, which again would be a substantial cut from Chicago. But the cost of living was less in Austin (which was then in a lull between booms, and yet to experience the high-tech explosion). And we'd have all of Texas as our backyard.

We'd be leaving friends and family and everything familiar behind, but I figured then (and still figure now) that we'd never lose that, it would always be inside us and available to us, and now we could add to it. Whereas if we stayed in Chicago at a job I felt I was outgrowing for a paper where I saw no future, we'd just be spinning our wheels. Maria had been to Austin with me for SXSW, and if her enthusiasm wasn't unbridled like mine, she knew how much it meant to me and was willing to embark on the adventure.

So everything about the second round just seemed like a formality. If there were other candidates, I never heard about them and never worried about them. I flew down (again), interviewed with everyone (again), sampled the nightlife and the musical attractions and returned home convinced that they would make an offer and I would accept it. Which they did, and which I did. My beat was the city's nightlife, the music clubs in particular, where there would always be friendly faces and free-flowing alcohol. I'm not that much of a party guy, but in Austin that spirit would extend to people my age and well older, who still went to hear music in clubs and often closed them down. What had been a younger person's scene in Chicago was integral to Austin's personality. And I would fit right in.

The only point of negotiation concerned Maria's pregnancy. We were comfortable with her doctors and care up north, and I wasn't about to shake things up with a move and change of benefits until we'd had the baby. So, though I took the offer in mid-September, I wouldn't change jobs until the baby was born. Which would be three months, a long time to keep a secret and for that beat in Austin ostensibly to remain open.

Molly Grace McLeese was born on November 25, 1990, after a few months of false starts and trips to the hospital. I was in Austin by December 1, as I had agreed to come as soon as possible after the birth, and that I would move my whole family down as soon as practical. Many of my Chicago colleagues thought I was insane, moving from a larger market to a smaller one, from more money to less.

Yet it was the best decision I ever made, other than marrying Maria. (Or finding my way to AA.) And it reinforced my sense of trusting my gut instead of conventional wisdom, for Austin would offer riches that couldn't be measured in dollars and cents. And gave me the assurance to know when it was time to leave, even though my friends there thought I was as nuts to leave Austin as my friends in Chicago had thought about my departure from the *Sun-Times*. I had gotten accustomed to trusting gut instincts in making crucial decisions, and my instincts have served me well.

There are some great books on Austin music and culture, and I'd love to write another one. But this isn't it. My beat now required an immersion in Austin music, 24/7, and any writing about the music world at large was secondary, an afterthought. The Austin club culture was different, and on a different clock, than the one I'd known in Chicago. Usually there were three acts—the first rarely starting before 10:30, the headliner starting around 12:30 and finishing just before closing time at 2.

So, this became my new routine, hitting the bars, often three or more in a night, maybe one that had an earlier set scheduled and a couple bands I wanted to see at different club across town. Since my drinking, drugging and sleeping were also subject to routine, I had to adjust that as well. As usual, I didn't subtract from the equation, but only added to it.

Drinking would commence with dinner as before, most of a bottle of wine or a couple margaritas. Then I'd go outside, do my reading, have my cigar. Then it would be time to put the kids to bed, maybe read Kelly a story, before my work night began. And once it began, the drinking would begin again, as if the first round hadn't happened, like I was starting fresh.

Every night I would be out for four or five hours, and over that stretch, one drink would lead to another. Maybe pints of Harp at the Cactus Café, or more margaritas at La Zona Rosa or Shiner Bock at the Continental or Antone's. I would pace myself, feel like I was nursing those drinks, but never letting them get too warm to drink. No less than one an hour, but usually no more than two. A nice, consistent buzz, but always in control. Or usually.

Until it was time to drive home, when a Breathalyzer would certainly have marked me as over the limit. But I was only stopped once, a few months after our move, having closed the Continental Club and heading home. South Congress (not yet the chichi SoCo) was a wide boulevard, one that could easily accommodate the U-turn that I made. I never saw the cop in the car, but he saw me, and he immediately pulled me over with lights flashing.

This was it, I figured. He started with the illegal U-turn, but then asked me about the Illinois plates and the Illinois driver's license, with an address that was no longer mine. I told him that I'd recently moved to take a job at the newspaper, just a couple long blocks north on Congress from where we were stopped. He took this under consideration, and went back to his car. When he returned, he didn't write me up for anything, but just told me to go home and drive carefully.

I have no idea why. Maybe the late hour and the infractions piling up meant that this was more paperwork than it was worth. Maybe he just decided to cut me some slack. If he'd bothered to test my alcohol level, I would have been busted bad, a DUI that would hinder my ability to cover my beat. And if he'd checked the glove compartment for the joint I had in there, I would have been busted worse.

So, I was very grateful and relieved. I had learned my lesson. About drinking and driving and drugs? Of course not. About U-turns. I never made another when I had been drinking, and I scrupulously adhered to speed limits. But I continued to drive drunk every night. And I continued to have a joint I could light so I was stoned by the time I hit the driveway. More efficient—so I could go right to sleep when I got home.

More than ever, my nighttime world was one of bars and drinking, the roadhouses and punk clubs and honky-tonks and blues bars where musical Austin flourished. And where Austin musicians lived nocturnally, not having the day job that I did. So many of them strove for peak creativity and intensity after midnight. Most of them recognized that their gigs depended on attracting drinkers and keeping them drinking. And then it was time for all of us to unwind, to come down, a process that often kept those who worked those bars awake past dawn.

If Austin was one of the nation's liveliest alcohol-fueled playgrounds for music lovers, the flip side was a strong sobriety network for recovery. Those on the alcoholic hamster wheel, often abetted by drugs that kept them awake to drink more, could find plenty of admirable examples of those who had hopped off, straightened out, and seen both their creativity and careers flourish.

Stevie Ray Vaughan, for one, perhaps the most beloved musician in Austin, at least this side of Willie Nelson. The guy whose untimely helicopter crash had proven timely in bringing me to town. A man who not only preached recovery to those closest to him, but whose renewed health and artistry testified to its benefits.

There's a saying that I first heard attributed to him (though, like every saying in AA, he likely heard it from someone else), "The elevator is broken. You've got to take the steps."

Not that I needed to, but I developed some of my closest friendships in Austin with those who had once drunk, likely more than I did, and now drank no longer. Some occasionally mentioned AA, but only fleetingly and in the vaguest terms. Most didn't; they just didn't drink. None suggested that I might have a drinking problem.

The farthest I would go is to recognize that I had a driving problem. When Maria and I were at a party, and I had drunk as much as I wanted (likely more than most), she would drive home. But most of my driving home was from the bars, when Maria was home asleep with the girls, and I would wing it. But drive very carefully doing so.

Everybody knew the real alcoholics on the Austin music scene, and my behavior didn't approach those. There were the legends, like the bluesy Texas troubadour Townes Van Zandt, whose performances could be a shambles if he'd drunk too much. There was the crowd at the Austin Outhouse, who seemed to live to drink. I interviewed one of them, living in way South Austin, his front yard filled with junk cars. In France, he was considered a superstar anti-hero of Texas music, more popular than Willie. In Austin, he was just another drunk.

But at least he had a permanent address. Others were on the couch circuit. Joke: "Q: What do you call a musician whose girlfriend breaks up with him? A: Homeless." I knew drunks who had written songs that friends had recorded on major-label albums, who were now stumbling around South Congress with brown-bagged bottles, slurring their words, the typical alcoholic cliché.

So, in Austin, I had plenty of eyewitness experience with both sides of alcoholism—the damnation to which drink could sentence the alcoholic, the possibility of redemption through recovery. Neither extreme seemed within the realm of possibility for me. I went to the bars nightly, and when I went to the bars I drank, after drinking plenty at home through and after dinner. But I wasn't a sloppy or noisy or a problem drunk. I could hold it better than most, a source of pride, a sign that I was no alcoholic.

There was a time or two when I was carrying on a conversation with someone and then realized this was actually someone else. I supposed I staggered occasionally, even stumbled a time or two. But if nobody else called me on it, I could convince myself that I was doing fine. Now I'm a little embarrassed in the presence of those who might only be half as much in the bag as I was back then. The slurred words, the repetition, the laughter over something that doesn't really seem funny. They probably feel like they're doing just fine as well. And if they don't do it nearly as often as I did, maybe they are.

Though I still considered myself a native Chicagoan, Austin had welcomed us as a second home, and I assumed that we were there for good. I suspect that if I had stayed in Austin, I wouldn't have stopped drinking. As deeply as I bonded with friends who had stopped, as much as I admired them, I figured that they had suffered worse consequences from their drinking—health or jobs or relationships or drunken-driving accidents or the whole shebang—and I had not. (At which point all the twelve-steppers will chorus in unison, "Yet.")

I was more of a social drinker, one whose job required me to be out and about every night. And my drinking when I was out wouldn't be seen as problematic in comparison with the boisterous drunks. Even when I was half-smashed, it was quietly smashed. It would have taken an accident or a drunk driving ticket on the way home to convince me that I needed to change. And I felt fortunate that I had never experienced either consequence. What was really fortunate is that I had never killed anyone else or myself. A ticket might have been fortunate—a wake-up call.

Meanwhile, my career was ascending, at least beyond Austin. As SXSW became more popular, it drew more attention to the city and its music, and I was the main chronicler of it all. I was perfectly positioned to write stories on Austin artists for national magazines, and I was becoming increasingly associated with roots-rock, alt-country and the like (whereas in Chicago I'd been known for covering it all). I even had a regular column in *Rolling Stone* highlighting the sort of music that would soon be known as Americana, as well as writing other reviews and features for them.

Life was good in Austin, and I figured we were there for good. But things change. The editor who had hired me was fired after repeated clashes with the publisher, who would soon move to the paper in Atlanta where I had interviewed—small world. There were a lot of moving pieces during the transition, with interim editors and people jockeying for position. During this process, they made me an offer I couldn't refuse—a high-profile column where I could write about anything I wanted, at a significant increase in salary. The promotion would hasten our departure from Austin, but I had no way to know that then.

My new position meant that I had to reinvent myself as a general columnist, hoping that the readership I had attracted and the reputation I had earned would follow me to the new role. Mostly, they did. And I gained some new readers and followers as well. The life in Austin that had been good became even better. I could still write about music and culture, but I could also write about politics, sports, family issues, media matters and whatever else struck my fancy. It was hard to beat, to be paid more than I ever had to write about whatever I wanted.

As with my music writing, I won statewide awards for the excellence of the column and attracted a loyal readership. But eventually a new editor was hired. And he was not a fan of my column. He saw himself as something of a power broker, where I saw myself as someone who would question and challenge those power brokers. He wanted more reporting and less opinion in the columns. And when there was opinion, he didn't want it to differ from the paper's official opinion on the editorial page. Which was difficult, because the editorial page was infamous for addressing issues late or not at all, and for pulling its punches when it did so. My columnizing was from the Chicago school, where the columnist's voice was all his own.

Eventually that editor brought in layers of other editors. Shortly after their arrival, I lost my column, a decision that the top editor insisted was solely that of his new hires. Which was nonsense, and I lost all remaining respect for him. It was only a matter of time before we left Austin, a city I still loved (and love), but with a newspaper where I felt I could no longer work.

In retrospect, I feel like my response was pretty petulant and typically immature. *I'll show them!* In some ways, I still had a really good gig, with the same salary, and the time and space to concentrate on ambitious features, magazine length and quality, that would run on the Sunday front of the features section. The editors to whom I reported were pretty much the ones who had appreciated my work from the start, and they did their best to shield me from the upper echelon of newer editors whom I resented.

But so much of my identity was wrapped up in my work, and my ego had taken a big blow. I started scouring classified ads in the journalism trades and sending out feelers. I engaged in some serious soul-searching over an offer from the family-run paper in Eugene, Oregon. Not only was this another university town and a comparatively radical city in another fairly conservative state, but they absolutely loved the columns that had gotten my column yanked in Austin. But I couldn't justify another pay cut with two daughters who would need college tuition, and I wasn't sure I had anything to bring and say to Eugene, in the way I had spoken to and for Austin.

So, I ultimately decided to go in a different direction entirely, both geographically and journalistically. I was sick of spouting opinions and making a living at it. I would become fairly anonymous in my new position, less an artist than a craftsman. An editor as carpenter—measuring twice and sawing once, devoted to making things fit while stifling any sort of self-expression.

Within a year after losing my column, I would take a job at a magazine I had never known existed before I applied. And we would move to Des Moines. Maybe another fresh start, and maybe the beginning of the end—of something.

18. No Direction Home

WE HAD MOVED TO AUSTIN IN the year of my 40th birthday. We would return to the Midwest on the cusp of my 50th. Nothing planned about all this, but I was beginning to see a pattern. What changes would my 60th birthday bring? Just as Chicago colleagues had thought I was nuts for moving to that smaller Texas market, Austin thought I was nuts for leaving the hippest city in the universe to live amid the cornfields of Iowa.

I wasn't exactly going into this blind. Though I had never heard of *Midwest Living* magazine before responding to its opening for a senior editor, I was very familiar with the Des Moines-based Meredith Corporation that published it. It was the biggest multimedia corporation not located either in New York or L.A., with tentacles stretching across the country—TV stations, book publishing and dozens of magazines, *Better Homes and Gardens* and *Ladies Home Journal* foremost among them. (It would later swallow the Time/Warner family of magazines, but spit a few of them out.)

They had also been one of my dad's biggest accounts during his mail advertising heyday, and I had fond memories of accompanying him on business trips to Meredith in Des Moines and then on to the office in Lincoln, Nebraska (before his whole company moved to the boss's home town). He had liked the people at Meredith, and had even vacationed with E.T. "Ted" Meredith, who still presided over this family empire. So I felt like this was coming full circle for me to take a job with Meredith. I had a hunch it would somehow work out.

I also had a pair of colleagues and friends who had come to the Austin paper from the *Des Moines Register*, which had once been regarded as the finest midmarket paper in the country, with a statewide reach and readership, before it had turned into just another money machine for the mammoth Gannett chain. They told me what they could about Meredith and about Des Moines, and though both had obviously succumbed to the siren song of Austin, nothing they shared discouraged me.

"Good place to raise a family," is what everyone says about Des Moines. I had a family. We needed a good place to raise it. Des Moines sounded as good as any—affordable, good schools, conveniently located between friends and family in Chicago and those in Lincoln. We would be right on the Interstate 80 bloodline. Perhaps the clincher was that the Chicago Cubs' top minor league team was in Des Moines, and it would be just like seeing developing bands in the bars before they established themselves as stadium superstars. I could do another whole book on the Cubs and baseball drinking, for after music and before books, my loyalty to this team has been my life-longest passion.

So, I went from one of the most vibrant music scenes in the country to one without much music to speak of. Or nightlife. Or restaurants. Des Moines has changed significantly since we moved here at the turn of the century, but the main attraction for the move was what we were leaving behind: a newspaper with an editor who had disrespected me, the daily grind of meeting deadlines and generating column ideas, the identity that had become so inextricably linked with Austin journalism and Austin in general.

In Des Moines, I could reinvent myself by shedding skin. Or something. I would submit to a new routine. And, boy, did it become routine, very quickly. I had always considered myself a 24/7 journalist, a part of me always at work. And now I found my work so structured that it was like trying to fill a house for which I didn't have nearly enough furniture. Unless I was out of town on assignment, a liberation I quickly embraced, I was expected to be in the office no later than 8:30 AM and to leave no earlier than 5.

It was the expectation that bothered me, not the hours. I had been accustomed to starting work well before this and working well into the evening. But this felt like grade school. Like someone was taking attendance. And maybe there would be detention for showing up late. And worse for leaving early—a trip to the principal's office. I still had all of my instinctual rebellious tendencies, and these strictures gave me plenty to rebel against.

Meanwhile, how was I supposed to fill all those hours? I had been accustomed to the adrenalin rush of daily journalism, to cranking out 500-word reviews on deadline and 1500 word features a couple times a week. At this bimonthly magazine, which spoke with a single voice no matter how many the bylines, I had to learn how to spend weeks, even months on end on a single piece, one that would likely be shorter than 500 words and never as long as 1500.

I would see it subjected to round after round of team editing, which I soon began to compare to dogs marking their territory, because even if you'd fixed everything raised by the last round of editing—often doing your best to mediate among conflicting responses from different editors—the next round would find the same editors pissing all over it all over again.

And since every writer was also an editor, I'd also have to do the same with the copy of others, make niggling corrections and suggestions that might make the copy more mine—or at least more institutional, in the magazine's voice—and less the writer's. Some style affectations we learned very quickly. You couldn't write "antique store" (and there were many of these in a publication aimed at female, well-to-do empty nesters), because the reader might think this was simply a very old store. So, "antiques store." And that store couldn't be "on Main Street," because that same reader might fear that the store was in the middle of the street. So, "along Main Street."

When not writing or editing copy, stretching a process that I had been accustomed to taking a day or two into a month or two, we would be expected to do "research" on assignments. Research typically took two forms—finding a version of the same story the magazine had previously done so we could do it as close to the same as before, and contacting the local visitors bureau to send a press kit and arrange a tour. I had done a few travel stories for the newspapers where I'd worked, and we had never involved the PR folks in our preparations. Never let the hotels, restaurants and attractions know we were coming there to write about it. And certainly would never accept the freebies that might influence our opinions. At *Midwest Living*, we were always making official visits, guided by whomever was employed to promote the city or region, and our expenses were more often comped than not. That is, complimentary, on the house.

Maybe this could explain the relentlessly upbeat and uniformly positive tone of the magazine, though that was also a matter of editorial philosophy. Our readers wanted tips on where to go and what to do. Why would we waste any space on places to avoid? If we'd had a bad experience or a bad trip, we simply wouldn't write about it. In my experience, this was never the case. The PR people had experience with the magazine and knew what we wanted. And we'd done our "research."

I often felt that it might have been easier, or just as easy, to write the stories from the brochures rather than fill our notebooks with all these details that would never find room in the tight formats. I always felt that there were two versions of the story I could write after doing my travel reporting—the really interesting story that would be too long and not relentlessly positive enough for the magazine, and the best version that could possibly be published.

Lest all this start sounding like sour grapes, I generally liked the people there, and I enjoyed the travel. The magazine and its parent company had perfected a formula that worked for them, and if there was a problem here, that problem was me. (Well, maybe not only me—of the three of us hired around the same time, I lasted the longest, though both of the others later returned to Meredith.) But I've always been one to gripe. And then to drink about my gripes. I had hoped that this might be the Midwest equivalent of *Texas Monthly*, or that I could help turn it into such a publication with literary flair, one that would explore and illuminate the region. Instead, it was a promotional vehicle, and I was a faceless cog in a machine.

But this is what I'd wanted, right? No longer living by my opinions. Stretching my resume in ways that would expand my employment opportunities. Measuring twice, sawing once, the same damn board, day after day. This felt like a transitional job, a stepping stone, in a way that no other job had for me. Early on, when my wife dropped by to pick me up, she looked around and said, "You really don't seem to fit here."

And I really didn't. Even colleagues who were younger than me seemed more like my parents' friends, 1950s holdovers from the days of bridge club and pride in one's lawn. I couldn't imagine dropping acid with any of them, not that I had been tempted to drop any acid, or even do any cocaine, since becoming a parent. Hell, I didn't even know where to score any weed in Des Moines, as I continued to rely on connections elsewhere.

Because, if anything, my routines had become even more rigidly routine. Wine beginning with dinner at night. Larger glasses, filled to the brim. And when we went out for dinner, it was increasingly to places with low or no corkage fees. Bring your own. Because glasses of restaurant wine cost too much for such skimpy pours.

Cigar after dinner, an hour of solitary respite, reading something for pleasure. Then back inside, drinking whatever would tide me over until bedtime. These were the empty hours, the ones that had to be filled, and I filled them with alcohol. Sips, but I discovered my capacity was increasing, that I could take more and more sips, for longer and longer. I was drinking cognac or even whiskey as if it were wine. I was no longer going out to hear music, which was in shorter supply in the bars of Des Moines, and I no longer had to concern myself with driving home. I already was home. Waiting for everybody else to go to bed. So I could continue drinking as much as I wanted without suspicion or challenge.

Then, nightly, a joint before bed. Taking the edge off whatever I had been drinking to take the edge off. Not only was the routine rigidly predictable, and not only was I drinking more than I had been in Austin, but I was drinking differently. I wasn't out, or working, or facing a deadline; I was drinking because I drank. Self-medication as an end in itself, no longer the means toward the end of doing a job. And I now drank alone, at home. Though I had never been very social, at least much of my previous drinking was out in public. Now I was an anti-social drinker, using it to isolate, with nobody to bother me, nobody to judge me, unless Maria was still awake when I staggered to bed.

From the perspective of hindsight, I can see that there's no way for this to end well, but at the time I saw no reason for concern. What had once been a coping mechanism—to cope with deadlines and other professional pressures—had become a numbing agent. My life had become like the movie "Groundhog Day," though it didn't seem like a bad life. The workload was lighter than it had been in a newsroom, and I was well compensated for the tedium. We didn't have any social life, but I didn't much like people anyway. I read books, listened to music, watched the Cubs, went to movies. The stuff that gave my life whatever meaning and purpose it had, the stuff I could access pretty much wherever I lived.

Yet this was the only job and city that had seemed transitional to me from the outset, and if I had one more move in me, I knew I had to make it soon. As I went deeper into my 50s, I suspected I would find opportunities narrowing from slim to none. Now that I had an editor's chops, at least on my resume, I started thinking that maybe I could return to newspapers as the book critic/editor for one of them, transforming the beat so I'd handle the biggest stories and reviews myself and assigning the others to freelancers.

I began discussing the possibility with a paper in San Antonio (soon to be another one newspaper city), where my reputation still had some currency, and the features editor there was intrigued enough to pursue it. Then the Austin paper had a situation where it wanted to improve its book coverage and dump the woman who had been providing it. Even though these were the same editors who had let me go, we all thought that the book beat would be less problematic than my column had been. And I was a known quality with a loyal readership.

None of it came to anything. I put San Antonio on the backburner when Austin decided to fly me back for a round of interviews. The friend and editor who picked me up at the airport cheerfully informed me that the paper had instituted a hiring freeze the day before, but had decided not to cancel the interview because they had already bought the plane ticket and it would be so good to see me again.

So, we all went through the motions, interviewing me for a job that they couldn't offer me (and thus ended up filling from within). I was pissed, but this reaffirmed my belief that leaving Austin had been the right thing to do. By the time I resumed discussions with San Antonio, the same sort of budgetary concerns were in place there. The idea that the entire industry was a sinking ship had yet to take hold, but plainly it had sprung some significant leaks, and I had jumped, without knowing it and planning it, at just about the right time.

Because I've never been much for long-range planning—proceeding instead by hunch, impulse, happenstance—I often only realize the full consequences of a choice in retrospect. If I had stayed at that newspaper in Austin, I would now be out of work, or at least out of newspapers. Almost all of my colleagues with whom I'd worked at the Austin paper, and at the Chicago paper, for that matter, are no longer there. Some have retired, not necessarily by choice. Others have retrained themselves for different jobs, different careers, perhaps taking steep pay cuts from the days when newspapers had been flush.

I somehow avoided all this, but not through any master plan. Call it chance, or luck, or fate, or just the way things were supposed to work out. Among the good friends we'd left behind in Austin were Frank and Gigi Durham, both music fans, both journalism professors at the University of Texas. I had taught a course in feature writing at UT as an adjunct—the academic equivalent of freelance—and had been having lunches with Frank and going with him to concerts.

A year or so after my family had moved to Des Moines, the Durhams had moved to the University of Iowa in Iowa City, 100 miles to the east. That fall, Gigi invited me to visit her feature writing class, similar to the one I had taught, to share the perspective of a working professional with students. She also told me about an opening in the department, for someone with my sort of experience, no doctorate required. Since PhD's are typically a prerequisite for tenure-track positions, which this was, it was a rare opportunity, one that seemed like fate with us living so close.

Maria wasn't enthusiastic, with good reason. She had moved for my job in Austin and then moved for my job in Des Moines. She was done moving. As were the kids, who were just settling in and getting adjusted. And I figured it was a longshot, that there would be other applicants with better academic credentials, or journalistic resumes, or both. But the process of application offered a formal opportunity to take stock, as I learned from Frank and Gigi.

The single-page cover letter with a resume (CV, or curriculum vitae, in academic lingo), and a bunch of clips wouldn't cut it. Frank advised that this letter or statement or whatever could well run 10-15 pages, and that I should study the job posting closely, follow its prompts and explain how my life and experience up to now had made me exactly what the university was looking for. In other words, justify myself and my curious decisions, tell how I had once intended to be a professor, during my University of Chicago days, but had instead run away to join the circus, as I had come to think of my decades on the rock beat. Now I was perfectly prepared to fulfill my grad-school ambitions, a prodigal son returning to the hallowed halls of academe. What a grown-up move! In my early 50s.

I wrote and polished the letter on New Year's Day, 2003, enjoying this ceremonial exercise in taking stock, in explaining myself to myself, not necessarily expecting this to lead anywhere. Why worry about the logistics of living a hundred miles from work unless we had to?

19. Back to School

I wasn't overly surprised about being invited to interview, because I knew I had two advocates within the department in the Durhams, and I figured I was cheap to take a chance on because it was just a two-hour drive over (plus a night in a downtown hotel). I felt fine through the interview process, thought I did well with the sample classroom lecture (in front of the faculty) and left knowing little more about the process than I had when I'd submitted the application. I didn't know how many other applicants they had or might be interviewing, how stiff the competition might be or how long the whole thing might take.

As we headed toward May, months after my winter visit to Iowa City, I figured that either I had been eliminated (and not informed) or that they were waiting to hear from their top choice. The semester would end soon and the courses that whoever they hired would be teaching were already posted. They had to do something soon, didn't they?

They did. After I had been counseled to sit tight, I received an offer right at the end of that spring semester, a slightly unusual one that helped account for the delay (though academe tends to move at a glacial pace in the best of times). I was being offered the position at the rank of Associate Professor rather than Assistant Professor as was customary. This allowed them to offer me a more competitive salary, though less than I was making as a journalist. It was a tenure-track position, but my clock was set at three years before the decision, rather than six, the time that an assistant prof is given. As with law firms and partnerships, I had three years to finish my provisional status, and then it would either be up or out.

What I didn't know, and didn't learn until after I had accepted, was that though they'd begun with only one job to offer, they ended up petitioning for two. It seems like they liked me and another candidate both so much, and figured our expertise was both so different and complementary, that they convinced the powers that be to make another tenure line available. I didn't realize at the time just how rare this was, as tenure lines kept diminishing, but the department knew it would soon have other openings (with retirements imminent) and why not anticipate filling another now rather than going through the expense of another search?

The other guy was an investigative reporter from the Los Angeles Times and had won a Pulitzer Prize. He was plainly their first choice, though he had yet to accept their offer before I did. When he joined the faculty and turned his investigative experience into a course called "Depth Journalism," I joked that I could offer "Shallow Journalism" as a counterpart, reflecting the stereotype of entertainment and celeb journalism as fluff.

I knew that I would regret it forever if I couldn't work things out to take this offer, but we had yet to address logistics. By chance, a former colleague at the *Sun-Times* was a non-tenured lecturer in the department, and he had the same logistical issues I did. He lived in Des Moines, where his wife worked, and commuted to Iowa City, where he would stay two nights and three days each week. He had found a family that would rent him a room for less than a motel would charge.

I pursued a similar arrangement and found it, with a guy who ran a (legitimate) massage school out of his house and rented rooms, mainly on lucrative football weekends. Not only did I have full kitchen privileges, but he was also a cigar smoker, with a three-season porch and wood burning stove to keep it warm, complete with cable TV. He was also an alcoholic who had stopped drinking, though I didn't know that when I moved in, and he had started drinking again by the time I moved out. Not that I had made it look like fun, drinking brandy after dinner, big glasses full, lost in my book and cigar. But I guess I had made it look manageable. It was the routine with which I ended every day there, after confining myself to my office and classroom throughout the daylight hours, then grabbing a takeout pizza or something to eat with the wine I had squirreled away in my room.

I didn't leave any of my other things there, since I had plenty of office space to hold whatever I would need regularly in Iowa City. But every week I would pack three days' worth of clothes, food, cigars, booze, whatever. And then I would repack to return home, and unpack again, always feeling like I was living out of a suitcase. Our courses were scheduled for Monday-Wednesday or Tuesday-Thursday, so I would pretty much pack a full week's campus work—committee meetings, office hours, publication research, class prep—time with students—into three days.

No matter what time I taught, I'd generally be in my office before anyone else, around 8, and be there through late afternoon or early evening. I had no social life in Iowa City and didn't want one (though the Durhams graciously invited me to their family dinners once a week). I was there to work, and I worked hard, knowing that the tenure clock was ticking. When my work day was over, I needed to relax hard, shift my mind that was in overdrive back to neutral, so I could go to sleep. I began drinking even more with dinner, and then drank till I dropped after my cigar. Maria wasn't there to keep tabs on me. Whatever bottle I'd brought on Monday—brandy or cognac or whatever—would be finished by Wednesday, to be replaced by another that I'd finish at home before returning to school. I'd usually try to gauge things so it might look to Maria that the level was staying pretty much the same, diminishing incrementally, when in fact I was going through bottles at an alarming rate, or one that she would have found alarming, keeping the new one close to the level of the old one.

Perhaps professors weren't the notorious drunks that journalists were, but the University of Iowa had a legacy all its own, as the Iowa Writers Workshop was foremost in the country at developing top talent into published authors and attracting legendary alcoholics to help them develop. You could still purchase liquor at John's Groceries—"Dirty John's"—which had supplied John Cheever and Raymond Carver during their Iowa City sprees, and drink at the Deadwood, or the Mill or wherever else student writers had gathered to grouse after workshopping sessions. Not that I participated in such social drinking rituals, but I appreciated the continuity and being a part of it. And I shopped weekly at Dirty John's.

Except for the back and forth of the 100-mile commute, everything about this decision to slide from journalism into journalism education felt right. I had been in some sort of identity limbo at *Midwest Living*, all but anonymous in Des Moines, the first time in decades that I hadn't had a regular byline in the newspaper of the city where we lived.

"Daddy, remember when you used to be famous?" ten-year-old Molly asked, referring to our Austin years. Not that I had been, but in our neighborhood, when I'd walk her to grade school, someone might stop us and tell me how much she'd enjoyed the column that morning. Or her teacher might make some reference to something I'd written. So, to Molly at least, I was once a public figure.

In Des Moines, I could hardly have been less public, barely even knowing our neighbors, having a couple friends at work that I didn't much see outside of it. Kelly was also having some trouble fitting in among middle-school girls who had known each other since the playground days. Molly found herself with a group of girls in her neighborhood, their allegiances and alliances always shifting. Our lives were different than they had been in Austin. Drinking helped take the edge off those differences.

Now I was establishing a brand new identity—tenure-track professor at the state's flagship university, with a closer connection than most Iowans to the school they had attended and/or the football team they still rooted for. So many had formative memories of Iowa City—where the university had recently been named the number-one party school in the country, and the tailgating before football games typically began around dawn. Many who participated in the ritual didn't even have tickets for the games, while others who did would be passed out before kickoff.

I never experienced that side of Iowa City, the one where the weekend began on Thursdays, or even Wednesday nights, when the bars were filled with underage students, many of the girls notoriously underdressed in next to nothing (even in winter), the cops notoriously vigilant to write public intoxication tickets at closing time.

When I was there, typically driving over Monday around sunrise and returning home Wednesday by dinner, the University of Iowa was more stereotypically studious, the best students serious about their work. I loved being in the classroom with them, and certainly found it more rewarding than the Meredith magazine offices. I was learning a new profession, and I was even more eager to learn than my students were. I'd been warned to avoid relying on "war stories," that any back-in-the-day reminiscences would be lost on students who had yet to be born back in that day.

But, in my case, the students themselves were the ones who most wanted to engage in such talk. They were particularly impressed by my connection to *Rolling Stone*, even though it had been severed a decade earlier and none of them read *Rolling Stone*. (But many aspired to work for it.) I had met a lot of famous people that even they knew—a Beatle, all of U2, the Rolling Stones, Madonna—and so some of that reflected aura stayed with me. Some of them aspired to the sort of career I'd had, an ambition that still seemed realistic when I started teaching, less so as digital technology accomplished its hostile takeover of media culture. And made it so hard to get paid a living wage for writing criticism, or writing anything.

Those three years after my hire would prove to be among the most transformational of our lives for everyone but Maria. And perhaps that made the impact of this period greater on Maria than on anyone, a different and darker sort of transformation. With my tenure clock ticking furiously, I had to balance the coursework demands of this new career with the only slightly longer-term focus of publishing or perishing. I had been told that a book would make tenure a slam dunk decision, and that all I needed to do was write and publish one. Is that all?

The end of this period would also mark Kelly's transition from high school into college, wherever she decided to go, and Molly's entrance into high school, and all that entailed. When I had taken the job, we had also decided that this would be the time we'd revisit our living situation, and the department assumed, as I had led them to believe, that we would be pulling up stakes in West Des Moines and settling down in Iowa City. We didn't. Maria's occasional visits to Iowa City had convinced her that it had even less to offer than Des Moines. I sometimes joked with my students that I had been following a course of downward mobility, bigger markets to ever smaller ones, Chicago to Austin to Des Moines to…Iowa City? Peoria? Podunk?

It was a joke to me, because I knew how well each move thus far had turned out, but it was no laughing matter for Maria. If anything, the three years would strengthen her resistance toward moving, though she had no increasing affection for Des Moines. We both retained strong ties to Chicago and an emotional connection to Austin, but neither one of us felt much either way toward Iowa. Nice place to raise a family. And our girls were definitely becoming Iowans, developing whole new sets of friends and cultural references.

I had secured a job here, one that would be pretty much guaranteed forever, with no retirement age, if I could just make it through the tenure gauntlet. Kelly and Molly both had lives here, and pretty much everything that enriched those lives, at least socially. Maria had nothing but us; she otherwise felt adrift in Iowa, like everyone else in the family was pushing forward to brighter futures and she was spinning her wheels.

She had always felt unusually close to the girls, who told her everything, but this was changing as well. Inevitably. The teen years can be tough on mother-daughter relationships, particularly when the mother remains so invested in that closeness, which makes the daughters even more determined to pull away and establish their autonomy. Which left Maria with me, only there half the time and not all there even when I was. As I had learned from the tension between my parents when I was growing up, the more Maria demanded, the less I responded. She started going upstairs to bed earlier after dinner; I kept drinking, more and more.

Cramming a week's academic schedule into two and a half days left me spent by the end of my two-hour drive home. It was about all I could do to eat dinner, feign some interest in conversation and then drink myself into oblivion before returning to the land of the living the next morning. Maria resented that she was just something else to fit into my schedule, and she was right to do so. My priorities were professional, because professional priorities would secure our personal future. Besides, I reasoned, a month off at Christmas, and a three-month summer break—these would be ours forever, and they were certainly worth the short-term trade-off until then.

We were verging on a turning point. Or a breaking point.

20. Breakdown

IN HINDSIGHT, IT WAS OBVIOUS that the center could not hold. But before things fall apart, you find it hard to imagine how they ever could. And once they have fallen apart, it seems impossible to put everything back together again. My routine-enforced stability provided scant protection from the dark chaos to come. And distinctions among physical, mental and familial health no longer seemed to mean or matter much.

This was uncharted territory.

Spring break of Kelly's senior year in high school provided the breaking point. Spring break was when high-school seniors were supposed to go wild, but Kelly was never really the wild sort, and we weren't about to subsidize Mexico or some other rite-of-passage bacchanal. So Maria had arranged for her brother in Florida to house Kelly and a few of her closest girlfriends for a beach week, with Maria shepherding them and Molly accompanying them. My spring break didn't coincide with theirs, so Maria would need to do all the things I usually did—rent the car, handle the driving and money, navigate her way from the Orlando airport to Vero Beach on the coast, a couple hours' drive. Traveling in the best of times made her a little anxious, and the closer we came to zero hour, the worse she felt.

On the day before their scheduled departure, she suffered sharp pains in her abdomen. She went to her doctor, who said she likely had an infection and shouldn't fly. Maria has long suffered from a nervous stomach, sometimes diagnosed as diverticulitis or colitis, but in its milder forms she has just called it "stomach monkeys." This was one area where we knew that the line between physical and mental health blurred, that relaxing would ease the stomach woes, that this too would pass.

But there was no way Maria wanted to get on that airplane, where she might have to keep running to the bathroom. Or, worse, strapped in her seatbelt when she needed to. And, besides, it wasn't her decision, it was doctor's orders. So we had to cancel, a day before everyone was to head for the airport. The girls had looked forward to the trip for months and their parents had paid for non-refundable tickets, but this was beyond anyone's control. Nobody blamed Maria, at least out loud.

Except Maria. She was down on herself for feeling she had let everyone else down, yet she would have felt even worse if she had gone. And this—the pain in the abdomen, the disappointment—was the start of the downward spiral that would quickly spiral out of control. Through the rest of that day, having made the decision not to go, she had no energy or motivation to get out of bed, yet she couldn't really sleep. She had no appetite. She had no spark. We had an appointment for tests at the hospital the next day, where she would need to drink a gallon or so (or so it seemed) of fluids she could barely stomach. It was tough enough to coax her out of bed for that.

I, of course, kept to my routine. This had been a tough day, and I would end it as I always had, with most of a bottle of wine, a cigar, some cognac, a joint. Having nullified the day as best I knew how, I came to bed, and passed out. At least for me, one day had ended, and I could start fresh in the morning. If Maria had been awake or semiconscious during this stretch, she had shown no signs of it. In hindsight, I recognize how shameful this might seem, to barely be there for her when she needed me most. But, in my denial, I'd thought

I was doing my best to hold things together while she fell apart. And my routines were essential to that, or so it seemed at the time.

The next day, things got way worse. At the hospital, the test results confirmed a colon infection, and the antibiotic came with instructions that seemed conflicting, or at least conflicted with the advice of Maria's doctor. To make things easier on her digestive system, he had prescribed a liquid diet. Yet these medications required that they be taken with a full stomach.

Meanwhile, Maria didn't feel like eating much of anything, and increasingly didn't feel much of anything at all. She seemed suspended between two states, never quite falling asleep but never really waking up—listless, almost lifeless—a suspension that would last for days on end. She worried about not eating, and not sleeping, which made her increasingly nervous and less likely to do either. I would hover in and out of the bedroom throughout the day, and disappear to go through my routine after my dinner. Day after day, night after night.

Realizing that we had gone well beyond abdominal infection, we made calls to try to find Maria a psychiatrist or psychologist who might coax her back from the abyss. Such services are woefully inadequate in Iowa, and we were told repeatedly that it would be two or three months before there was an opening. For Maria, seven or eight days of this had become an eternity; even two or three hours were hell. She just felt totally drained—physically, psychologically, emotionally—and exhausted.

It was like a war of attrition, and it wore her to the nub. She felt like she couldn't take it any longer, and that nothing would ever change. She started thinking about starting the car with the garage door closed, sitting there and killing herself. So she told Kelly, when she happened to come home from high school for lunch, something she hardly ever did. Maria was glad to see her, and called Kelly her savior, her angel. Kelly was as alarmed as any dutiful teenaged daughter would be over her mother's thoughts of suicide, and she tried to call me. Over and over again.

Unfortunately, I was now in the mode of my weekday routine, driving to Iowa City for class. There was a dead zone on our cellphone service of about an hour on the drive. By the time she reached me, Kelly had called my brother, Richard, who had urged her to take Maria to the hospital, where the psychiatric ward was now processing her admittance. I drove right back.

There was a pragmatic benefit to this crisis escalation. In the hospital, she could receive the psychiatric care that had been unavailable as an outpatient. She would be monitored around the clock, receive medication that would have to be tweaked a couple of times for her anxiety, depression and sleeplessness. She would feel safe there, and she seemed happier when we visited, more like herself.

That long weekend in the hospital left her feeling that she was making some sort of progress, seeing some light and hope, after her depression had boxed her into such a dark, claustrophobic space. She could recognize that she had more of a spark to her than most of the other patients, those who were heavily medicated or perhaps beyond medication. We talked of her coming home as soon as they would let her, and she was eager to do so. She was eating, and she was sleeping. She was smiling, at least occasionally, even laughing.

And so she was released after that weekend's observation, home with prescriptions to fill and a psychiatrist who had her under his care as a patient. She also went home to an uneasy limbo, feeling like the outside world bombarded her into sensory overload, that everything was too bright, too loud, too quick. She had felt well enough to leave the hospital, but didn't feel quite as well once she was out, particularly outside the house. If she didn't belong in the hospital, and she didn't feel right in the world, where did she belong? She retreated again into the bedroom, lights off, shades drawn.

Working toward a transition, we took baby steps—walks around the block, drives to the park. She didn't necessarily want to get out of bed, but she knew she had to. When we talked a little about what had happened, what would happen, her tone was flat, though occasionally she would tear up. It was if she were a bystander to her own life, that she had seen something happen, rather than done anything or had something happen to her. She had no more understanding of what she was going through, what we were all going through, than any of us did. It was as if somebody else needed to flip the switch, and things would be over, things would be better.

But things remained the same. Intolerable for Maria, a familiar routine for me. The kids had to go back to school, and I had to go back to teach. But there would be no staying half the week in Iowa City. I would be home every night to make or microwave or bring back something for dinner, and we would all be together, like a regular family. Then the kids would go to bed and I would continue to drink. Maria softly insisted that she was no danger to herself, that she would be fine alone, that closing the garage and turning on the car was something she would never do. No one in her right mind would.

Meanwhile, we were in limbo, and I was pretty much on autopilot—drive a hundred miles to school, teach a couple of classes, drive home. Leave before 8, home before dinner. The girls needed some semblance of order, of routine. They asked if their mother would be okay, and I assured them she would, that this was something we had to get past, get over, work through. And that we would. I guess I believed it, because what other option did I have, did we have? To think that things would not get better was unthinkable. This was just a long nightmare from which we were all trying to awaken.

From dinner through bedtime, I drank. Every night. More and more, once the girls were asleep or at least in their rooms. Enough to dull any doubts or uncertainties or resentments. Enough to drown my consciousness into unconsciousness. I needed to sleep so I could awaken to do my work. And if I didn't drink, I couldn't sleep. I was sure of it. Often I would fall asleep on the couch, glass in my hand, the brandy or whatever else, what little of it was left, spilled on my shirt. Drinking helped me manage my life, hold it all together, or so I thought. It would take years before I realized how deep in denial I had been.

Maria mostly remained in bed, never fully asleep, or so she believed, and never quite awake. It was hard not to hover, to monitor her, which made her uncomfortable. As did being left alone. She seemed to want the comfort of knowing someone was near, but not too near. And during the long days at school when each of us was away, she knew at least that we would be home soon enough.

For a month or more, we lived like this, tenuously, looking for signs of improvement, fearing that things could get worse. Walking on eggshells. The line between physical and mental health seemed so tenuous, and so did the distinction between sick and well. She had long been well, well enough, as well as any of the rest of us. And now she was sick, with the light that had been in her eyes barely flickering, with no motivation or even energy, just staying in bed, often with the covers pulled over her head.

We looked for signs, small victories, like when she would eat something for which she plainly had no appetite. A bigger victory was when she would leave the bedroom and walk downstairs, maybe for just a change of scenery. Even bigger, when she would shower and get dressed, and we would take a short walk, around the block, not talking much, for talking and listening threatened to disturb her. Something had to give, somehow, someday.

On a sunny Saturday in May, when Maria seemed to be having one of her better mornings, she came downstairs and we had coffee together and read the newspapers, like we once had. She said she was going to go upstairs and rest, take a nap, and she encouraged me to go work out. I did, for a little more than an hour.

When I returned, the bedroom door was closed, so I left her alone. Until I heard her calling me. And went upstairs to find her on the floor of the master bathroom, her wrists all bloody, the big kitchen knife next to her. She had taken her suicide intentions to the next step, though not the final one. As I walked her downstairs to rush her to the hospital, Kelly opened her bedroom door, just getting up, and saw her mother and the blood. I told her I'd call, and that mom would be all right.

Maria's mood when we checked her into the hospital for return was lighter, almost serene. There was some deadpan joking during the paperwork, and it seemed she felt better now, safer. The way the ER attendant interpreted it, her medications had been out of whack, and this was like a cry for help. He told her that she could come to emergency any time she felt her meds were off kilter and her doctor wasn't available. She didn't need to slice her wrists to get the attention she needed.

During this second, longer stay at the hospital, Maria received a lot more help on what to do the next time, or to prevent a next time. Meanwhile, I learned a lot. One thing I learned was that her slight improvement after her first release from the hospital had made it more likely, rather than less, that she would attempt suicide. Because such a major step required more energy, motivation and sense of purpose than she'd had during the initial dark period.

The other thing I learned, mainly from talking with Maria, who seemed to have some perspective on her crisis that she hadn't had (or hadn't shared) before was how tough it was to be feeling so awful when the weather was so nice, when it was so warm and sunny, when everyone was feeling better and every sign was that she should be too. Everyone knows that the holidays are tough for the depressed, and that the winter's cold and gray brings seasonal affect disorder, but spring apparently carries a cruel emotional irony for those who can't share its spirit. The warmer and brighter it was outside, the greater the gap between how Maria felt she should be feeling and how she actually felt.

Maria received a lot of advice through workbooks and group sessions, on how to recognize the warning signs, the triggers, and what to do about them or how to avoid them. She needed to feel more connected, less alone, and the hospital was good for that. And when I picked her up and took her home the second time, a few days after we'd celebrated Mother's Day in the hospital, a couple of weeks before Kelly's high school graduation, we knew that it didn't mean she was "over" anything.

We would need to be careful, vigilant; she would have to ease back into some sort of daily life. And we would receive a lot of crucial help, from family and friends, who would let Maria know that they were there for her, that they loved her, that she didn't need to make it through anything on her own. And neither did I. For months, we had somebody coming to visit and staying for awhile—my sister and sisters-in-law, Maria's dad—nobody there to judge her (which Maria generally feared everyone was), just to love her and help her and be with her.

Maria never did make it back to where we were before. Instead, the experience took her, and all of us, to a different place, where I think she is in a stronger position than she had been. We now know how easily the rock can crumble, how the stability we had taken for granted can be temporary, illusory, that conventional notions of the mind-body dichotomy are just an artificial construct.

And she learned that there are tools and resources, triggers to acknowledge and anticipate, support groups, exercise and fresh air and connections that could help her from feeling trapped in such a dark and claustrophobic place, the place that her very self had become. She would always have this memory, this experience of how bad things had been, and she would never feel that she was entirely free from the possibility of returning there. It was like cancer, in a way, in remission. But she now knew she could live through it, or at least that she had.

Coincidentally, while I was immersed in writing this chapter, revisiting such a fragile time in our lives, a delicate balance that we feared would either last forever or end way too soon, it seemed that depression had permeated the consciousness of the culture at large. In quick succession designer Kate Spade and multimedia foodie Anthony Bourdain had both died by hanging themselves, and it appeared that suicide itself was on the rise, as if an epidemic. It was the topic of the times, for weeks on end.

The question of "Why?" went viral across journalism and social media, as if there were some sort of pat answer that could put borders around this abyss, make it manageable. And then the focus of attention shifted elsewhere, as it always does.

By happenstance, I was also immersed in reading *Spring* by Karl Ove Knausgaard, the Norwegian novelist celebrated for his autobiographical, multivolume *My Struggle*. This new, nonfiction series of books was seasonal, commemorating the birth of his youngest daughter, and this third book was different than the previous two. It blindsided me, just like Maria's hospitalization had blindsided me. In fact, the story he told of his wife's depression and attempted suicide could have passed, word for word, for Maria's.

"It had culminated in a severe depression," he writes to his daughter, who is still far too young to read this, "with your mother lying motionless in bed, unable to perform even the least demanding of actions, such as listening to the radio or reading, much less get dressed, get up and face the day."

Exactly. And, then, after things got worse, they eventually got better:

> "Life stabilised, even though these events stayed alive within her, like a kind of reverberation, for the oscillations between high and low were still noticeable even if no longer unmanageable, and they gradually became smaller and smaller."

In Maria's case, the scars grew fainter, but they never disappeared. It was the worst of times, the darkest. But it made Maria stronger, knowing that whatever she was going through, this too shall pass. And in a way none of us could have anticipated, it led to my sobriety.

21. The Other Shoe Drops

WE TELL STORIES TO OURSELVES, about ourselves, to try to understand ourselves. The way I've told Maria's story isn't necessarily the way she would tell it. And it's her story to tell. My story, in this book at least, is about drinking and then not drinking. Maria's story proved pivotal in this, at least as I now understand it, in the story I tell myself. At the time, I didn't understand much of anything. What had happened to Maria seemed out of the blue, but in retrospect it was easy to render it as a chain reaction of causes and effects, starting with the trip that she hadn't wanted to cancel, but hadn't wanted to take. And then everything just went haywire. And dark, very dark. Eventually, things got brighter, as they often do with the passage of time, the healing of wounds.

Though Maria's nervous stomach, her "stomach monkeys," had been a condition of our lives since I had known her, what subsequently happened with me was without precedent. I had never experienced or anticipated anything like it. I was tempted to title this chapter "My Turn," but that would have seemed like I felt entitled, that now that she had had her chance to fall apart, and I had been there for her, it was my turn to fall apart.

And I guess I feel that way, but only in retrospect, because I've only been able to connect the dots after the fact. At the time, what was happening made no sense whatsoever. I still occasionally reviewed music as a freelancer, now that my full-time employment had shifted from journalism to academe. I was reviewing a solo show by Wilco's Jeff Tweedy in Iowa City, staying over on a night before I would be teaching the next morning. I had asked for the assignment because I wanted to see the show. Nothing out of the ordinary, nothing I hadn't done many thousands of times. I watched and listened, took notes, had a pretty good idea what I would be writing the next morning. I had drunk my drinks before the concert, and I smoked a joint on the drive back to my room. Went to bed, oblivious, woke in the morning, drank my coffee, started typing. Piece of cake. Almost like automatic pilot.

I must stress that I was consciously feeling no stress whatsoever. The review was going well. I was all but done with an hour and a half to go before class, one which on this day didn't require much prep. I was typing my last paragraph before emailing my review. And then, all of a sudden, I couldn't. My left arm was dead, and I had no movement in my fingers. I was terrified. I thought I was suffering a heart attack, but I wasn't sure what I could do, what I was capable of doing. Sit still? Lie on the floor? There was no one else in the house where I stayed in Iowa City, and I don't know that I would have had the strength to shout if there were. I didn't know where my phone was, and I didn't know if I had the strength to call Maria and talk to her if I could find it. I was afraid that the numbness in my arm and hand would spread to the rest of my body. But since it hadn't, I walked downstairs.

Not "decided to walk downstairs," because my brain was pretty fuzzy, and I wasn't deciding anything. Not even thinking "this too shall pass," because I had no idea what "this" was and I was scared it would spread. But walking helped, somehow, as did breathing while I was walking, focusing on these essential processes. Maybe 15 minutes after my arm had gone numb, I started regaining some feeling in it. My fingers started working again, and I somehow remembered that last sentence I had been about to type, so I typed it, sent the story, drove to class and everything seemed fine.

So that was that. Everything seemed fine, as if this hadn't happened. But it had, and I had to tell Maria, knowing she would tell me to go to the doctor, which I was always more hesitant to do than she was. Especially when things seemed fine. So I promised her if anything else felt even a little bit off, I would call the doctor right away, and I would be sure to mention this to him the next time I went in any case.

No harm, no foul, as they say in basketball. But that weekend, after I had returned home, a whole different strain of inexplicable invaded my nervous system. We were at a fast-food style restaurant, where you order at the counter and find a table, when I experienced a sensory overload of voice and vision that I might have considered an acid flashback, if I had any experience with such, or was in any condition to consider anything.

We quickly wrapped our food and took it home, because the cacophony of voices, all these different conversations, was driving me crazy. I wasn't sure what was wrong with me, but I was desperate to make it right. Maria had experienced something similar during her fragile recovery, when a trip to Target had made her want to flee because everything had been too loud, too bright. Among her pharmaceutical cocktail that she continued to take daily was Clonazepam, an anti-anxiety medication, a benzo. She thought this might help me, and I was desperate to try anything, so I took one of hers. It worked. I felt calm; I felt fine. So now I had additional impetus to see the doctor, not only because I had experienced two incidents in short succession that would have otherwise seemed to me unrelated, but because I wanted my own prescription.

When I saw him on Monday and described what had happened first, and then second, he said that both of them sounded like panic attacks. He agreed to write me my own prescription for Clonazepam, which I continued to take daily (and continued to take, though in a minimal dosage, for almost a decade afterward). I told him that I also planned to consult a psychiatrist for the medication and a therapist for talk, which struck him as a sensible course of action.

This was a turning point for me, though I wouldn't realize the significance of the turn until a couple of years later, or address all of its implications until I fashioned a narrative for this book. I would return to therapy, which I hadn't done since leaving Chicago, and had felt no need for since my second marriage. Maria was the one in therapy, first for postpartum depression and currently for a much deeper depression. She was the sick one; I was the healthy one. Or so I had thought.

And I would begin taking psychotropic drugs, for the first time in my life, at least on a prescription basis, and perhaps for the rest of my life. I had often joked about "self-medication"—the substances I relied on to go to sleep, the jolt myself awake, to get high, to fill the void in my life—but this would be the first time I would be using anti-anxiety medication, and, soon, anti-depressants, to address the working model of chemical imbalance that psychiatry had begun to favor, a genetic predisposition that plainly ran in my bloodline.

Pills came with instructions, and the instructions, I had always figured, were there to ignore. I considered them lawyer talk, with the cataloging of possible side effects and activities and other substances to avoid. I mean, I was fine with not operating any heavy machinery while taking the drugs, and I wouldn't be doing any breast feeding. But "avoid drinking alcohol while taking this drug"? I figured that was the pharmaceutical company covering its ass, with legal boilerplate.

I had taken plenty of other drugs with this admonition, and had never followed it. I drank daily, rain or shine, in sickness and in health. If I'd really thought that starting down this pharmaceutical path meant no more drinking, I would never have taken the first step. Weird things had been happening with me, but I would barrel mt way through them. Panic attacks? Me? What panic?

So I kept drinking like I had been drinking, and "like I had been drinking" meant drinking progressively more. Progression can be a slippery slope, but the sort of limits I had once put on myself were long gone, or at least significantly extended. I had no problem with averaging a bottle of wine a night, now that I was away from journalism and deadline writing, and my snifter of after-dinner cognac, or whiskey or whatever, filled to the brim, was now two or more.

I was drinking alone, with no one watching, and nothing to do beyond making my way to bed. And I wasn't suffering the sort of morning repercussions that had once kept me in line, the queasy stomach and dry mouth and headache. My body now seemed to be able to accommodate what had once given me a hangover. I could drink as much as I wanted, and I wanted to drink a lot. I was not a normal drinker, nor did I want to be. I was an exceptional drinker, with an exceptional capacity.

I will always associate Templeton Rye with the penultimate chapter of what AA would euphemistically call my "drinking career," as if the progression of thirst were a matter of professional promotion and escalating salary. Whereas it was more like a spiral of demotion that had me spending more and more to support my habit. Anyway, Templeton Rye briefly became quite the phenomenon in Iowa—a small-batch product made from a rediscovered Prohibition-era recipe. It was like the craft beer of rye, but even more exclusive.

"Enjoy the good stuff!" exhorted the promotional campaign, which claimed that it had been Al Capone's drink of choice. And the low production meant scarcity, in Iowa at least, so that there were sign-up sheets at local liquor retailers for the few bottles that became available. I had never before tasted rye, and likely couldn't distinguish it from whiskey, but the exclusivity and forbidden-fruit element made me take to it as if it were mother's milk, and I bought as much as I could wherever I could (it became easier to find outside the state, where it wasn't such the rage), and drank it as if there was no tomorrow.

Since my early days as a record obsessive, I would be drawn to buying things when they were available, with less regard to cost, and also to buying in bulk as a bargain. So cases of wine and bottles of the hard stuff made every trip to the liquor store a three-figure transaction, which could push well beyond a couple hundred when I was out of town, particularly in Chicago, where I could find stuff that I wouldn't in Iowa. (It turned out, by the way, that Templeton Rye was something of a sham, blended at a distillery in Indiana rather than the homegrown Iowa product it had promoted.)

I never thought of it this way at the time, but I was always spending at least $500 a month on alcohol, with many months closer to a grand. And what I bought, I drank, averaging almost a bottle of wine a night and a bottle of something—Templeton, Grand Marnier, Makers Mark, Remy—every two or three. At Costco or Sam's Club, those bottles might be quarts or larger rather than fifths, but I stuck to my bottle rate, which increased my fluid intake, if I'd been thinking about such things.

I was also taking Clonazepam daily, not because it gave me any sort of boost or euphoric feeling, but to avoid feeling what had started me taking the drug, popularly known and feared as a "benzo." And I was not only disregarding the injunction to avoid alcohol, not really thinking it applied to me, I was stepping up my intake. I was plainly headed for a fall.

Literally.

On July 20, 2007, I was heading toward bed after my bottle of wine, a couple full snifters of Grand Marnier and nightcap joint. It wasn't even 10PM, but I think I had already stumbled once in the kitchen, maybe fallen. Maria had the lights off in the bedroom, and all I had to do was climb the steep set of 17 stairs to make it there. And I almost made it, because I have a hazy image of being on the top landing.

But absolutely no recollection of tumbling down, hitting my head, and then finding myself at the bottom of those stairs, my forehead bleeding, my brain foggy, knowing I'd been up there and was now down here but no real idea what had transpired. Had I tripped? Blacked out? Passed out? I hadn't been drinking appreciably more than usual or feeling appreciably different than usual, but this was plainly new and dangerous territory. As with the panic attack that hadn't been preceded by anything that felt like panic to me, this was one of those split seconds between before and after, when everything had become different.

The commotion of my fall woke Maria, and she asked me what had happened. I really had no idea. She called an ambulance and they took us to the hospital. And she called Molly, who joined us there. By this point, I was more embarrassed than anything, as if I had done something stupid rather than had something happen to me. I know now that I could have died from the fall, or at least suffered a concussion, but in my haze I just wanted all this to be over. Or to have never happened.

The hospital kept me overnight, gave me a CT scan, did all the blood work. As always when the doctors ran my numbers, the drinking didn't seem to pose any serious health risk. My liver was fine. My blood alcohol level was higher than the legal driving limit but not approaching anything toxic. My blood pressure was great. I could stand to lose a few pounds, but who couldn't? I went back a few days later for a treadmill stress test, and those results were fine as well. I worked out daily. I was in pretty good shape for a guy in his mid-50s.

Nobody even suggested that I had to give up drinking, though common sense would dictate that when you start falling down flights of stairs some reassessment might be in order. So I decided that I would limit my drinking to dinner, a couple glasses of wine, with nothing later as a nightcap. I would learn from this near-catastrophe.

I had dodged a bullet.

22. End of the Road

I WOULDN'T QUIT DRINKING FOR another two years, but I had turned some sort of corner, apparent only in retrospect. Because I couldn't then imagine a life without drinking, I didn't, or hadn't. I fully expected that fine wines and harder liquor would be an integral part of the rest of my life—an enhancement of it, not an escape from it—but there was no denying that tumbling down a flight of stairs and ending up in the ER was some sort of warning sign. I needed to change my ways.

So I vowed from then on to limit myself to two glasses of wine with dinner, and to reserve anything after dinner for special occasions, not part of the daily ritual. I tried to adhere, but since I was the one enforcing the rules as well as making them, I allowed myself some leeway. Limiting myself to two glasses inevitably led to larger glasses. "Special occasions" could encompass just about any time that was somehow out of the ordinary.

Trips to Chicago were the first and the best special occasions. I had shared the Templeton Rye phenomenon with my friend, John Soss, who was gracious enough not only to put me up at his Lincoln Park three-flat whenever I would come to town, but who would have a bottle of what was somehow easier to find in Chicago than back in Iowa. He would make a fire in his pit at night, bring out the bottle, I'd grab a couple of cigars, and we could talk for hours. I was likely drinking more than he was, but neither of us was keeping watch. And all we had to do was climb the stairs back to his flat. If this didn't qualify as a special occasion, what could?

Within six months or so of my fall, I had reverted to my old routine and upped the ante. They say alcoholism is a progressive disease, and though I wouldn't even consider the possibility that I was an alcoholic, I understood the progressive part. I was drinking more and more to achieve the same buzz, and feeling no ill effects the next morning. Maybe a little foggier, needing a little more coffee to cut that fog, but none of the debilitating headaches or even the dry mouth that had once followed drinking to excess.

I did my best to hide the increase from Maria, but when I was at school, no one was keeping watch. By now I'd bought a condo to use during the nights I was there, and for Kelly and her boyfriend (now her husband Ryan) to share full-time. It was about as cheap as paying rent separately for a place for me and a place for her, and I'd get some tax breaks and eventually some investment profit.

I'd have my wine with dinner with them, smoke my cigar on the deck, and then retreat to the bedroom where I had my bottle stashed. And I'd drink and read until I passed out. Pretty much every night. Kelly would say goodnight and I would reply through my closed door. Sleep, wake, repeat. Kelly and Ryan probably had some suspicions or even concerns about me, but they kept them to themselves, just as I kept my progressive intake to myself. No harm, no foul. Just my way of getting through the end of the day and putting it to sleep.

My only real concern about my drinking was projecting into the future, in retirement. I didn't drink during the day because I had work to do. My drinking at night was my reward for a full day's work. I never started before dinner. What would happen when I had no work to do? Would I change my rule to no drinking before lunch? Would I start drinking instead of lunch? If there was nothing governing my drinking, how would I proceed and how quickly would I spin out of control?

Idle speculation. I had no immediate plans for retirement (still don't), and as long as I was working and functioning, I wasn't really worried. I've often maintained that I never considered quitting drinking until I actually quit, and on a conscious level I still believe that. Yet what do I make of my reading during this period, when I was drawn to dozens of books about alcoholics and their deterioration, their recovery or both? Some of this might be that a spate of good books received a lot of attention, and a few of these resonated even more with me because of our shared Iowa experience.

Biographies of John Cheever and Raymond Carver topped that particular subsection of the list, of their days howling together at the Iowa City moon and banging on the door at Dirty John's as soon after dawn as they could. Both of them were great short story writers and really bad drunks, and both got sober before writing some strikingly redemptive work. (Carver would continue to depend on what some 12-Steppers derisively refer to as "marijuana maintenance.")

As a journalist, I found another subset of vocational glimpses into the abyss through the memoirs of David Carr, Pete Hamell and others, who also shared some of my belief that alcohol had helped them work. (Until it didn't.) And since I loved literature almost as much as rock, there was a deep pool of literature concerning alcohol among the literary, with John Berryman, Mary Karr and David Foster Wallace among those whose stories might serve as cautionary tales.

So I was reading a lot about alcoholism and its effects, and it never occurred to my conscious self, the one that I now feel was deep in denial and defensiveness (and hadn't even been able to recognize the stress that had brought on my panic attack), that I myself was suffering from what they had, even in a milder form. Or what AA might call a "higher bottom." To the contrary, reading such books reinforced my sense that if this is what it meant to be an alcoholic,

I wasn't one. I wasn't losing jobs, sacrificing my health, abusing my personal relationships, risking my life. My hands didn't shake until I'd gotten my fix. I simply drank a lot. Daily. And the reason why was that I liked drinking. A lot.

I nevertheless experienced some freakish symptoms that might have scared someone who was less in denial. On more than half a dozen occasions, though never in such succession that I felt it was anything but an aberration, I would awaken from a deep sleep gasping for breath, loudly, and terrified. It was like I wasn't even aware that I had been asleep until I was awake, and now trying to breathe as if my life depended on it. Which it did. It felt as if my throat had been coated and sealed by whatever I had been drinking after dinner, particularly if it had been the sticky sweetness of Grand Marnier.

After maybe four or five gasps, I would calm down and breathe more easily. If I were home when this happened, the commotion would wake Maria, and she would be as scared as I had been. She thought maybe it was sleep apnea, and that I should go for testing. She also attributed my snoring to the same. (Since I have quit drinking, this has never happened again. And I don't snore, at least not like I used to.) Then a week or a month would go by and it would all be forgotten. Until the next time.

Maybe you'd have to be nuts not to take this seriously. Maybe this is what the 12 Steps are getting at with that "restore us to sanity" stuff. Maybe I just liked to drink too much, or was too addicted, to worry about any consequences. I now suspect that tumbling down stairs, bleeding all the way to the ER, waking up breathless and gasping are not the usual experiences of the so-called "normal" drinker.

Though there were no more dramatic, life-threating, head-bleeding falls down the stairs, there was the occasional crash of my body into something, a piece of furniture, or even the floor. If I were home, Maria would hear the loud noise and call down the stairs, "What's wrong?" And I would get up or straighten up and say (or slur), "Nothing." Again, it didn't happen much or many nights in a row, so it seemed like an anomaly to me.

Then there was the one night that had seemed like a mystery to all of us, at her brother's place in Vero Beach, the destination for that spring break that had started the downward spiral for Maria. We had finished a rich dinner with a lot of wine, which was our usual routine there, even more convivially excessive than my usual routine, when we went upstairs to our quarters and I experienced the most severe vomiting of my life. It felt nothing like the vomiting that overdrinking might bring on, preceded by "the spins" when lying down which would lead to queasiness. This was more like extreme flu, with chills and fever, and with repeat performances throughout an hour even when it had felt like everything had been drained out of me.

It was so extreme that I was sure I'd had food poisoning, something that my cast-iron stomach had never experienced. But everyone else had eaten the same food as I had, and nobody else had felt anything like this. It seemed like a mystery, one with alcohol perhaps at its root, but nothing like any previous nausea I'd felt from overdrinking. I now think it was just another sign of how medication and alcohol might mix within me, but back then it just seemed like one of those things. Another aberration. I felt fine the next day. Again, no harm, no foul.

When I now consider the insanity of my alcoholism, my road trip with Molly to take her to college that summer, a year before I would stop drinking for good (or for now, one day at a time) hit some sort of peak. I wouldn't feel comfortable with my usual routine of after dinner drinking and dope when she and I were sharing a motel room, so I doubled down on the wine. I bought boxes of it from

Target, a house-brand red that had been well reviewed and where each box had the equivalent of four bottles in it.

Since we'd be driving for less than a week, one box would have been enough for my more moderate drinking days. But better safe than sorry. I packed three or four. Where once a bottle of wine would last two nights, one of the great features of the box is that I couldn't really tell how much I was drinking by a bottle level. It was only when the box got appreciably lighter that I would know I was close to finishing it. And as soon as I was that close, I would finish it.

Why would a father taking his daughter to college require so much wine in the way of provisions? I'd driven those endless stretches before, through Nebraska and beyond, and I could only imagine what we'd find in Utah. I figured there would be plenty of nights where fast food or carryout pizza would be our only options. And I never ate dinner without wine, even when dinner was a Wendy's double cheeseburger, a Subway footlong or a cardboard pizza from Domino's. I knew that when those were the options, the wine selection wouldn't be any better, even if there were liquor stores. So, this was prudent planning. Self-sufficiency.

At the time it made perfect sense to pack my own wine to accompany dinner from the Wendy's drive-through, as if I couldn't have had a fine time with my daughter without it. And Molly and I did have a great time, lots of talking and listening to music on the long drive through lunar landscapes, the cinematic emptiness of Utah. We made her first visit to the Grand Canyon, and then turned right toward Las Vegas, which would be both of our first visits there. And every night, after dinner, I'd pretty much shut things down with more wine than usual, my post-prandial cigar and early to bed.

Vegas proved to be a whole 'nother world. On the advice of my brother-in-law, a gambler and horse player who goes there a few times a year, we'd booked the Bellagio, with its balletic fountains in front. When we checked in, the clerk addressed my daughter and me as if we were husband and wife. I'd been 40 when Molly was born; I was now 58 and she'd be turning 18. A few years earlier, when she'd accompanied me on a travel story in Wyoming, I'd been asked if I were her grandfather.

Here in the land of anything goes, I decided to go looking for a store where I could buy liquor by the bottle, to resume my after-dinner drinking ritual. I'd done well by suspending this on our drive through the emptiness, rather than packing more than enough for the trip (as I had with the wine) or searching through Bacchus-forsaken Utah for something I could drink. But now we were back in something like civilization, Vegas tonight and Los Angeles tomorrow. I could get back to normal.

Finding a package store on the strip isn't all that easy, in a town where bar liquor flows freely. I found one at last in a mall, of all places. I purchased a bottle of Armagnac, which I'd had first and last in France. Not that I could tell the difference between this and cognac, but it sounded more refined. As it turned out, I could have saved myself some trouble if I'd settled for a pint of something rather than this fifth, but by this point a pint looked to me like an airplane bottle, a single serving and not enough of one.

Maria would be flying to meet us in Los Angeles, where there would be even more mother-daughter tension that usual. It comes with the territory, particularly with such rites-of-passage. Molly couldn't wait for her emancipation. Maria dreaded the prospect of our empty nest, with only her occasionally available husband for company. We had to find Molly an apartment that her best friend from Des Moines would be driving out to share. We had to furnish it. And we had to stick to a budget.

Every decision provoked a new argument, or a series of them. Maria couldn't wait to fly back. Molly couldn't wait to be rid of us. But the day before we were to leave there was the biggest argument, when an incredulous Maria looked at the quarter of a bottle left in the Armagnac and realized I was about to drink it all. What choice did I have? Couldn't take it on the plane. It seemed like a manageable amount to drink to me, maybe even less than I had drunk on nights when no one was looking or measuring.

But to her this was insane. I wouldn't quit drinking for another full year, and nothing would get appreciably worse. Nor in any way better. But the tension between us was palpable, and the drinking was just a symptom, in my mind at least. By the next summer, Molly would be done with Los Angeles, ready to return to Iowa after her freshman year on her own. I would fly out, pack her car with what we could fit in it, toss the mattress and whatever else we had bought the year earlier, put her on the flight so she could make it for new student orientation in Iowa City.

Drive back alone. Same empty stretches, fast food, motels that seemed sadder because I was lonely. And I looked forward more to drinking at the end of the day, my full stash replenished for the road, my dinners earlier because I still didn't start drinking until dinner. Or stop until I was falling asleep or passing out, which was now happening with plenty of daylight left.

A couple of weeks after I made it home was the night I collapsed in the rain, the night that Maria called the cops and then packed her bags, the night from which I awoke with shit all over my legs and the sheets, vomit on my shirt, and a kitchen sink into which Maria had emptied a whole bunch of bottles. That night marked the end of something, but it was more profoundly the beginning of something. The beginning of this book, for anyone who wants to circle back. But really the beginning of a new life that I had never imagined or anticipated. And which I wouldn't have wanted had someone promised it to me. It was the life I found, or that found me, from working the 12 Steps of Alcoholics Anonymous.

Part IV:
Stepping Up

23. The Promises

WE HAVE NOW ARRIVED AT THE point where this book finds both its purpose and it focus. *(About time!* you might say.) I didn't write this because I thought a book about me would have any intrinsic interest, and, if I had, I could have made that part way more interesting—rock stars, journalism gossip, whatever. My purpose all along was to write about how sobriety can change your life, or at least has changed mine.

But to do that, to write in specific detail about recovery and what has changed within me, I had to write about what my life was like before, and what little I knew about Alcoholics Anonymous when I stumbled into it. Because I'm sure there are readers out there who might feel like I did, who think that real alcoholics are the ones who live under the bridge and have lost their jobs and families. The ones with the shakes that can only be calmed with that morning fix. The ones with the bloodshot eyes, the gin blossom nose, the slurred speech.

That wasn't me. Well, maybe, on occasion, it could have been, but in the depths of my drinking, alone with my bottle, nobody was looking at me, and I wasn't talking to anyone. So I was fine, comfortably numb in my isolation. I had no problems from drinking with my job, with our kids, with my friends. My drinking was definitely adding to tension in our marriage, but so was pretty much everything else. As I've said before, Maria thought I had a drinking problem. I thought she had a nagging problem.

I now realize just how unavailable I was to those I loved, and how I marginalized them into compartments. I didn't drink during work, but I was so focused on it before, during and after that I barely had time to acknowledge anyone else, especially my family. Drinking started with dinner, and dinner was pretty soon after I got home from work. Often our daughters were elsewhere, with schedules and priorities of their own. After dinner was "my time," with the cigar keeping everyone else away and the alcohol driving me deeper into myself, while I was ostensibly reading a book. Then I would surreptitiously sneak a joint and pass out, either making it up to bed or not.

What kind of life was that? For the family, let alone for me. It hadn't always been like that. I had been an attentive dad, reading to the girls at night, helping with schoolwork, attending all their sporting events. Maria and I had once shared a lot more—concerts and movies, dinners out, family outings. Now that the girls were no longer as interested in sharing family time, Maria retreated to her TV and latest obsession (jigsaw puzzles, crocheting, cozy mystery novels) and I would retreat to my booze and dope. When there was tension between my mom and dad—and when wasn't there?—he would head to the basement. And the tension would escalate. You'd think I would have learned something.

During the daylight hours, in my interactions with those outside my household, there was no indication that I had any sort of dependence on alcohol. I rarely drank before dinner, nor did I miss a day's work or assignment or obligation from drinking the night before. It was at night that I couldn't imagine being able to live, sleep or function without alcohol, and when I'd sedate myself into a stupor after the girls had gone to bed and Maria was no longer downstairs to judge me. By the time the drinking had led to the nightly marijuana, I had closed myself off, compartmentalized, no longer answering the phone or seeing and talking to anyone. By my standards, I was doing just fine.

So, the first illusion that AA dispelled for me is that it is only for derelicts, for life's losers. In the early days, toward the end of the Great Depression, it was. Because alcoholism had been stigmatized as a moral failing, and no one except those who had fallen to the lowest bottom would admit to being one. If you needed to stop drinking and needed help to do so, you lacked moral fiber, will power. You were the dregs of humanity.

What surprised me at my first meeting and has continued to impress me ever since is the quality of the people I have met, and the quality of life enjoyed by so many of those who have been going to meetings for ten, twenty, even forty years after achieving sobriety. Some of them are smarter and more successful than I have ever been; plenty of them are very funny, with the gallows humor of the reprieved. All of them want to connect with each other and help anyone else who needs it, without any hidden agenda or payback. There's a generosity of spirit within the program that I have rarely encountered elsewhere.

These people have kept me coming back to meetings, four or five or even seven times a week, though I'd figured at the start that my going to meetings would be a very temporary phase. I've never liked meetings, or people, or small talk. There is very little small talk at AA meetings, where the talk is about the best way to make it through the day, or the year, or this life. And you do so, as songwriting sage Ray Wylie Hubbard wisely put it, by keeping your gratitude higher than your expectations. Be grateful for each breath, and don't put too much worry into things you can't control.

Which means, in AA terms, "letting go," or "turning it over," which is where we run into what I could call the second illusion, but is really more of a misconception. It's the idea, which is prevalent among AA members, that a belief in God is the key to sobriety—the

God of the Bible, the Christian God. And skeptics who don't share that belief often dismiss AA as some sort of religious cult. But there are determined atheists and wavering agnostics in the program who have found what AA calls "a faith that works" without making a leap of faith into the supernatural. And there are devout Christians who have relapsed in the program multiple times and even left it.

Besides, if this were Scientology or Jim Jones or your typical cult, somebody would want something from you—your money, or your life, or your blind allegiance or whatever. AA doesn't. It loves and accepts you unconditionally, knowing that, as you benefit from the program, you will do the same for others. It changes your perspective from inner-directed selfishness to outer-directed usefulness. It frees you from what AA calls "the bondage of self."

Friends who are self-styled Buddhists—or "Buddhish," as one of my fellow meditators puts it—can see as much Eastern mysticism as Western duality in the program. The idea that the self is a construct, that change is the only constant and that clutching and grasping at that impermanence is the root of suffering is at the crux of AA. It's a program of paradoxes, or Zen koans, that finds power in powerlessness, triumph in surrender, serenity in letting go. There is no creation mythos in the gospel according to AA, and no afterlife. AA simply doesn't address those tenets of faith. It's all about the present, one breath at a time.

Let's go back to the "Big Book," the cornerstone of the program, the Bible for recovering 12-steppers. AA fundamentalists treat it like holy scripture, in particular the first 164 pages, mostly written (evidently but anonymously) by Bill Wilson. This is Bill W.'s account of the hopelessness of his own alcoholism, his descent into despair, and his "spiritual awakening" that would find him "catapulted into…the fourth dimension of existence."

It also introduces the program's essential tenet about drunks understanding other drunks in the way normal people can't. The origin story of Alcoholics Anonymous involves Bill sharing his "experience, strength and hope" with Dr. Bob, credited as AA's co-founder, and a more conventionally religious physician who had found that God alone couldn't save him from his own alcoholism. "Dr. Bob's Nightmare," the first of the personal testimonies that follow Bill's opening gospel, explains how a long conversation between these two men, on June 10, 1935, started Dr. Robert Smith down the road to recovery and planted the seeds for a program based on spiritual awakening and one drunk helping another.

For the AA devout—the thousands who have made pilgrimages—Akron, Ohio, is Jerusalem (or even Bethlehem). It's where Bill W. and Dr. Bob talked for hours, where the program subsequently was developed (an outgrowth of the Oxford Group, an esoteric Christian sect) and its principles articulated. It arose during the depths of the Great Depression, and it focused totally in the beginning on what were subsequently termed "low bottom drunks."

Those were the ones who were threatened with losing it all—their jobs, their marriages, their homes, their bearings, their minds. Their lives. They were pariahs, because society considered alcoholism a moral failure, a lack of resolve and self-will. Only the men who had sunk the lowest would be open to the "cure" provided by AA. And it was predominantly men at that time, because only the loosest of women would similarly succumb to alcohol, and then to whatever else. When Dr. Bob met Bill W., each knew he had found a kindred spirit.

"This was a man who had experienced many years of frightful drinking, who had had most of the drunkard's experiences known to man, but who had been cured by the very means I had been trying to employ, that is to say the spiritual approach," writes the doctor.

AA insists that alcoholism is a physical disease with a spiritual cure, which initially sounded borderline wacko to me. I have always been on the lookout for hidden agendas, and I was wondering what and when I would have to believe to be truly accepted by these people who had been so welcoming to me. Was this a quasi-religious cult like Scientology? It seemed to have that Zen quality—"those who knew don't tell, and those who tell don't know"—and I wondered what and why those folks who I'd known in the program weren't telling.

Yet the people I'd met at that first meeting didn't seem like zealots or cultists. They had laughed easily, particularly about the tragic ridiculousness of their drinking. They had seemed like passengers on a lifeboat that had avoided some great calamity, and still had room for others who needed a helping hand to come aboard. For all the talk about "God" and "a higher power" that I would hear, I took comfort from these words I remembered from the start of that meeting, and would hear at the start of every one after: "The only requirement for membership is a desire to stop drinking."

At my first meeting, I had lacked even that. And I still wasn't completely sure whether I desired to stop drinking *forever*, or just long enough to get the heat off with Maria. Again, here's where "one day at a time" proved particularly helpful. I wasn't making any life decisions about alcohol, which had been my habitual companion for more than four decades. But I wasn't going to drink today. And not tomorrow, when I'd take another Antabuse and go to another meeting to discover more and bolster my resolve.

So, one day at a time, it was easy to decide which one of the dozens of meetings I would attend as my next, that day after my first meeting.

There was a noon meeting listed at the Des Moines Register building, and I figured that these would be my people. At least I'd meet a few fellow journalists. At the *Chicago Sun-Times*, my colleague Roger Ebert, the movie critic, had once been one of the local newsprint community's most notorious drunks and had then become one of the most celebrated (and least anonymous) members of AA.

Journalism tended to attract those with big thirsts, as well as those of us who romanticized the image of the hard-working, hard-drinking, deadline-driven reporter. We worked hard and then we played hard. Once when I'd finished a late-night review and was waiting for the editor to sign off, I looked down the offices of my fellow critics and realized that every one of us was alcoholic, divorced, or both. (I was then divorced and a nightly drinker, yet decades from admitting to alcoholism.) It was not a profession that promoted stable family lives, with the hours and single-minded focus it demanded.

As one of the nation's best-known movie critics, a regular presence on national TV, Roger had become almost evangelical in his praise of AA, whose meetings he had first attended in the same newspaper building where we had worked. He called AA "the best thing that ever happened to me." His career had flourished, as had his personal life and sense of well-being. He remained a wise-cracking humorist, particularly in his banter with TV partner Gene Siskel, his counterpart at the rival *Chicago Tribune*.

As I took my first baby steps into AA, Roger's example provided inspiration, mainly because of how sobriety had transformed his life and given him strength after a very public series of health setbacks. I also knew that Roger had never been a conventionally Christian believer and had likely identified as an atheist. Yet here was someone who believed in AA absolutely and had made his peace with the spirituality and the "higher power" part of the program.

As he wrote about the way "God" and "higher power" are invoked within the program, "(Its) critics never quote the words 'as we understood God.' Nobody in A.A. cares how you understand him, and would never tell you how you should understand him." I would meet those in AA for whom the group itself remained their "higher power," and GOD an acronym for "Group of Drunks" or "Good Orderly Direction." They had remained sober.

Attending my second meeting broadened my horizons, doubling my experience. I didn't meet a single journalist, at this meeting that I have attended pretty much every week since then (or did until the pandemic). At least none that self-identified as journalists. I've since realized that downtown noon meetings are mainly populated by the working professionals who work in the city, and that many of these are lawyers. I'm still unsure whether this is because law, like journalism, tends to attract or breed alcoholics, or whether lawyers were just more likely to tell the group that they were lawyers.

The feel of the downtown meeting was different than the one the previous day at a suburban church (I would subsequently discover that some of those who aren't churchgoers prefer the more secular settings for meetings). Instead of the more nurturing warmth, this was more like a business club. The guy running the meeting was apparently a retiree in his 70s, a crusty, bald, occasionally profane gentleman with a sharp tongue. He would soon become one of my best friends in the program. I had worried a little about losing my edge; he showed that you could stay sober without going soft.

I thought he was in charge of this meeting, the leader of the group, in the same way that the woman who had given me the Big Book was in charge of my first meeting group. I soon learned an essential truth about AA—nobody's in charge. Most groups rotate leaders on a volunteer basis each month. Some have guidelines about who can lead—maybe you need to have a year's continuous sobriety or more—but mainly what the month's leader does is handle the preliminaries, select a short reading from "program approved literature" for the day, start the discussion and pass the basket. Each person throws in a buck, some put in two, some make their own change for a five or a ten, some contribute nothing. There is no shame attached to this.

Some of that money goes for the room's rental (usually nominal). Some goes for coffee and candy (recovering alcoholics notoriously crave caffeine and sweets). The rest goes to the Central Office, wherever that is, which covers its expenses and then sends some to the national office. Each group has a volunteer treasurer, who handles the money, and most others give it no thought whatsoever. The storytelling, therapy and collegial bonding of an AA meeting can seem like the best value in town for a buck.

When you are attending your first meetings, you might think that you and any other newcomers—"the most important ones in the room," as others are quick to tell you—are at the gate of sobriety, where all the others have long since passed through. Stick around, and you'll discover that some woman who sounds so smart and calm has only been there a month (though you'd never think *only* a month at the start, when a month without drinking might seem like an eternity).

And, inevitably, dozens of members who seem to be models of sobriety and even inspirations to you, some with years or even decades under their belts, will suffer a relapse. If you come back, AA will dismiss this as a "slip," and so might you, even if that slip has seen you drinking for weeks, months or years.

When you stop going to meetings and start drinking again, it is said that you have "gone back out." Some never return. Some decide that this whole AA thing was a mistake, that they just like to drink and that they can handle it. Some drink themselves to death. Some commit suicide, believing that they can no longer live with or without drinking. Those who go out and come back almost invariably confess that it was worse than the earlier times, that they picked up right where they had left off, and that the return to drinking had only brought them misery. Some will say, even with a laugh, that AA ruins drinking for you, takes all the fun out of it. (And I'm sure there are some who go out and handle their return to drinking much better. They just don't come back to meetings to talk about it.)

Though I still wasn't sure what the rest of my daily routine would be like, I now knew that a meeting would be as much a part of it as my morning coffee. I liked this community of sobriety I had found, and I liked hearing their stories and comparing them with mine, focusing, as the program advises, on "the similarities, not the differences." I felt I was taking baby steps on a very long journey, and that these people could not only serve as my guides, but would be eager and happy to do so.

As I would later read from Roger Ebert, "Before I went to my first meeting, I imagined the drunks would sit around telling drinking stories. Or perhaps they would all be depressing and solemn and holier-than-thou. I found out you rarely get to be an alcoholic by being depressing and solemn and holier-than-thou. These were the same people I drank with, although now they were making more sense."

At the end of every meeting, everyone stands to make a hand-holding circle and recite the Serenity Prayer or the Lord's Prayer or whatever else that particular meeting has decided. Then, still holding hands, you raise them up and down and chant, "Keep coming back, it works if you work it."

Having followed the lead of everyone else at the first meeting, I had a better idea of what to expect at the end of the second.

Something seemed to be working for those who kept coming back. I would continue to come back as well. And learn about whatever "working it" might mean.

As it turns out, there are as many ways of working the program as there are drunks who enter it. What you do and how you do it, and at what pace, can be as varied as our backgrounds, our experiences, our deepest beliefs. Yet underneath all that, we are all the same, broken individuals, looking to be made whole. Or as AA puts it, "We aren't bad people trying to become good; we are sick people trying to get well."

And what does getting well entail? There's a passage in the Big Book on working the program. It is informally known as "The Promises," and it is also read at the start (or the end) of some AA meetings. It refers specifically to Step Nine, but you don't need to know what that step is to share the spirit of hope in the promises. I didn't. And the promises did sound unlikely to me, or "extravagant" as they put it. But another thing that connects pretty much everyone in AA is their belief that the promises have come true in their lives, are coming true or will come true.

We call it "waiting for your miracle."

Here are "The Promises," from pages 83-4 of the Big Book:

If we are painstaking about this phase of our development, we will be amazed before we are halfway through. We are going to know a new freedom and a new happiness. We will not regret the past nor wish to shut the door on it. We will comprehend the word serenity and we will know peace. No matter how far down the scale we have gone, we will see how our experience can benefit others. That feeling of uselessness and self-pity will disappear. We will lose interest in selfish things and gain interest in our fellows. Self-seeking will slip away. Our whole attitude and outlook upon life will change. Fear of people and of economic insecurity will leave us. We will intuitively know how to handle situations which used to baffle us. We will suddenly realize that God is doing for us what we could not do for ourselves. Are these extravagant promises? We think not. They are being fulfilled among us—sometimes quickly, sometimes slowly. They will always materialize if we work for them.

Even those of us who don't believe in God—or God as we understood him before entering the program—find that these things are now true for us that wouldn't have been true before. That we have come to experience serenity, a word I had previously been able to define but had never truly felt. It isn't that economic insecurity ever leaves us, but the fear of it, that we won't have what we need tomorrow, or next week, will no longer haunt us. We learn to trust that things will work out, things that are beyond our control. And even though they may not work out the way we wanted them to, we can live with this, even benefit from it. As someone who had spent decades complicating my own life, overthinking it, getting in my own way, the program from the start offered early glimmers of clarity.

24. Meeting Makers Make It

After my first week of meetings, I knew a whole lot more about AA than I had when I began. Which had been nothing. Or very little: 12 Steps. Don't drink. Something about God.

I now knew that pretty much every meeting started with a moment of silence "for the alcoholic who is still suffering." (Sometimes there'd be an acknowledgement that those alcoholics still suffering might include some in this room.) Then there'd be an opening prayer and the reading from the Big Book's "How It Works," including those 12 Steps.

Each meeting ended with another prayer and that "keep coming back" chant. Each meeting, at least in the Des Moines area, lasted an hour—almost never longer, but sometimes shorter, if there were few people there and they ran out of things to say. Or "share," as I'd learned to say in AA parlance, with which I was becoming more familiar, though a long way from fluent.

In between the beginning and the end, there'd be some sort of reading, depending on the meeting's format, with each person sharing some reflection or experience for a couple minutes, and then "passing" to the next. If you didn't have anything to say, you would just pass. "Cross-talking" was discouraged; you weren't supposed to talk about what someone else had shared, certainly not challenge it, but restrict your comments to your own reflections and experience.

Those attending these meetings didn't look much different than a cross-section of the metro's demographics as a whole. At the downtown noon meetings a lot of men wore suits and ties, or work dresses for the women. A few dressed in shorts and T-shirts, like me. Some of what the program calls "old timers," based on the length of their continuous sobriety, were half my age. I'd meet some who had determined that they were alcoholics before reaching the legal drinking age.

I had trouble figuring that out. As a student and now as a professor at the University of Iowa, long ranked with the nation's top party schools, I wondered how you distinguished problem drinking from normal college behavior. Yet these kids had discovered that their bingeing had a darker, aberrant side. Or maybe some court had ordered them to attend.

On the whole, however, those attending the meetings tended to be older rather than younger, middle class rather than lower, male rather than female (though not by nearly as much as in AA's early days), white rather than not. There were meetings specifically for black alcoholics, Hispanic, gay, even atheist/agnostic, as well as meetings that were for men only or women only. Most of the meetings were "open"—anyone could attend—while a few were "closed," which meant only members of AA were permitted. Now that alcoholism had lost much of its stigma—and was more commonly considered a disease or affliction than a character failing—open meetings were the rule. There was less reason why alcoholism couldn't be discussed openly.

I'm as agnostic and increasingly open-minded about "disease" as I am about "higher power." Whether it's physical or psychological, genetic or acquired, the "curse of alcoholism" extends across gender, class, race, ethnicity. If it's a disease, as modern medicine now approaches it, it's one that I'd much rather have than terminal cancer, where my behavior can't change it, and which doesn't seem to respond, as alcoholism does, to a "spiritual cure." My attitude toward my experience with alcohol abuse is like what you hear in "Amazing

Grace": "I once was lost, but now I'm found/Was blind but I can see." You gain clarity, perspective and vision in AA, if you stick around long enough.

At any open meeting, anyone who wanted to attend could. Some were visitors from nursing or social work programs. Some were there to provide support for the alcoholics they accompanied. Some weren't sure if they had a problem with alcohol, but wanted some perspective to figure out if they did. Or, better yet, confirmation that they weren't. AA lets you decide if you have the problem, though, as members sometimes joke, "We don't get a lot of tourists around here." In other words, if you think you might have a problem with alcohol, you probably do.

There were almost 200 meetings in the Des Moines metro area each week, 25-30 every day. The variety of choice was enough to overwhelm a newcomer, yet after each meeting someone would take me aside, make sure I had the booklet schedule of all the meetings listed and circle a few that they had found useful. That way I would be likely to know at least one person when I attended a new meeting, though I found that the more meetings I attended, the more people I recognized. Lots of people went to lots of different meetings, so there was inevitable overlap.

With schedules also online, you could structure your own program. Most of us who fit this addictive profile benefit from some sort of structure, or at least some routine. We needed a new routine to help replace the old one of going to bars or daily drinking at home. Beyond going to meetings, there was no litmus test or attendance requirement or card that confirmed that you were an AA member. You learned more about being in AA by going to more meetings.

You adapt to AA through experience and osmosis. You stick around and you catch on. You learn that members are expected to have a "home group," which was the one meeting most important to them and the one they regularly tried to attend. Some veterans of AA were once-a-week meeting goers, and that meeting was their home group. Having a home group that you attended regularly helped keep you accountable. If you didn't show up, folks would worry about you.

How many meetings did others attend? And for how long? There was a standard stipulation for those starting their sobriety journey that you should strive to make "90 meetings in 90 days." You need to immerse yourself in the program to counter the powerful lure of alcohol. Some desperate souls went to two or more meetings a day, with meetings scheduled from before dawn until after dark. Some, like me, settled into a routine of one per day. One old-timer with decades of sobriety maintained that the weekly formula for attending meetings was "three to maintain and four to grow."

Another old timer with a bit of an Ozark drawl would always end his sharing with the pronouncement, "Meeting makers make it." Maybe if you were dedicated enough to keep going to meetings you were dedicated enough to stay sober. Though it was an article of faith in the program that you couldn't do it alone, that you needed the help of some "higher power." And that attending meetings wasn't enough—you needed to work the steps. Yet for some, the group itself, the collective spirit of AA, would serve as their "higher power" or "power greater than yourself."

Many would attend meetings when they were out of town, and feel welcomed wherever they were. And even more would confess that when they hadn't been to a meeting for a while, whatever their own personal schedule might be, they would feel a little twitchy, like the meetings had become as important to them as alcohol had once been. Even if they felt no desire to have a drink, they felt a little off. Edgy. Almost invariably when someone would return after suffering a "slip," or "going out" for longer, their explanation would start, "I stopped going to meetings."

A lot of those who had quit drinking with AA stopped going to meetings. You wouldn't know whether they had started drinking again or just felt they no longer needed to attend meetings to stay sober. One of the high points of most AA meetings was the announcement of "birthdays"—as members referred to the day they had quit drinking—which were commemorated with a "chip," a poker-chip sized coin with the Serenity Prayer and the Roman numeral for years of sobriety on it.

Early on, you'd get a new chip every month, in recognition of how much of a struggle it could be to resist those urges at the start. After your first year, you'd get a new chip on every sobriety birthday. And there would be big applause for those announcing they now had 30 or 40 or more years of sobriety. And for those with a few months or a few years. But you'd notice there weren't as many announcements in the middle, in the teens, say. Maybe they'd gone out; maybe they'd just quit coming back. Some would return, either because they'd messed up their lives again with alcohol—and would start all over again, with a new sobriety—or because they had felt something missing despite staying sober.

There were a variety of standard meeting formats, and participating in different ones could help keep your program fresh. The format typically referred to the opening reading that would provide the topic for the sharing.

Some meetings were "Big Book meetings," where they'd read the Big Book from beginning to end (either the whole thing or the first 164 pages), and then start over again. A few pages each week, a paragraph or so read aloud by each attendee, followed by discussion.

Others were "Step meetings," a discussion of a single step each week, in order, and then starting over. Often these meetings began with a reading from *Twelve Steps and Twelve Traditions*, through which Bill Wilson (anonymously) expanded and elaborated on principles introduced in the Big Book.

Some were "Speaker meetings," mainly devoted to one alcoholic sharing his story with others. Those stories were informally called a "drunkalogue," and were just as informally formatted into three parts: *What we used to be like. What happened. What we are like now.* Speakers were expected to share their "experience, strength, and hope." (Remember, AA seems particularly attuned to the power of three, whether describing alcohol as "cunning, baffling, and powerful," or describing the life you could live without it, as your higher power wanted, as "happy, joyous, and free.")

Most of the rest of the meetings, like the first two I'd attended, just let the leader for that month pick the reading, or the topic, from some book of daily meditations, or from the Big Book or from other literature approved by the program. A few that I came to love followed discussion with a silent meditation, lasting 20 or so minutes, a stillness that eventually came to calm my mind in a way that I'd once depended on the self-medication of alcohol to do. I would come to depend on it as much as I had my daily drinking. Every bit as obsessive, but easier on the liver.

Some meetings might attract a couple hundred members, though most numbered more in the dozens, and a few would proceed with just a handful of members each week. Sometimes meetings would just discontinue for lack of participation. New ones would be introduced when someone saw a hole that needed filling—a new location or demographic or hour of the day or format.

What I now consider my home group is a meditation meeting that didn't start until I had been sober for a couple of years. Those who founded it no longer attend it, but a core group of 4-6 has kept it going, and it generally attracts a dozen or more to a meeting every Friday night at 6. It is one of four meditation sessions I attend each week.

Some people go to the same meetings on the same days for decades. Others frequently vary their meeting schedules to keep the program fresh, meeting new people and gaining new insight. If some people at some meetings start to annoy you—talking for too long or repeating too much, week after week—you might replace that meeting with another. As I heard someone joke early on, "If you say you love everyone in AA, you just aren't going to enough meetings." Sometimes you need to back away, take a break from daily or even weekly meetings, to gain some perspective on what you really value when you return.

Meetings allow you to get acclimated to the program. And the process. They ease you in. They reinforce the sense that those in recovery had found a new life that was better than the one they'd left behind. The Big Book served as the operating manual, with the 12 Steps and how to apply them to every facet of one's life, along with stories in which the reader could see his own experience reflected in that of others.

The crucial third element of a successful program—perhaps the most important thing about AA that no one tells you coming in, but that everyone soon learns—is that you need to find a "sponsor." Initially this seemed as nebulous in concept and value to me as a home group. This is someone of the same gender as you who has more sobriety and experience, and who will serve as your personal guide through the 12 steps, the program and as much of life in general as you might want to share with him. You pick him because "you want what he has."

When I entered the program (i.e. went to my first meeting or two), I was in no hurry to find a sponsor. Like I needed an amateur therapist, after decades of counseling with professionals, at least some of whom had asked about my drinking and listened to my lies. Sponsors and home groups aren't part of the program as delineated in the Big Book, but they have become essential elements of the catechism. I wasn't sure how I was supposed to make a decision on either, and I wasn't in any hurry, so I left those decisions in limbo.

You can keep going to meetings as long as you'd like without anybody ever asking you if you have a home group and a sponsor. Some go for years. A week or two in, I found myself enjoying the meetings and the people in them a lot more than I had anticipated, missing my former routine of drinking and drugging a lot less, but not really ready to make a commitment that would involve other people more deeply in my program, one that would make it more difficult to extricate myself if I wanted. I still took "one day at a time" to heart, not letting how I felt about drinking today suggest how I might think about it in a month.

In any event, I figured that I'd find a home group and a sponsor when I needed to, when I felt like it, if I had to. And that the right choices would make themselves plain, reveal themselves through osmosis, as so much of the program had. *Keep coming back, it works if you work it.*

And, in my own way, I was working it. You enter AA thinking that you've succumbed to a life of abstinence, an existence defined by denial. You feel empty, facing all those hours every day, with no idea how to fill them. AA helps you fill them, shows you how. You could go to a meeting every morning, noon and night if you wanted. And then what so many call the "meeting after the meeting," going out with a group for coffee or lunch, dropping the restrictions against "cross-talk" and maybe even gossip.

You could spend your off-hours reading the Big Book, learning more about the program that was becoming the focus of your life. Once you'd found a sponsor, you might check in with him at the same time every day. And he might suggest daily rituals of prayer, meditation, maybe a "gratitude list" (a few things each day for which you felt particularly grateful).

And your sponsor would guide you through the 12 Steps, which provide a structure for living. You come in wondering how you were going to fill all those hours, and, as you become adjusted to sobriety, you start to wonder how you will make time for all that you wanted to do, all that was enriching your life.

You came in thinking that you'd been filling the big hole in your soul with alcohol, and that you'd be empty without it. You discovered that your drinking had been digging that hole even deeper, and that you could fill it by forming a connection with these other recovering alcoholics, seeing how they lived their lives, how they'd found the serenity and spiritual enrichment you'd never experienced.

I had yet to find a sponsor or decide on a home group, decisions that might mean I was in it for the long haul. I hadn't really even decided if I was done drinking forever, though every day, week or month without a drink would mean that I was feeling better about not drinking. Because, knowing me, if I hadn't been feeling a whole lot better than I had anticipated, I would have returned to drinking and rationalizing my return. At least one day at a time, not drinking felt both way different and way better than I'd ever anticipated. As long as I stuck to my new routine, I would be fine.

25. If You Want What We Have

As the section from "How It Works" that opens every meeting advises, "If you have decided you want what we have and are willing to go to any length to get it—then you are ready to take certain steps."

I was ready, but I'd been told from the start that a real commitment requires taking the steps under the guidance of a sponsor. Because if you were emerging from a fog of denial and self-deception, you needed somebody who had been through this before, who had sustained the clarity you had started to experience. Who should that sponsor be? A lot of initiates turned that "How It Works" quote around—you wanted to find a sponsor who has what you want. In other words, someone you admire, and think you could learn to trust and emulate.

The other decision was less important, but I figured I needed to find a home group as well, the one that seemed most significant to me among my weekly schedule. It's likely that no one will ever ask you if you have a home group, or what your home group is, but you might at times feel compelled to declare it to the meeting you have selected, letting them know that this is the one you've selected, the one where the sharing hits deepest, the one you try never to miss, the one where you feel most accountable. The one where, if you aren't there, they'll miss you, and maybe someone will call to see about you. You let these folks know that theirs is the meeting where you feel most at home.

For me, these two searches ultimately became one, as I suspect they might for many initiates. One of the AA adages I'd accepted early on was that "it's your best thinking that brought you here." In other words, *you think you're so smart and look where it got you.* So I wasn't about to allow reason or intellect rule the selection process. This would be more about what felt right, a gut decision.

The most popular meeting I attended was Saturday morning at 9, in the largest mega-church in Des Moines, maybe all of Iowa—it was supposed to be the fastest-growing evangelical Lutheran church in America. I had attended a few times with Maria, who had found help through one of the church's many support groups for her depression, a depression which I later figured had had a pivotal role in my jagged path toward sobriety.

A lot of AA meetings are held in churches, which generally charge nominal fees at most for the use of the room. And many atheists and agnostics have some trouble with this, because it reinforces the sense that the program's "higher power" is just a euphemism for "Jesus Christ, our personal savior." And a lot of people who went to this meeting were also members of the church, but most of them refrained from much proselytizing.

It was a meeting for the many, more than a hundred on good days, who wanted to start their weekends in a different manner than they had long spent Saturday mornings—hungover, bleary-eyed, easing into the day's harsh sunlight. A meeting would get the weekend off to a good, fresh, comparatively early start. It was a step study meeting, and I recognized many who attended from other, smaller meetings. A nice balance between men and women, younger and older, with a lot of insightful, articulate and some surprisingly funny people there.

One of them became my sponsor. Until the morning I had asked him, on impulse or intuition, this hadn't been my plan. Selecting a sponsor seemed fraught with peril—there had been stories shared at meetings about sponsors who were like drill sergeants, demanding their own version of strict adherence, insisting that even those who didn't believe hit their knees in prayer at least twice a day. "Fake it until you make it" was their litany; "my way or the highway" was their attitude.

There were others, maybe most, not quite so strict, but who still wanted you to check in with them daily, call at the same time, and meet at least weekly. And there were some who themselves "went out" after decades of sobriety, returning to drink, leaving the sponsees who looked for them for guidance devastated.

Just as there were potentially as many ways to structure your program as there were people in it, there were many different sorts of relationships between sponsor and sponsee. Good sponsors often had multiple sponsees, and some of the best would have slightly different relationships with each. It was a matter of intuition, of feeling each other out.

And as I tried not to turn the selection of a sponsor into an intellectual or checklist process, to rely more on my gut and less on my brain, I was also nervous. I am shy, an introvert, someone who fears rejection, and this felt a little like asking a girl I didn't know very well to the prom. And having no idea how she would respond, but fearing the worst.

I'd had a few potential sponsors in mind—that first guy who had been so nice to me at my first meeting, though it turns out he wouldn't have been right. He soon showed himself to be a very evangelical atheist, one who eventually began turning every meeting he attended into an argument over God's existence and role in the program. I might have even agreed with much of what he said, but I was less interested in debating about God than staying sober.

Another potential sponsor seemed, like me, somebody who was spiritually open to possibility but not necessarily a true believer. He might have proven a good match for me, but he would die of cancer when I was two years sober. Yet another was a political bigshot and a man I admired quite a bit, though our politics were different and as a journalist I was something of an adversary (his final drunk had landed him on the front page of the local Des Moines Register). I knew he had a lot of sponsees and that some of them were prominent citizens, but I decided against a celebrity sponsor.

I'd had no intention of asking my sponsor to be my sponsor until I acted on impulse, following a Saturday morning meeting that he was leading, a step study on a particular step—the Fourth—that he'd advised should not be taken without a sponsor. For those of us working the steps would need some outside perspective, some experience and clarity, to lead us (or at least me) out of the fog of denial and defensiveness that working the program would clear.

So, when he said we needed a sponsor to proceed, I took that as an invitation to ask. I need one, will you be one? He said we should get together, have coffee, talk things over, see how it felt. Like a trial basis. He wasn't rejecting me, but he wasn't recruiting me, as some of the more aggressive sponsors might. (And a couple had.)

He was and is very Irish—once drunkenly, still proudly—with a wiry frame, flowing silver hair and a gift of gab. Only five or six years older than me, he nevertheless seemed like something of a father figure, a surrogate program father. And something like a priest, to whom I could confess. We would meet for coffee, and take this one step at a time. If we sensed a connection, we'd proceed. It would take me awhile to realize how mismatched we were, and yet how perfect.

He had more than 40 years of sobriety, and that earned my respect. With his black, Buddy Holly horn rims and his longish hair, he talked of himself as a rock and roll kid, a child of the 1960s. Like me, he'd spent most of his career in media—as a TV news reporter and then as news director, before launching some public relations companies that would make him more financially secure than I would ever be.

Unlike me, he is devoutly Catholic and very politically conservative, agreeing with his church on most social issues and with the Republican Party on fiscal policy. He fancies himself something of a ladies man, which I most certainly am not. When I'd hear him say "put the plug in the jug," at meetings, I'd cringe, because it's one of those clichés that newcomers find so corny.

It turned out that he and I have rarely discussed politics, and when we do it is more like fellow journalists than as opposing partisans. Beneath his surface extroversion, he tended to isolate, as do I. His Catholicism has a strong mystical bent, owing much to Thomas Merton, the sort of Christian with whom non-Christians such as myself believe we share a kindred spirit.

If I was making a leap of faith with him, so was he with me. As he admitted early on, I was someone he hadn't given much chance to stick around. Most don't stick around, and I had admitted from the start that I was there to save my marriage rather than out of any deep spiritual desire to get and stay sober. He had been around long enough to know that if you don't get sober for yourself, you won't stay sober.

But, one day at a time, he was willing to take me on, to help me. We would get together every week or two, at a supermarket dining room where the quality of the food wouldn't draw much of a crowd, and we could eat and talk in privacy. No rush for our table. He was very flexible about our relationship—never demanding that I call or pray daily—but very literal about his adherence to the Big Book. We would analyze it page by page, as he helped me work my program step by step.

He would always ask about my "spiritual fitness," and the advice he gave me that became almost a mantra was "embrace the mystery." I was starting to sense that my life's path had somehow led me to Des Moines to become sober, and led me to him to show me how to stay sober.

26. Step by Step

To join the program, which has the most open admissions imaginable, you need only one thing. And it isn't a belief in God or an embrace of any sort of spirituality. Those can come later, if at all. **"The only requirement for membership is a desire to stop drinking,"** as it says in the AA preamble, recited at the start of almost every meeting. That's it. Hell, you don't even need to have stopped drinking, and some haven't, as long as you have the desire to stop. And I didn't even have that, when I started coming around, until the program worked its osmosis on me. I was there to show my wife I could stop, after which I fully planned to start again.

But I didn't. Or I haven't. Because meetings kept me coming back to the program.

So, what is this program?

The program is the 12 Steps of Alcoholics Anonymous. And working the program means working the steps, pretty much in order, with a couple of notable exceptions. Some rush through the process, as if they could graduate from alcoholism. Others spend a couple of years hanging around, maybe relapsing between short stretches of sobriety, until they are ready to commit fully and start working the steps.

Everyone who works the steps does so imperfectly, because, as AA insists, "we believe in progress, not perfection." Here is how I worked the 12 Steps of Alcoholics Anonymous.

Step One: *We admitted we were powerless over alcohol—that our lives had become unmanageable.*

Everybody knows that AA is a 12-step program, but I'd never known what any of the steps were before attending my first meeting. I knew vaguely that they insisted you stop drinking—abstinence, not moderation—and that they had something to do with God. Even after I had read them, and heard them read dozens of times, at the start of every meeting, it was like they were written in a different language than the one I spoke.

I mean, "powerless over alcohol"? How could that be, or what could that signify? I liked drinking. A lot. And so I drank a lot. Saying I was powerless over alcohol was like saying I was powerless over pizza, or sex, or baseball, or music, or any of the other elements I valued in my life.

It is with the very first step that one encounters the first paradox in a program full of them. According to Des Moines legend, an old-timer who was quite the quotable AA character (yet had trouble sustaining long stretches of sobriety) would proclaim, "There's a lot of power in being powerless!" This first step also introduces the concept of "surrender," the means by which we ultimately triumph over our demons.

If the first part of the first step made no sense to me, the second part contradicted my experience. Sure, there was the occasional tumble down some stairs and the humiliating vomit and excrement all over me, ensuring that I would never forget that last drunk, but in general I used alcohol to manage my life, to compartmentalize effectively what would otherwise overflow into chaos.

My mind tended to run on overdrive until my first drink with dinner served as the shut-off switch, the signal that the workday was over and that play time had begun. Without drinking, or so I'd thought, if I'd thought about drinking at all, my mind would still be whirring with recriminations from the day just passed—what I should have done in class, how I should have phrased something—with ideas for the writing assignment that was due or the lesson plan for the next session.

This would not stop on its own. I had to stop it. Drink had to stop it. So I used alcohol to manage my life, to maintain the balance of productivity and rest for maximum efficiency. One of the questions that had long stumped me was why I consistently felt some sort of emptiness, a mild depression, between the dinner hour and bedtime, as if this were the time of day that was hardest to fill. It wasn't until I stopped drinking, and that feeling went away, that I realized that this was the feeling I risked after having a couple of glasses of wine and then stopping. The wine had made me too hazy to concentrate on anything, and it was too early to go to bed. So I was in limbo, lost.

I found the answer before realizing I had the question. If I continued to drink, I would not feel that emptiness. If I smoked a cigar, I could delay it. If I continued to drink and then smoked a cigar and then drank a little more (brandy, cognac, whiskey, whatever) and then smoked a joint, I would fill those hours, that emptiness, and it would be time to go to bed. Early, maybe even still daylight, but time to pass out. I had finished that day, and when I awoke I could start fresh on the next.

Once I had stopped drinking, if only for a week or two, AA started to work its inscrutable ways on me. In my head, my behavior had been perfectly normal, drinking a lot because I like drinking so much. It was normal to drink. Everybody drank. Well, everybody I knew did, though few drank nearly as much or as routinely as I did. AA offers a different sort of normal, one in which you're surrounded by people who once drank but now don't, and whose lives seem better because of it.

Not that these lives are perfect, by any means. *Progress, not perfection.* But they seem capable of living, as AA calls it, "life on life's terms." Crucial to this acceptance is the realization that, no matter how bad things might get, drinking won't make it any better. Not for people who drink like we do, or did. Numbing, or masking, or self-medicating, or any of the ways we had thought we were using alcohol to manage our lives had turned on us. The cure had become the disease.

I had never thought of myself as an alcoholic before I came to AA, and didn't really identify until I was months into my new routine. At that point I had stopped twisting myself into knots over words and definitions. It really made no difference whether somebody else would diagnose me as "alcoholic" or not. I knew deep down that my life was better, richer, now that I was not drinking daily. I knew that, for me, not drinking daily meant not drinking at all. Because I'm an all-or-nothing kind of guy. And if that makes me an alcoholic, so be it.

Powerless? If you say so. If they say so. What I discovered in AA is that my problem wasn't necessarily how much I drank, that I had trouble with the fourth or the eighth drink. My problem was the first drink. Because that first drink would necessarily lead to however many others, and inevitably back to drinking daily. And then my life would be Groundhog Day all over again.

However others might interpret "powerless," I knew that I had some power, or choice over that first drink. I didn't need to make that choice forever, to resolve that I would never drink again. But one day at a time—or one hour or one breath—I could decide not to take that first drink. Because I knew that one would leave me emptier than none. Because I had learned that one is too many and a hundred aren't enough. I had discovered just how thirsty I had been, and that the only way to quench that thirst was to transcend it.

While I was still wrestling with "powerless," another concept that turned my head inside out was "freedom." When I'd previously thought of freedom in conjunction with alcohol, I'd thought that, as a responsible and fully-functioning adult, I had the freedom to drink as much as I wanted. As long as I wasn't hurting myself (as my medical tests had assured me) or anybody else.

When I came into AA, "freedom from drink" simply would not compute. Just like "powerless over alcohol." I had to ease into it, or let it seep into me. Once the fog started to clear, and sobriety had begun to seem to me like not only an option, but a better way of living, I realized that, yes, now I felt free in a way I hadn't before. Free from the tyranny of that daily ritual, the drinking and drugging myself into sleep every night. I didn't need it. Didn't want it. I could feel more comfortable in my own skin without it.

I was free, or at least a little freer, from what AA calls "the bondage of self." If this meant admitting that I was powerless over alcohol, I would do so. Though I was by no means ready to do so right off the bat. I had come in thinking I would go back out within a matter of weeks or months. I wasn't ready at the start to work any of the steps, let alone the first one.

But I had already surprised myself: I enjoyed these meetings, and looked forward to going to them daily. I enjoyed not drinking, something I had never previously considered. Maybe the program had other surprises in store for me, one day at a time.

Step Two: Came to believe that a Power greater than ourselves could restore us to sanity.

What I now choose to minimize as semantical issues seemed at the start to be insurmountable obstacles. I was still less than comfortable with "powerless over alcohol," and here it seems that such powerlessness had rendered me insane. For why else would I need to be restored to sanity?

And what about this "Power" that would do the restoring. Plainly this was God, as the capital P indicated, the God in whom I did not believe. Now I was asked to believe that this God would restore me to a sanity I felt I had never lost. In terms of my work, my family, my life, I had always been pretty rational, very reliable. Even when drinking, as I did every night, I was generally quiet, and I usually felt lucid. I was no raving lunatic alcoholic.

Old-timers in AA are fond of using the step's first three words as a way of easing into the step, of easing into a program where "easy does it" is something of a mantra. So, first:

(We) came: We started attending meetings. We showed up. We entered AA.

Came to: We came to our senses. The fog lifted, and we were finally able to see our drinking life for what it had been.

Came to believe: In something greater than ourselves.

Maybe most who enter AA aren't quite as suspicious as I am (or was), but I had to be convinced that there was no hidden agenda, that this whole 12-step program wasn't some sort of bait-and-switch for a cultish Christian fundamentalism.

While there's no question that AA has changed my perspective on Christianity and softened my resistance, I have never felt any pressure within the program to embrace a particular religion. There is no mention anywhere in the AA literature of two of the primary tenets of the Christian religion—the creation mythos or the afterlife. Make that three, for I've never encountered any insistence in AA to accept Jesus Christ as your personal savior.

Even among the churchgoing Christians, and there are plenty in AA, most of those in the program make a sharp distinction between religion and spirituality. The former is a matter of dogma and tenets, of rules made and interpreted and enforced by mankind that supposedly reflect the will of God. Spirituality is more of a direct connection with a Higher Power, however the individual perceives that power and that connection.

At its most elemental, it is a recognition that there is something greater than the individual, that the individual is not the center of the universe. Through such a recognition, selfish, inner-directed alcoholics can be transformed, or restored, into compassionate, outer-directed, spiritually-minded beings.

The sense of connection is crucial, as you grope your way toward some sort of belief. Early on, you'll be advised that if you struggle with faith, you can accept the group itself as the higher power, this Group of Drunks as your G.O.D. Another acronym frequently employed is Good Orderly Direction. AA loves word games and playful phraseology, but these are all signposts that point in the same direction: There is something beyond your individual will that can heal the disease within.

12-steppers joke of the distinction between religion and spirituality that "Religion is for those who don't want to go to hell. Spirituality is for those who have already been there." Not only is hell something you've been carrying around inside of you, the seeds of salvation just might be as well.

I'd long since decided that I would slide past Step Two as well—after all, I wasn't planning on sticking around very long—when I encountered another paradox within the program that would turn my perspective inside out. At one of the meetings I intended, one of the old-timers was fond of selecting a reading from the very end of the Big Book for us to share and discuss. It was from the second appendix, and it concerned the varieties of spiritual awakening, how not everyone needed to experience a "burning bush" moment, and that the process might be so gradual we'd barely be aware of it.

In either case, the appendix insisted that *"With few exceptions our members find that they have tapped an unexpected inner resource which they presently identify with their own conception of a Power greater than themselves."* (pp. 567-8).

It wasn't until I'd heard it a few times that the implications staggered me. I still wasn't convinced about this "restore us to sanity" business (that would come), but here was the suggestion that the Power greater than ourselves was actually an "unexpected inner resource." Just let that sink in. Something within us, something we hadn't known was within us, was the Higher Power. We didn't need to go searching for faith in something beyond ourselves; it was flickering right inside. And what was inside me connected to what was inside you, and perhaps to what was inside everyone and everything.

AA gives us the latitude to perceive this however we'd prefer. There is a spiritual dimension to life, something within our existence beyond meat, blood and synapses. We are all part of something bigger. Even if our first inkling of belonging to something bigger than ourselves was within the group of AA itself, our existence could begin expanding along with our faith.

It was already bigger than what I'd remembered, sitting in a room every night, with the door closed, alone with a bottle. It was like I'd found a key to something that was not only way bigger than that, but way richer.

Step Three: Made a decision to turn our will and our lives over to the care of God as we understood him.

This should have been the deal breaker, the step that I couldn't even attempt. It was the biggest paradox I'd encountered in a program full of them. *God as we understood him?* If I didn't reject the basic concept of God, my understanding was that I couldn't understand Him. Or Her, or It, or Whatever. Any God worth worshiping was just too big and amorphous for me to wrap my tiny brain around.

Yet Step Three became the key to my program, the step that allowed me to return to one and two with a fresh perspective and to move on to all the rest. I determined that my incapacity to understand God as I understood him allowed me to concentrate on the first part of the step, the part that would change my life.

"Turn it over," as one old-timer kept repeating. He would summarize the step as "Let go, and let God." In practice, I would just let go, and not worry about letting God. Or, in other words, I would turn it over, without regard to Whom. Or What. In principle, it just didn't make any difference as far as my program was concerned. The important thing was recognizing that my will, my control, had landed me where I was. My clutching and grasping. I hadn't even believed that sleep could occur on its own, without my controlling the process through drinking and doping myself, pretty much every night of my adult life.

There's that other common saying in AA, "Our best thinking is what brought us here." Many of us thought we were smart, maybe too smart for our own good. Our brains were always whirring, always complicating matters, requiring that "off" switch that alcohol provided for me. Another control, another micromanagement.

What if I could just let go? What if I could fall asleep and wake up without willing it, just as I inhaled and exhaled without thinking about it. (And if I started thinking about it, the process would become labored.) Turn it over. Trust that things will take care of themselves. Just let go…

Where most AA-ers would complete that sentence with "…and let God," I just didn't need to worry about that. I was being true to my program, knowing that I couldn't understand God as I understood him, that not understanding was the essence of my understanding. And this was fine, for now and maybe forever. Letting go would be the key for me, turning it over. Trusting that things would work out just fine if I could just get out of my own way.

As Christian as the underpinnings of the program might be, Step Three is as Eastern as it is Western, reflecting the understanding that grasping and clutching is suffering, that change is the only constant. Letting go, turning it over, realizing that I'm not in the driver's seat or at the center of the universe. If I could just concentrate on what was at hand, one breath at a time, doing the next right thing, things would work out just fine.

Maybe not exactly as I had planned them, but we've already seen the value of my "best thinking." Sometimes things would work out much better than if I had micromanaged. Take the move to Des Moines. I hadn't planned on leaving Austin in order to get sober, but Des Moines turned out to be a great place to do just that—lots of meetings, plenty of good people, a pace of life and values that didn't push me toward extremes. I could lead a rich, sober life here, one that I had never anticipated or known I'd wanted.

Similarly, my transition from journalism to academics had seemed serendipitous, or at least never part of my master plan. I wasn't that sort of master planner. But the field in which I had earned a living for decades was about to collapse, leaving a whole lot of my peers unemployed, looking to make the sort of jump I already had. When you're trying to bridge middle age into retirement with so little job security, a tenured position with no retirement age looks all the more attractive.

I couldn't have planned things any better if I'd tried. But I hadn't planned much at all, other than moving from a newspaper where I didn't see a future and then from a magazine that bored me to death. Even if I had no conception of the divine, maybe some divine providence had been lighting the path.

Once I opened the door to the "maybes," I could return to steps one and two with a fresh perspective, working them provisionally. It's worth noting here that Step One is the only one of the twelve that so much as mentions alcohol or makes any reference to drinking. The rest of the steps are more of a guidebook for living, a way toward a "faith that works."

By Step Three, this was working. My head was clearing, my very existence felt lighter, now that the weight of responsibility for planning and controlling everything, worrying about everything, had been lifted. Most pertinently, I no longer had to worry about how much I was drinking, how much was too much, how I could get away with drinking as much as I wanted. I wasn't drinking at all, and I didn't want to. My obsession had also been lifted.

Now that I was letting go, I could let go of some of my earlier reservations concerning the steps. Maybe I had thought I was using alcohol to manage my life, but I was now doing a much better job without it rather than with it. Maybe a life in which I shut myself in a room, in no condition to answer the phone or interact with others, drinking until I passed out, had been a pretty piss-poor way of managing. From this perspective, it appeared to be so.

Maybe "unmanageable" isn't the word I would have selected, but the emotional essence of the step felt right. I knew now that I had been "powerless" once I'd had that first drink, and that I'd had that first drink and many more every night because I had been powerless to make the decision not to.

Now that I had "surrendered," as the program put it, I discovered where my power was and where it ended. Now that the obsession had been lifted, I had the power each day to decide whether I would take that first drink or not. And if I took it, I would sentence myself to a life of daily drinking, because I was powerless to resist that ritual. Some people could. They could have a drink or two with dinner one night and then decide not to the next few nights. I couldn't. I was an alcoholic.

So, Step Two: I was now more comfortable with "restore us to sanity" than I had been, because once the fog had started to lift and my life seemed lighter and brighter, the thought of returning to that old life seemed truly insane. Why would I give up this for that? I no longer felt like I had given up drinking. I felt that I had received the gift of sobriety, and that this is what I would be giving up if I permitted myself even a single drink. Because I knew myself even better now, knew the extent of my thirst, and knew that one drink on one night would simply whet an insatiable appetite.

But what about that "Higher Power" that was doing the restoring? I didn't need to have to work that out now, have a definitive grasp of the ineffable. I knew that I wouldn't have done this on my own, that maybe I couldn't. Even if I had for some reason decided to stop drinking, I would have been what the program calls a "dry drunk," a guy who was still so obsessed with the alcohol he wasn't drinking that he was "white knuckling" it. I would have been living a life of denial.

Instead, I felt blessed. By whom or what I had no idea. But I had found a program filled with kindred spirits, whose lives added connection and meaning to my own. I was no longer alone in a room, obliterating myself. I had received this gift of sobriety that I had done nothing to deserve. It didn't make much difference whether I used the group as my higher power (as many did, early on) or thought that God was talking to me through the members of the group (as many others did) or simply felt spiritually awakened (as we pretty much all felt). I was a changed person by the time I had finished Step Three, and those changes were just starting.

So here's how I managed "came to believe," and perhaps still do. I heard the stories of others who had come into the program with doubts as deep as mine about God, or their Higher Power, or whatever term they chose. And I saw how they had managed to stay sober while committing themselves to some sort of spiritual path, one that often turned and broadened as their program progressed.

What I "came to believe" is what these former skeptics had come to believe, despite their initial doubts and resistance, and that possibly I would as well. Or maybe not. It didn't really make much difference, as long as I kept coming to meetings and working the steps, remaining open. And not drinking. One day at a time.

Step Four: Made a searching and fearless moral inventory of ourselves.

For me, this was the step where I really committed to the program, where there was no turning back. It is the first of the so-called "action steps," the ones that require us to do something other than acknowledge, believe or accept. And it was the first one I knew I couldn't do without selecting a sponsor, a term I had never heard in this context before attending my first AA meeting.

The term "sponsor" never appears in the Big Book but it has subsequently been considered an integral part of the program. You don't need a sponsor to join, like you might a country club. But if you're really going to work the steps, all of them, you can't do them on your own. Your sponsor holds you accountable. Your sponsor serves as a sounding board. Your sponsor provides clarity when your perspective seems distorted or cloudy, even to you.

As I described earlier, I didn't intellectualize or rationalize my sponsor selection. I went by impulse, by feel, trusting that something was guiding me (that "higher power" toward which AA was already softening me) and that whatever choice I made would somehow be the right one, for reasons that I might not immediately understand.

Just as leaving newspapers and moving to Des Moines had come to seem in retrospect like part of some sort of divine plan toward spiritual sobriety, so did my selection. He was only a half-dozen years older than me, but he seemed from the start like some sort of "father confessor," and the fact that he was more politically conservative than I was didn't bother me in the slightest—so was my dad, or so he had been.

And the fact that I wasn't the believer that he was didn't bother him. None of those he sponsored were as Catholic as he was, and few were as Christian. His concern was that we were "spiritually fit," that we had a defense against the alcoholism that still lurked within us—"cunning, baffling, powerful," as the program put it.

The whole sponsorship issue doesn't always go so smoothly, because alcoholics have a tendency to be a willful, difficult lot, ones who don't respond well to authority. Since part of the program is letting go, realizing that you're no longer in charge, some sponsors feel duty bound to approach their role like they are drill sergeants.

If I'd had one of those "hit your knees twice a day and call me every morning" sponsors, I might have been out of there.

Fortunately, mine was a "wear the program like a loose garment" kind of sponsor, giving his sponsees the latitude they needed, never insisting on a one-size-fits-all regimen. One of his other sponsees, who has become one of my best friends in Des Moines, took a full year before he was ready to start on Step Four. My sponsor didn't care—my friend was staying sober, he was committed to the program, and he'd be ready when he was ready.

To my mind, Step Four is the most dated, anachronistic of the twelve, one that reflects the Depression-era origins of the program and Bill W.'s business background. The "moral inventory" is an attempt to assess the damaged goods, to see what we've got and what can be salvaged. As the Big Book explains, "A business which takes no regular inventory usually goes broke. Taking a commercial inventory is a fact-finding and a fact-facing process. It is an effort to discover the truth about the stock-in-trade. One object is to disclose damaged or unsalable goods, to get rid of them promptly and without regret." [pg. 64]

Not the analogy I would have chosen, though perhaps it helps explain why my career as a record-store retailer (where we never once took inventory) was so short-lived. But tackling the inventory under the direction of my sponsor was definitely a turning point in my program, the pivotal step. Because it forced me to reflect, assess and turn inward, to think about expansive stretches of my life that seemed like someone else's a lifetime ago.

The process that AA calls a moral inventory is to me more like a housecleaning, or the start of a purification process, one through which you'll never get clean, but at least you'll get cleaner. It's a process that introduces the overriding concepts of "Fear" and "Resentment," which turn out to pretty much run the lives of even those of us who may not consider themselves especially fearful or resentful.

But the thing about fear is that it is so pervasive that it's like the water the fish doesn't recognize as such, because it is all he knows. From early on, well before drinking, I feared talking with other people, I feared sharing with others, I feared that my parents' love wasn't unconditional, a word I wouldn't know and understand until later. I feared striking out in baseball. I feared losing a girlfriend, or not having one in the first place.

By the time I was heavily self-medicating, I feared not being able to get to sleep, not being able to procure the alcohol and dope that would allow me to get to sleep, not being able to wake up fresh and rested enough to allow me to do the work that would ensure me a steady supply of the dope and alcohol that would allow me to get to sleep. I feared that, with each story I wrote, the well would run dry.

I am barely testing the waters of the ocean of fear I faced. On their own, things weren't right, or so I feared. They couldn't take care of themselves. My basic needs would go unmet—sleep, shelter, food, sex. I feared that, at my core, I was a fraud. As Randy Newman wrote and sang in "Guilty," "It takes a whole lot of medicine, for me to pretend to be somebody else."

Fear breeds resentment, and resentment becomes as pervasive as fear. You resent the girl who you fear is going to leave you, who won't give you sex, who doesn't seem satisfied with the sex she has with you, who must be faking it, faking everything. You resent people who won't do what you tell them to do, let alone what you want them to do, who can't read your mind and give you what you need. You resent those who seem to be more successful than you are with less talent than you believe yourself to have. They are better with people, it comes easier to them. They are networkers, backslappers, ass-kissers. Your lack of comparable success in those areas is a sign of your integrity.

Again, just scratching the surface. What Step Four forces you to acknowledge is your role in this twisted, complex web of emotions and relationships that is your existence, and which you have partly been drinking to sustain. The "character defects," as AA calls them, are the ways in which these black holes of existential dread manifest themselves. Most of us 12 Steppers, to one extent or another, can be categorized as "Egomaniacs with an inferiority complex." Step Four represents a big step toward getting us right-sized: not greater than, not less than.

It's easy to recognize how we've been hurt or wronged by others, but much tougher to see how we've been complicit. Most of the time, we have in some way been complicit, as a flawed human being dealing with other flawed human beings. Step Four forces us to shift perspective, to concentrate on our own character defects, recognizing that we can't change other people or past actions. Rather than wallow in the self-righteousness of the wrongs done to us, we have to move on. We have to clean house. We have to see where the dirt is and recognize it for what it is.

So, character defects. How might our character be defective? Let us count the ways. Start with the Seven Deadly Sins— pride, greed, lust, envy, gluttony, wrath and sloth. The point is that once you get started, there's no stopping. There are some worksheets available for the step (online, of course, where everything now is) and some of them catalog the myriad options of personality flaws that manifested within us, the jealousies, angers, insecurities that warped our relations with others, that bred our resentments and fears.

The time had come to turn the tables. Make a list. Check it twice. In the first column, include everyone whom we felt had wronged us, and whom we feared or resented as a result. In the second column, after each name, the specific incident or cause of that wrongdoing—the boss had treated you unfairly, the former friend had made a play for your wife, a colleague had gotten an award or a promotion that you felt you deserved.

Then the third column, the crucial one, how did this manifest itself in us? Or, more simply, what was our part in this? We couldn't change the past or another person, but maybe through recognizing our own weaknesses, flaws, character defects, we could come to terms with them, temper them, even eliminate them. Maybe if we hadn't been so insecure, or jealous or competitive, the resentment wouldn't have festered. Maybe if we can admit weakness in ourselves we can accept it in others, have some compassion and connection.

Maybe if we can see ourselves as something other than the center of the universe, we can stop playing the victim and the blame game. We might even discover that others hadn't intended to hurt us at all. Maybe they were oblivious to the resentment that continued to burn within us.

Here's what they say about resentment in AA: That it's like drinking poison and expecting the other person to die. That it's like letting another person live rent free in your head. That it will kill you. Or at least drive you back to drinking. Which will kill you.

As skeptical as I had been about Step Four, I found it illuminating, how character defects tended not to be random traits but would cluster and connect. How those clusters and connections could provide a map of not only my personality but my way forward. How they showed the ways in which I had been a bad son, a bad older brother, a bad friend, a bad boyfriend, a bad husband, a bad employee.

Not singularly bad or especially bad, but flawed in the way we all are. I had been fixated on myself, my fears, my needs. I needed to be more outer directed, more understanding, more accepting, more compassionate. I needed to let go, the same lesson I had learned in Step Three.

I remain a work in progress. At the start of this process, what others might consider my character defects were what I considered my character, my personality, my ineffable charm. I was and am pretty caustic, using words as weapons, employing sarcastic humor to cut others down and thus, in my mind, build myself up. These days, however, I'm at least less likely to say anything and everything that pops into my head, to take the cheap shot at someone else's expense. I'm no longer the "fuck 'em if they can't take a joke" sort of self-justifier. I recognize how this kneejerk tendency makes me the jerk—how it hurts them and reflects on me.

Many sponsors encourage you to include your good qualities in that inventory as well, so as not to use it as just another excuse to beat yourself up. I had never lost sight of my good qualities, tarnished though they had been, brighter now through the polishing process of working the steps. My self-esteem had long been reinforced by professional success, a loving family, a verbal facility that allowed me to express myself and make a living. I valued all this, and was grateful for it, yet the program helped me put these qualities in better perspective.

Some stop or stall at the Fourth Step because "inventory" suggests a thoroughness before which they feel incapable, inadequate. So they procrastinate. The keys to the fourth step are getting it down on paper and doing the best you can. You'll have more chances when you've been sober longer and have discovered more about yourself. If you get a new sponsor, he'll likely want you to go through all the steps all over with him. You might just want to do a new Step Four at crucial stages for your own well-being.

By now, you're starting to recognize how interconnected the steps are, how they aren't discrete, individual suggestions but a way of transcending what the program calls "the bondage of self" so you can "bask in the sunlight of the spirit." Step Four is not an end in itself, but the necessary prelude to Step Five.

Step Five: Admitted to God, to ourselves, and to another human being the exact nature of our wrongs.

Everyone has heard that confession is good for the soul. It says so in Psalms 119:26, where the reference actually begins, "Open confession…" and the passage continues, "Nothing brings more ease and more life to a man than a frank acknowledgment of the evil which has caused the sorrow and the lethargy. Such a declaration proves that the man knows his own condition, and is no longer blinded by pride. Our confessions are not meant to make God know our sins, but to make us know them."

But you don't need to be a Bible thumper, a Christian, or much of a believer of any sort to experience the value of pouring out your soul to someone else, and letting your higher power eavesdrop, whoever or whatever your higher power might be. Most of us who are not Catholic and have never run afoul of the criminal justice system have never had the opportunity for such a formal confession.

The closest I had come was in some therapy sessions, ones in which I had done all the talking and felt drained and changed in the aftermath. Initially therapy was one of the reasons I had resisted this step, before I had a sponsor or much intention of getting one. I figured I had already talked all this stuff out with professionals, so what was the sense of doing it again with an amateur.

Once my sponsor and I had bonded, after going through the first three steps fairly quickly and taking more time with Step Four, I found myself actually looking forward to Step Five. It is the step that many fear the most, or at least in the top two, because not only do you have to admit your transgressions to yourself, you have to share them with somebody else. They are out there in the open, things you'd vowed you'd never tell anyone.

There's a reason why confession is sometimes called "coming clean," why even those who have committed a crime feel some relief at confessing to it. Most of those making Step Five confessions had to admit to some pretty shameful behavior, or at least behavior for which they are still ashamed. Maybe they'd cheated or stolen or borrowed with no intention of paying back. Maybe they'd done things drunk that they never would have done sober. Some seem to have drunk in order to do things they wouldn't have done sober, loosening the inhibitions that had kept them in line.

Many couldn't remember exactly what they had done, suffering blackouts through which they continued to function on some level but had no conscious memory of it. Only the fallout they had to deal with the day after, when they had to pick up the pieces, after others told them just how they had embarrassed themselves.

No matter what you have done and how bad you feel about it, chances are that an experienced sponsor has heard it all before, and perhaps can even top (bottom?) yours with his own misbehavior. My sponsor had been sober for more than three decades when we met, but I also learned early on about his multiple stints in rehab facilities, more than a dozen in his teens alone, before sobriety took hold.

I knew enough to recognize that the stuff I felt bad about would be chump change to him. I had committed no high crimes or misdemeanors, never lost a job or underperformed because of drink. My sins were mainly sins of omission, not being there as fully as I should have been for my wife and daughters, using friends as a supporting cast rather than equal partners, living my life selfishly.

What you discover in Step Four about your character defects lays the groundwork for Step Five. Where the former is more of a connect-the-dots map, the latter is generally more of a chronological narrative, predating your drinking while including the sorts of fears, resentments and character defects that would lead to your drinking and continue through it. Whatever you've done wrong, whomever you've hurt, whatever you remember, spill it—and get beyond it.

Some fifth steps are marathon sessions lasting four or five hours, which seems obsessive to me, like the drinking that preceded them. Mine clocked in at less than an hour, though no one was keeping time while I was talking, and I couldn't have told you how long it was taking. I knew nothing I said would shock my sponsor; instead, I was scared that I might bore him.

We had driven to the parking lot of a nearby nature preserve and sporting complex, otherwise deserted with the approach of winter. It was a gray and chilly afternoon. When I was finished, I did feel lighter, unburdened, as if a weight had been lifted from my shoulders. My sponsor might as well have told me to do ten "Hail Mary's, two "Our Father's" and to go in peace and serve the Lord.

Instead, he gave me a different sort of absolution, instructing me to go do what it says in the Big Book, to go home and "find a place where we can be quiet for an hour, reviewing what we have done." We're over the hump and ready for a little breathing space.

Step Six: Were entirely ready to have God remove all these defects of character & Step Seven: Humbly asked him to remove our shortcomings.

Big Book purists, the strict constructionists and absolutists, will be aghast at my daring to combine two steps into one. There is some crucial distinction between these two, but I remain convinced that 12 was something of a magic number for Bill Wilson, and that this program could just as easily been edited and compressed into fewer steps. (Or, it could have been more, since pretty much everyone agrees that Step Twelve has three different components.)

Here we have reached a turning point, a turning inward, toward a place where contemplation and resolve will take us up the ladder to the next steps. There has been a cleansing and a lightening, a confession and a catharsis, an acknowledgement that useless and damaged goods need to be removed from our personal inventory.

But how?

As we've discovered through working the steps, the powerlessness over alcohol that we've admitted extends to so much else. Pretty much everything, in fact, except the power to decide whether or not to take that first drink. We've lived with these character defects forever, and most of us likely aren't "entirely ready" to have "all" of them removed.

As I've said, what you call my character defects are what I called my character, my personality, my ineffable, inscrutable charm. Remove them all, and I'll be just as bland as the next guy. I'll lose my edge. Yet I've surrounded myself in the program with some of the brightest, funniest people I've ever met, and they don't seem to have lost much of anything except their thirst, the obsession to drink.

So maybe I can become a kinder, more empathic, more loving version of myself, warmer and more open, someone who isn't always calculating what's in it for me. Someone who isn't trying to control you to meet my needs. But according to these two steps, I can't do it on my own. I need God, or my higher power, or the God of my understanding, who remains beyond my understanding, but I've come far enough to quit playing semantical games.

The Big Book, which devotes pages to the completion of each of the earlier steps, compresses steps six and seven into a couple of paragraphs. Sit still, think about what you've done in the previous steps, and say a prayer. You're ready to move on to the next steps, the ones that require the really heavy lifting.

Why are these two steps? What's the distinction between six and seven? It really comes down to two words. The first, in Step Six, is "ready." The paradigm has shifted sufficiently where we are ready to let go of the qualities that we have long used to defend ourselves and which we have felt defined us. We know that there's a better life for us, and we are ready to become worthy of it.

In Step Seven, the key word is "humbly," and I won't argue with those who believe that humility is so crucial to the process that it merits its own step. It may well be the key to the whole program, a recognition of where you fit in the cosmos, the limits of your power and control.

As the stereotypical "egomaniac with an inferiority complex," I am not naturally prone to humility. But the program has made it easy for me to connect the dots: I believe in grace, the quality of mercy that is not earned but bestowed. I haven't earned my good fortune, or even my seat in the program—I had to be dragged in virtually kicking and screaming. So I connect grace to gratitude, to the blessing that I have not gotten what I deserved from decades of drunken driving and living recklessly, heedlessly, mindlessly.

Humility necessarily follows, because I know I have done nothing to deserve the life the program has given me. And I've learned that I cannot will these character defects away, any more than the stories of the alcoholics around me suggest that will power alone could have stopped their drinking. We need to rely on something beyond us, or which could even be what the Big Book calls "an unexpected inner resource" that is somehow a power greater than ourselves.

I've become comfortable enough with the paradoxes of the program that I can live with that, and with the leaps of faith that these two steps require. My readiness is crucial, but my humility recognizes that the timetable for the removal of these defects may not be my own. I can ask, as Step Seven requires, but it may not be on my timetable when I receive.

It wasn't until I had eight years of sobriety that I encountered another paradox at a step-study meeting, one that I don't think the program really addresses. If the God of my understanding (whatever that may be) can remove all of my defects of character, why can't he/she/it just go ahead and remove my alcoholism? The program tells me that I will always be an alcoholic, even in recovery and decades of sobriety. Couldn't this higher power just remove that along with my other shortcomings, just as my obsession/compulsion to drink has been removed.

It's a stumper. But I'm not going to drink over it.

Step Eight: Made a list of all persons we had harmed, and became willing to make amends to them all. & Step Nine: Made direct amends to such people wherever possible, except when to do so would injure them or others.

As with the sixth and seventh steps, Step Eight is where you show the willingness to do what Step Nine requires. Pretty much everyone agrees that Step Nine is the toughest in the program, the most uncomfortable and the one that takes the longest. Step Eight, by comparison, is one of the easiest, though perhaps you have to delude yourself that Step Nine doesn't exist in order to proceed with Step Eight.

You've pretty much done Step Eight by the time you arrive here. If you've kept your notes from the fourth and fifth steps, every person you have harmed is in there somewhere. All you have to do is list them. And become willing to make amends.

Sponsorship is crucial for these steps. Your sponsor will assure you that Step Eight is just a list, and that there's nothing difficult about making one. It is only when you realize that every name mentioned in the eighth step requires some sort of encounter and confession and pledge in the ninth step that you might be tempted to edit yourself.

Your sponsor should hold you to account with Step Eight, because he's seen your fourth step and heard your fifth step, and he should know if you're being evasive. As should you. You make that list, and you become "willing to make amends to them all." Which does not mean that you will, or that you do. Having completed Step Eight, you review the list with your sponsor, deciding which amends you should make first and which people you should not contact, because "to do so would injure them or others."

This wasn't the case with me, but what you hear so often in step-study meetings, usually accompanied by laughter, is that old girlfriends/boyfriends are the ones that so many 12-steppers want to approach first, and the ones that sponsors advise against approaching at all. Because they know you have a hidden agenda, that you want to tell your old flame that you are sorry, that you have changed, become a new person, and that you have some vague fantasy about rekindling some sparks.

The ninth step is not about saying you are sorry, and it is most certainly not about picking up where you had left off. It is about what the program calls "cleaning up your side of the street." You're not here to revisit who did what and why. You're doing this step to make things right and to keep yourself sober.

To "amend" is not to apologize. It is to change. If you are truly a changed person, you will repay your debts, even confess your embezzlements, show those you love most that you understand how self-centered you have been, how you weren't there for them in your obsession with drinking. And show those you have harmed through your bad behavior when you were drinking or because of your drinking that the sober you has become a changed man.

Your sponsor will stress that it doesn't make any difference how the other person responds. Some might have trouble remembering the wrong you have done to them or think that it wasn't so wrong. Others won't want anything to do with you and will refuse to forgive you. A few will allow this to open the door to a deeper discussion and a renewed relationship. The old girlfriends would really prefer to be left alone; they've long ago moved beyond you.

The ones I would make were all close at hand: Maria and our two daughters, Kelly and Molly. Once Maria had heard about Step Nine, she might have preferred an "all amends, all the time" program. She had been warning me about my drinking for years, until we had gotten into a vicious cycle of nag, deny, resent.

I don't mean that "nag" pejoratively, because she was right, I was in the grip of a progressive disease, and it had been getting worse. But I had been so sure that there were control issues that extended well beyond drinking, that she was trying to treat me like a child. I hadn't changed, she had, because she had once enjoyed drinking and everything else as much as I had. Or at least she hadn't put any moral restrictions on such behavior.

But she was right, and I was *wrong, wrong, wrong*. I couldn't say it enough. Moving forward, I had to be more open to following her lead, to accepting the possibility that she might be right even when my gut instinct or best judgment said she was wrong. Like the dog she had spent more than a grand on, the one I had led outside in the thunderstorm on the night of my last drunk.

She had been right on that; Rosie has enriched our life for longer than I have been sober. Where my first instinct had long been to question Maria's judgment, not because it was hers but because it wasn't mine, I now was more likely to follow her lead. Our lives went better when she felt better. And, as the program had taught me, "Our best thinking is what brought us here."

With the girls, there were few such recriminations, because they generally thought I had been a good, loving dad. Or at least that's what they have led me to believe. My amends with them involved sins of omission rather than commission—the nights that I had brought alcohol in an unmarked cup to their softball games or couldn't wait until they were upstairs so I could smoke a joint to get high. They had been standing in the way between me and what I had really wanted to do. And which I no longer wanted to or felt compelled to do.

In such familial relationships, the crucial element was what the program refers to as the "living amend," and which I admit I consider the great loophole. I'm not very comfortable with setting up appointments, confessing to people what they may be equally uncomfortable at hearing, who may have no interest in hearing anything from me at all. The buried past can weigh on you, but what's really important is moving forward, living your life as an embodiment of how you should behave with others.

So I'm lighter on the formal amends that most people make, preferring the day-to-day of living amends. But I've heard the stories, in meetings, of devoting a day in the office to making amends to everyone you work with. Of making amends where the other person has no idea what you're doing or why. Of making amends to a person who wants nothing to do with you, who tells you to get lost or get fucked. And of making amends where it truly heals a relationship, perhaps one that has been broken decades ago.

Some make amends by writing letters to their dead parents. Otherwise, letters and now emails are discouraged. You need the face-to-face. And such readiness and willingness are the keys here, as they were in six and seven. You must be ready to encounter anyone to whom you might owe an amend at any time, and some of these encounters may not transpire until years after you've started your ninth step.

I had such an opportunity, one that would never have happened, certainly not with the same outcome, had I not been in the program. Some might not consider this an amend, but it felt like one to me. Some thirty years after my first marriage had ended, I received a letter from an insurance company addressed to me and my first wife, with a name she no longer used, at an address where she had never lived (because, of course, it had been decades since she had lived with me). It concerned some sort of policy that I didn't remember, and it needed to be cashed out. The money wasn't life changing but it wasn't chump change—somewhere around ten grand.

It required both of our signatures for payoff, and I had had no contact with my first wife since our divorce, and wasn't eager for any. It had hurt a lot then, and even though both of our lives had benefited from being apart, why open old wounds? So my first inclination was to forge the signature for the name she no longer used and have them send me the check. This would have been, in the words of the program, "the easier, softer way."

It would not have been the right way, and I knew it. So I brought it up at a meeting, where there were a number of lawyers in attendance, and they were unanimous in their opinion that tracking her down, getting her to sign and splitting the money was not only the right thing to do, but the legal imperative. If I'd planned to follow my own instincts, I would have never brought it up, because I knew without asking that they were right.

It wasn't the money so much as the stirring the pot, the revisiting the past when things in the present were going just fine. She had cheated on me, and so I had felt entitled, after all these years. The money was the least I deserved. And the way it was addressed to her, in a married name she hadn't used in decades—that person didn't even exist.

All my rationalizing and self-justification couldn't unravel the twisted facts that this was a policy purchased mutually by the two of us, when we were married to each other, and that we were equally entitled to the disbursement. The rest doesn't really matter, because it's pretty easy in this internet age to track down anyone. When I emailed her about this out-of-the-blue windfall, she was glad to hear about it, and, I suppose glad to hear from me, though we pretty much kept our exchanges focused on the matters at hand.

Sending a bunch of documents and checks back and forth took longer than it would have if I had simply forged the original, and it became more complicated, in terms of taxes and such. But it was the right thing to do, and I was glad to do it. And move on. The Promises that are meant to accompany Step Nine bear repeating here. They *did* sound extravagant, when I first heard them, at my first meeting. And they still do. But every one of them has come true for me:

If we are painstaking about this phase of our development, we will be amazed before we are halfway through. We are going to know a new freedom and a new happiness. We will not regret the past nor wish to shut the door on it. We will comprehend the word serenity and we will know peace. No matter how far down the scale we have gone, we will see how our experience can benefit others. That feeling of uselessness and self-pity will disappear. We will lose interest in selfish things and gain interest in our fellows. Self-seeking will slip away. Our whole attitude and outlook upon life will change. Fear of people and of economic insecurity will leave us. We will intuitively know how to handle situations which used to baffle us. We will suddenly realize that God is doing for us what we could not do for ourselves. Are these extravagant promises? We think not. They are being fulfilled among us—sometimes quickly, sometimes slowly. They will always materialize if we work for them.

So, as they say at the end of every meeting, "Keep coming back. It works if you work it."

Step Ten: Continued to take personal inventory and when we were wrong promptly admitted it.

One of my favorites, this is the floss-and-brush step. Do it daily, and you won't have that buildup of plaque—or in this case guilt, shame, resentment, fear, whatever. This step is central to incorporating the 12 Steps into our daily lives. I practice it pretty much every night.

Sometimes, I compare my consciousness to a tuning fork. If it's vibrating weirdly, I know something is off. I figure out what it is. I make it right. If there's a slight I perceive that I might once have resented, and stewed in silence over, I try to interact with that person, have a cordial conversation, often discovering that what I had perceived wasn't what the other person intended at all.

Typically, my transgressions involve Maria, and it's easy to read when she feels there's something off between us. I try my best to make it right, not by doing what I might have once done, attempting to convince her that she isn't justified in feeling the way she does, because you can't argue someone out of her emotions. She's right to feel however she feels, and I do my best to make things right between us.

This step combines Step Four (inventory) and Step Nine (amends), the two that most of us consider particularly arduous. Once you've done the heavy lifting of coming to terms with years or even decades of obliviousness and denial, you can maintain your balance by doing this daily. You won't need another root canal.

Step Eleven: Sought through prayer and meditation to improve our conscious contact with God as we understood Him, praying only for knowledge of His will for us and the power to carry that out.

Years before the Beat Generation and fellow travelers brought their versions of Eastern consciousness to Western civilization, meditation found its way into AA. Bill Wilson was a spiritual seeker, and the spirituality that suffuses the program makes it so much richer than a "how to quit drinking" regimen. He details his own spiritual epiphany in the Big Book's "Bill's Story," and he continued his spiritual explorations through Jung, through William James' *The Varieties of Religious Experience* and through experiments with LSD.

Even so, "meditation" as mentioned in Step Eleven wasn't intended as we now understand it. It was more like daily contemplation, spurred by a homily or a quotation, from a book such as *Daily*

Meditations that many meetings use to spark discussion. It was a means of aligning yourself with God's will.

The eleventh step has become my favorite, the cornerstone of my program as connected to step three. For meditation as we now understand it, a spiritual discipline that need not be aligned with any specific religious practice, provides a perfect template for a program of "letting go"—of our obsession to drink, of our fears and resentments, of our need to take control and micromanage not only our own emotional selves but the actions of others as well.

So, the "turning it over" in the third step manifests itself in the letting go of the eleventh. Eastern spirituality informs us that change is the only constant, that grasping and clutching after what we desire only leads to pain and that letting go, of even the artificial construct of self, leads to serenity, to the state of being "happy, joyous and free" that the Big Book insists the universe wants for us.

As my sobriety has deepened, I have sometimes joked that I entered a program to stop drinking and discovered meditation as a side benefit, but now I feel as if I am in a meditation program with sobriety as a side benefit. Drinking is pretty much off my radar; I spend almost no time thinking about drinking, or about not drinking. My favorite meetings every week are both meditation meetings, what are sometimes referred to as Eleventh Step Meetings.

I would go to more if there were more to attend. I have found myself attending Centering Prayer Meetings that have nothing to do with AA and which are specifically Christian in orientation. I also attend meditation meetings that take a Buddhist-themed rather than 12-step approach to recovery. Yet these sessions are all very much the same—twenty minutes of meditation, of breathing, of letting thoughts drift through without judgment, of letting go.

You'll often hear in step-study meetings or other discussions of Step Eleven that "Prayer is talking to God; meditation is listening to him." I don't make such a distinction. For me, meditation is what AA calls "opening a channel," and I've gotten beyond being too concerned with to whom or what that channel is being opened. To everything, maybe. To "bask in the sunlight of the spirit," in AA parlance.

In meditation, I feel like I'm breaking free of what AA calls "the bondage of self," that I'm connecting with something bigger than myself. It feels like prayer. Not a prayer in which I'm asking for anything, which always seemed to me more like a Christmas list, with God deciding who has been naughty or nice, who gets his wish and who gets the lump of coal. But a prayer of gratitude, the warmth of which permeates my being.

A dirty little secret: I don't meditate because of this, and I don't always attain it. But I have gotten higher meditating than I ever did smoking dope, with an expansion or breakdown or whatever of consciousness that is more akin to tripping on LSD. I rarely feel better than I do when meditating, but I don't meditate in order to generate any specific feeling. I meditate to breathe, to let go, to feel as alive as I've ever felt.

As a creature of habit, I meditate daily, or try to, just as I work out, read, listen to music, go to a meeting, drink coffee in the morning and have a cigar after dinner. If I miss any of these, I get a little edgy and can feel a little squirrelly. I'm still in some ways the same obsessive that I was when I was drinking, but my habits seem healthier (except for the cigar, which I don't inhale). My head is clearer, and I'd like to think my soul is richer, my heart more open.

According to the instructions in the Big Book, our Step Eleven process should have us beginning each day by asking God to guide us to do His will, and end each day by reviewing that day, asking where we could have done better, asking for God's forgiveness. For those of us whose understanding of God is that God is beyond our understanding, recognizing that opening a channel affords a serenity beyond our will, our desires, our plans, our grasping and clutching can truly bring a peace that surpasses all understanding.

It's a peace that now allows me to sleep better without drinking than I ever did when I thought I had to drink myself into a stupor in order to sleep. Even one who remains skeptical about organized religion and "God's will" can find himself sharing the spirit of letting go, of turning it over, that permeates Step Eleven, as detailed in the Big Book:

> *"As we go through the day we pause, when agitated or doubtful, and ask for the right thought or action. We constantly remind ourselves that we are no longer running the show, humbly saying to ourselves many times a day, 'Thy will be done.' We are then in much less danger of excitement, fear, anger, worry, self-pity, or foolish decisions. We become much more efficient. We do not tire so easily, for we are not burning up energy foolishly as we did when we were trying to arrange life to suit ourselves."*

"It works—it really does."

It really does, though for me it works best when I replace "Thy will be done" with "This too shall pass."

Step Twelve: Having had a spiritual awakening as the result of these steps, we tried to carry this message to alcoholics, and to practice these principles in all our affairs.

The final step, within a process that never ends, has so much packed into it that it could just as easily have been three steps. So, let's, as the academics like to say, "unpack" it.

The first part is the spiritual awakening, the concept that forced Bill W. to add a second appendix to the Big Book, which he titled "Spiritual Experience." With a nod toward William James, he explained that one need not experience that illuminative flash, the life-changing epiphany, the cosmic orgasm of the soul, the proverbial "burning bush," in order to have had this experience.

No, claims the final step, working the steps will inevitably have given you this "spiritual awakening." And not merely is it "a" result of these steps, it is *the* result. In other words, everything culminates in this. Whatever brought you here, however you have worked the program, you have arrived here, at a point of spiritual awakening.

What is this awakening? It is the recognition that I am not the center of the universe, that I have limited control over what has happened and what will happen, but that things will work out if I trust that they will. That the best I can do is the "next right thing," one day at a time. And the next right thing typically involves helping others, getting outside of my own head so I can connect, as one broken human being, with another broken human being. In order to heal.

I have learned, as the program says, to keep my head where my hands are, to immerse myself in the task at hand, trusting that tomorrow will take care of itself. I have learned that 90% of the things I have worried about never happen anyway, and that the other 10% could even lead me somewhere better than if I'd followed a plan of my own devising. I have found peace through the Serenity Prayer, changing what I can (me), accepting what I can't (you and everything else that is not me) and aspiring toward the wisdom to know the difference.

Bill references James in referring to the awakening for many as being of "the educational variety," coming slowly, over time, through the program in general and working the steps in particular. Some in

AA believe they've experienced a miraculous transformation, where others see such transformation mainly in retrospect, the great difference between who we are now and how we felt when we came into the program. No one who has made it this far would trade the life he has found for the one he had before. (Though this doesn't prevent relapses, for any number of reasons, even after decades of continuous sobriety. It forever remains a "one day at a time" program.)

Part two is carrying this message to the alcoholic who is still suffering, or, in the parlance of the program, 12-stepping those who want and need it. You'll notice that this is the first mention of "alcohol" or any form of that word since Step One, suggesting that the ramifications of this program extend well beyond not drinking liquor. And they do. But those in AA are repeatedly reminded that they need to put sobriety before all else. Before your spouse and family, because if you lose your sobriety, you'll lose them, too. And your job. And your freedom, once you have that drunken driving arrest. And, eventually, your life.

As the hardliners with a penchant for alliteration put it, drinking leads to one of three inevitabilities: the brig, the bughouse or the box. I've met plenty at meetings who have served time behind bars, or who have been hospitalized as part of their treatment. Everybody who spends any time in AA knows somebody who has died from this disease, who either went back out and drank and drugged himself to death or who committed suicide, no longer able to live without it or with it.

Those hardliners would say I am in denial because I still don't believe that I put sobriety above all else. Put a gun to the head of my wife and daughters and tell me to drink or you'll shoot, and I'll drink. If I felt I were trapped between a drink and suicide, I'd drink.

I've never lost a job, or even a day of work, to drink. I'm not like those others.

Yet. That's what the hardliners would tell me. You may not have experienced any of those tragedies yet, but if you had kept drinking, you would have crashed the car, maybe killed someone, lost a job, lost your family. Maybe so. What I envision more if I returned to drink is more like a death-in-life, a return to that ritual of Groundhog Day numbness. And because I know that this is a progressive disease, if I were ever to retire, I am convinced that I would drink more and more, earlier and earlier. So, yeah, maybe the worst would happen.

Meanwhile, one day at a time, I prefer the richness of my sober life to the sleepwalking of ending each day drunk, passed out. But the program has taught me that this isn't all about me, that my sobriety now allows me to carry the message, to help others who want and need that help. Just as my life has been transformed, so can theirs.

This is perhaps the most crucial paradox of a program that is filled with them. You hear it often: "To keep it, you've gotta give it away." Sobriety, that is. If you're going to stay sober, you have to help others. You have to get out of your own sorry head, stop drowning in your own misery, and be of service. This has been the spiritual awakening, the change in perspective that has always been the purpose of the program, the shift from inner obsession to outer directed.

From the start, the rationale behind the program has been that an alcoholic will listen to another alcoholic where he might not listen to anyone else. There's a common bond, experience, frame of reference. The alcoholic in recovery still remembers that thirst, that desperation, that insanity. He knows what it takes to get past it, and he knows you can't do it alone. He's there to help, to introduce you to others who can help, to show you a way of life that is better than any you have imagined. If you want what he's got, he can show you how to get it. One day at a time.

The result of that spiritual awakening is a recognition that your prime purpose, if not your only purpose, is to help others, as others have helped you. And as those you help can help others to come. That is the purpose of the program, to restore you to sanity, so that you can carry the message to the alcoholic who is still suffering.

Which brings us to the third, the inevitable and the most difficult part of the step—"to practice these principles in all our affairs." If we truly have changed, if we've been transformed, even reborn, some might say, such practice should be perfect. But it never is, because we have learned along the way that we remain imperfect, broken, *alcoholic*.

We turn our will and our life over, and then we snatch it back, perhaps many times each day. We admit that our lives have become unmanageable, and yet we still try to micromanage some situations, to direct others to do our bidding. In some ways, we find it easier to practice these principles within meetings, showing empathy and compassion toward other alcoholics, refusing to judge them. Here, we all play by the same ground rules, speak the same language. It is the rest of the world that provides the real test.

That is why, in the words that close every meeting, we "keep coming back." There is no graduating from this program, completing the steps and then moving on, as I'd thought when I first started to consider the remote possibility that I might never drink again. We keep coming back to help the newcomer, struggling to come to terms with what we have accepted, sitting uncomfortably in that seat we occupied at our first meeting. We can not only tell him that his life will get better, we can show him how.

We also come back because we've heard stories from those at meetings on how they had been sober ten, twenty years or more, and were as confident as we are now that they would never drink again. Yet they did. Alcohol, as we have learned in the program, is cunning, baffling and powerful in its hold on us. The threat of complacency requires vigilance renewed, one day at a time. In another of those paradoxes that the program loves so much, there's a common saying that the farther we are from our last drink, the closer we are to our next one.

I still remember my last one vividly. I hope never to forget it. It keeps me from taking the next one.

27. Epilogue: What We Are Like Now

AA DIVIDES THE NARRATIVE OF the recovering alcoholic's life into three parts: What we used to be like. What happened. What we are like now.

Somewhere along the path to serenity, I started to apply that narrative structure to the even bigger picture, to life on earth as it preceded me and will continue after I'm gone:

What we used to be like (life before me). What happened (my very brief existence, a cosmic blip). What we are like now (after my death, another eternity). In other words, ashes to ashes, dust to dust, peace to peace.

In the meantime, I'm not sure what I believe, and I'm no longer sure that whatever I believe makes much difference. Maybe there's a grand cosmic plan to things that seem to have happened by coincidence and serendipity, like my coming to Des Moines, which proved to be such a good place to get sober, long before I had any idea that I would ever stop drinking and live a sober life. Like connecting with my sponsor, who has been my guide all along this unlikely path.

Or maybe I believe that, whatever happens, we can find a way to turn it into something positive, like life is a series of choices, or options, and neither is necessarily the right or wrong one, but each choice leads to different possibilities, and each option has some potential of its own. Maybe there's no guiding force, no overriding fate, but serendipity somehow becomes destiny. Here's where you are, and now what are you going to do? And who you are is determined by where you are and what you do. Or vice versa.

I'm not sure that there is a higher power that recently put an analysis about alcohol consumption on my Facebook feed, and put it into fresh perspective. A *Washington Post* Wonkblog posting from September 2014 opened with this startling observation:

> *Do you drink a glass of wine with dinner every night? That puts you in the top 30 percent of American adults in terms of per-capita alcohol consumption. If you drink two glasses, that would put you in the top 20 percent.*
>
> *But in order to break into the top 10 percent of American drinkers, you would need to drink more than two bottles of wine with every dinner. And you'd still be below-average among those top 10 percenters.*
>
> *The top 10 percent of American drinkers - 24 million adults over age 18 - consume, on average, 74 alcoholic drinks per week. That works out to a little more than four-and-a-half 750 ml bottles of Jack Daniels, 18 bottles of wine, or three 24-can cases of beer. In one week.*
>
> *Or, if you prefer, 10 drinks per day.*

If I'd read this when I was still drinking, it would have had the same effect as reading all those recovery books. The top ten-percenters drink more than two bottles of wine a day? Or a 12-pack of beer? Those folks had a drinking problem, it would have seemed to me, but I wasn't nearly that bad. Sure, I had more than two glasses of wine daily, so I was somewhere in the top fifth of American drinkers, but that was fine. And if my drinking got worse, because I knew I was progressively drinking more, certainly more than most of my friends, few of whom expressed any concern about my drinking, I could deal with it then.

What I knew then and know now is that I have what I called an "addictive personality." If I liked something I wanted more, and more, and that liking would become a habit and a ritual. Maybe a borderline obsession. Is that alcoholism? I wouldn't have thought so then, and I don't care much now. I know that I am an all-or-nothing kind of person, that it's easier for me to live a life without alcohol to one where I'd be obsessed with measuring and moderating my intake, and that my life is richer since I stopped drinking. I had never once thought of stopping drinking during the decades I had been convinced that drinking enhanced my life.

Now I know I would have made it into that top ten percent, and that every last one of them has a drinking problem. Nobody's that thirsty. You drink to feel something or to numb something or to blur something or just to chase that buzz that is gone almost as quickly as you catch it. You drink because you like it the way that smokers like smoking, for the one that tastes really good and makes you feel really good, accompanied by all the others that are force of habit or some kind of disease.

AA insists that alcoholics wish they could drink like normal people. I never once did, if by normal we mean a glass of wine or less per night. What would be the point? Why stop at one? Or two? Why stop until you feel like stopping? And that goal line keeps moving. For the kind of alcoholic I am, though it took me years of sobriety in AA before I was convinced that I had become one, not drinking at all is so much easier, better, lighter, less complicated than drinking any amount could ever be for me.

I don't know about you. Maybe your drinking is fine, manageable, under control. Maybe you occasionally have too much, more than you'd planned. Maybe your head hurts the next day, though not enough to keep you from drinking again that night. Maybe you're fine with moderation. Maybe you're kidding yourself. Maybe you're not.

What I've learned over the last decade is that though my brain may lead me astray, my gut rarely does. And when my brain tries to offer one of those half-assed reasons why I could have another drink, why I should—because a hundred or a thousand years from now, who's gonna care one way or the other—my gut knows just how much I'd be giving up. Giving up drinking had been a piece of cake. Giving up the richness of the life I've found in sobriety would be closer to tragic.

At the end of the first section of the Big Book, the original section, the one that has remained unchanged through the various editions of "Personal Stories" that follow, there are a couple of paragraphs that some groups read at the end of every meeting. This is on page 164, and is known as "A Vision for You":

> Our book is meant to be suggestive only. We realize we know only a little. God will constantly disclose more to you and to us. Ask Him in your morning meditation what you can do each day for the man who is still sick. The answers will come, if your own house is in order. But obviously you cannot transmit something you haven't got. See to it that your relationship with Him is right, and great events will come to pass for you and countless others. This is the Great Fact for us.
>
> Abandon yourself to God as you understand God. Admit your faults to Him and to your fellows. Clear away the wreckage of your past. Give freely of what you find and join us. We shall be with you in the Fellowship of the Spirit,

and you will surely meet some of us as you trudge the Road of Happy Destiny.

May God bless you and keep you—until then.

I still have my issues with conceptions of God, and God's will, but AA has given me a depth of feeling for something greater than myself. The rest is just semantics. So I'll continue to put one foot in front of the other, do the next right thing, one day at a time, and "trudge the Road of Happy Destiny." This sounds like a paradox, this happy trudging, but I've made my peace with it. And the serenity that comes with it, to anyone who really wants it.

28. Pandemic Postscript: Lockdown Serenity

Up to here, most of this was written in the summer of 2018, updated in the summer of 2019, and then revised in the summer of 2020. I have never lost the habit of compartmentalizing that had carried me through decades of drinking. Now I was no longer using drink to switch from the compartment of work to that of play, or smoking dope to ease from that of numbed semi-consciousness into sleep. But there was no time or space to open the compartment labeled "book manuscript" while teaching occupied my energies during the school year. During the summer, I could switch back, return to this labor of love.

The summer of 2020 was like nothing that anyone could have anticipated. There has been all sorts of talk about the "new normal," but nothing has seemed normal about the way we have been living—masked, isolated in our familial pods, working from home. And it got old pretty quickly. We had to get used to it. Until it became something different.

So, how does a recovering alcoholic navigate his way through a pandemic lockdown? Same as before. One day at a time. Those of us who have been 12-stepping our way through recovery have some practice at this, realizing how little control we have over most of everything, recognizing what we can control, trusting that things will somehow work out if we continue to do the next right thing one day at a time, one step at a time, one breath at a time.

How will things work out? No idea. When? Who knows? But one of the many precepts the program emphasizes is "first things first." Whatever I might think about long-range projections or big-picture developments is conjecture, somewhere way beyond where I am now. Closer to home, here and now, the first thing is to remain present, retain clarity, recognize that there is nothing I am going through that will be improved by taking a drink. Because I know my drinking, I know the progressive nature of it. I know that if I drink today I will drink tomorrow, that I will inevitably drink more and earlier as the days progress, and that the sober life I have come to love in all its freshness and richness will revert to the Groundhog Day numbness I have done so well to escape.

Yes, I remain a creature of habit and obsessive devotion to routine. Many others I know have the luxury of having a drink or two today—to take the edge off—and not develop a daily reliance on alcohol. I do not have that luxury, nor do I wish I did. I can eat chocolate on occasion without needing to eat it daily. I cannot do this with alcohol, or with marijuana. So I fill my daily routine with things that are better for me—reading, writing, exercise, listening to music. I have my coffee ritual in the morning and my cigar after dinner, and though one of these may be worse for me than the other, and neither would be advisable if I were starting from square one, I have made my peace with these. For now.

I know I am better prepared to live through this sober than I would have been as an active alcoholic. I know that I have little control over so much, and I feel more comfortable than I would have over how I can't control or predict the future, can't even guess how long this will last, when it will end and something else will start. Can't even begin to imagine what that something else might be.

What recovery has instilled in me, more than anything, is a commitment to process, one day at a time, without a fixation on the goal. The journey, not the destination.

29. Coda: Me and Paul

(I'LL ADMIT IT: THIS IS MY THIRD [and final] attempt to end a book about a process and program that stress that there really is no end. But death still seems kind of final, even as the dead whom we loved still live on within us.)

A Facebook cliché lets you define a relationship as "It's complicated." If Tolstoy had been on Facebook, he might have posted that "Each relationship is complicated in its own way." Yet I had never thought of my relationship with Paul as complicated, until he died. Only then did I realize just how much I had lost, and how much I had left to unravel.

Time blurs; so do boundaries. He was my therapist for more than a decade, starting a few years following our move from Austin to Des Moines in 1999, and then he was my friend for many years after. Actually, I'd thought of him as more of a friend all along, and I suspect he'd thought of me that way as well. At least I'd hoped he did, particularly after we had begun to see so much more of each other outside the office and less by appointment. (Even those appointments had seemed like something other than a professional transaction to me. I had never paid for them—my employer's benefits did.)

I had started seeing him following my out-of-the-blue panic attack, one that felt as serious as a heart attack. Literally. I hadn't been experiencing any panic that I was conscious of, nor even any stress. Instead, during my ritual coffee one morning, as I was typing a review on my computer, a numbness started traveling from my fingers and up my left arm. My breath grew short. I felt like I was becoming paralyzed. I'd thought that maybe this was it, the Big One, though I seemed incapable of making a phone call or otherwise alerting anyone from the empty house. Instead, I kept moving what I could, kept breathing, kept conscious, fighting to keep it from spreading. Within a half-hour I felt back to something like normal, but still pretty shaken.

To recap, my wife had previously been hospitalized for clinical depression and had remained on anti-anxiety medication as well as anti-depressants. When I subsequently had a second, lesser attack, she gave me her Klonopin and it seemed to work. So I went to a doctor for my own prescription, my intro to pharmapsychology. I also decided to resume talk therapy for the first time in decades, to see if that might help me figure out what was going on. How could I have felt so consciously free of panic, or even stress, yet have started to suffer from panic attacks? My wife had a therapist she liked, and her therapist recommended that Paul, one of her partners, would be a good fit for me.

He was. He was very smart and warm and funny, maybe the most appealing combination of those three qualities of any man I'd ever met. He made our therapy seem more like friendship, or at least like equals hashing things out, even though all we ever talked about was me. He was very good at his job, and if his job suggested that one of his patients (clients? guests?) needed a friend, he would be a very good one.

Here is how he was most like my therapist: During the time I was seeing him professionally, I never knew his home address or telephone number. Never asked. Maybe he would have told me, maybe not. We didn't see each other socially, go out for dinner or anything. I had no contact with him except in his office, at the appointed time, once a month. I didn't know whether he was married or single, straight or gay, late 50s or early 70s. Bald, trim and immaculately dressed, he may have been a decade older than me. Or a few years younger.

He was taut, wiry, in good shape for whatever age he was. His smile twinkled; he had a very light touch. He was the Fred Astaire of therapists, if Fred Astaire had been bald. And Greek. He had a cosmopolitan, European courtliness to him. He was a gentleman, a very dapper one.

Here is how we seemed more like friends: We had a lot in common culturally, and bonded over the sort of things my friends and I do—music and movies and books. He introduced me to the novels of Lily King; I suggested that he read *The Maytrees* by Annie Dillard. We both loved Anne Tyler, her psychological acuity and plain-spoken insight. (Her husband was a psychotherapist.)

We also discussed male novelists, and a lot of books that blurred the border between Eastern spirituality and Western psychology. He would have never been so presumptuous to consider himself a Buddhist. He was, he said, an atheist. But he described his spiritual tendencies as "buddhish."

We talked about movies that were in town, the ones we wanted to see, or had seen. We acted on each other's recommendations and then discussed ones we had both seen. Friends do this, and so did we.

Music went deepest with both of us. He knew I had worked as a rock critic for much of my career, before I became a journalism professor, and he felt some sort of validation when my professional opinion confirmed his personal passion. He was nuts about Prince, and he was delighted that I considered him the most multitalented, virtuosic visionary in popular music, some sort of ungodly mix of Ellington and Hendrix and so much else.

Leonard Cohen was another mutual favorite, and a Buddhist to boot, with his dapper charm, droll humor and dark acknowledgement of death's inevitability. He was, in fact, a lot like Paul. We differed over Dylan; he didn't get him, thought he was a phony. Dylan wasn't anything like Paul, not warm or refined or gracious.

Paul made me feel like I was living a normal life, or normal enough, if there was such a thing, while recognizing that even the most well-adjusted psyches had some peculiarities. After my wife's hospitalization and my episodes, I no longer believed that there was any sort of absolute distinction between sick and well, between crazy and sane. It was all a continuum, a very fluid one.

Then our relationship underwent a significant change (from what to what?), and so did my therapy. We had long discussed my drinking, mainly because it bothered my wife, how much I was drinking, through dinner and then after, and how regularly, every day. I didn't see it as a big deal. I never drank during the day or missed work. She thought I had a drinking problem. I thought I had a nagging problem.

So Paul and I talked about this problem in my marriage, along with others that related to my comfort with routine, my discomfort with change and transition. Pretty much everything I did—from my coffee in the morning through my exercise regimen in the afternoon to my cigar while reading after dinner—I did routinely, inflexibly. And so much of everything I did routinely I did to excess.

I had long admitted to having an addictive personality and to be suffering from some form of obsessive compulsive disorder. He corrected me. I wasn't suffering, I was managing, and I seemed to be managing things just fine. Rather than OCD—with "disorder" implying a value judgment—why didn't we just agree that I had obsessive compulsive *traits*? If anything, those traits didn't seem to be hindering me but aiding me in a successful, productive career. The habits and routines helped me to compartmentalize. Though plainly they weren't helping my marriage.

Long story short, after things came to a head with my wife over my drinking one night, she had her bags packed the next morning, ready to move out, after pouring all my alcohol down the drain. She suspected that I cared more about my drinking than I did about her. I feared she was right, and that this was an admission I could not make.

So I quit drinking, cold turkey, started going to 12-Step meetings, and after a couple weeks of this, I had made a surprising discovery: I really liked being sober, starting and ending each day with a consciousness unfogged by alcohol. This was a startling revelation. It was nothing I had ever considered in therapy, or outside it. For someone who tends to overthink absolutely everything, how could I have failed to think about this?

I mean, one of the reasons I drank and drugged myself into unconsciousness every night was that I felt it was the only way to shut my brain down, to quiet the incessant chatter, to stop those wheels from spinning. But I had never once considered that not drinking at all might be the way to a better life than drinking as much as I did. Astonishingly, I was soon sleeping better without drinking at all than I ever had when I'd felt I needed to drink so much in order to sleep.

I was still a creature of rigid routine, but those routines had changed radically. Instead of drinking daily, I was daily not drinking. And I was going to 12-step meetings daily. At the ripe old age of 59, having been a drinker since my mid-teens and a pot smoker since shortly after that, I was a changed man. Or at least one whose habits had changed.

Just as Paul had supported my drinking, he encouraged my sobriety. So did my other friends, though few of them had thought I'd had a drinking problem. The bigger surprise came a year or so later, when Paul told me at one of our monthly sessions that he had also just quit drinking and started going to meetings. He had also quit smoking dope daily. Hell, he and I had been the same guy! No wonder he had never thought I'd had a drinking problem. He'd apparently had one as well, one that we'd never discussed, since all our talk was focused on me, not him. And now, like me, he felt that his life had changed and been enriched significantly.

Did the changes he saw in me influence his own decision? I have no idea. You'd think a friend would have told a friend that. And I suspect he had other patients/clients in the program, and other friends as well. He seemed to be well-connected, socially and professionally, where I was not. Our experience reinforced each other's sobriety in our sessions, changed some of our dialogue into 12-step speak, as we began discussing his recovery as much as mine, and how much better we both felt.

Paul's commitment to his sobriety led him to launch a weekly meditation session for those in recovery. He asked whether I'd like to attend, and I was eager. I had tried meditating before, even when I was still drinking, but meditating with him soon became a highlight of my week. It also marked a turning point in our relationship. We still hadn't begun seeing each other socially—I still didn't have his address or phone number—but we were now meeting more frequently outside his office for a purpose that wasn't part of his profession or part of my therapy.

There would usually be somewhere between a half-dozen and a dozen of us, some more regular than others, none more regular than me. They all knew Paul from somewhere. My wife sometimes joined us, as did Paul's girlfriend, though I didn't know she was his girlfriend then. There was another guy who I later learned had been a therapist, like Paul, though he seemed no saner than any of the rest of us.

I didn't know any of the others, at least at the start. Those of us meeting to meditate weren't his friends, necessarily, though maybe some of us were. And we weren't his patients, necessarily, though some of us were. But we met each week for a purpose that left us feeling even more deeply connected. And it made me feel so much more connected to Paul.

Not talking with him, during meditation, and talking with him casually before and after began to feel even more therapeutic than our therapy sessions had been, even though I'd felt I'd gleaned a lot of insight from those. I started thinking that maybe seeing him every week made those professional sessions superfluous. He always left the interval to me, so we began scheduling for once every other month, or even two months, between sessions.

Every time before one of those infrequent sessions, I wondered whether I should quit therapy altogether. Yet I never did. No matter how I'd felt going in, I left feeling glad I had seen Paul and talked with him. Talking with him like a friend, and like a brother in recovery. There was no real reason to quit—I wasn't paying anything. And I'd always had issues with any sort of change or transition, which had been one of the issues of my therapy all along.

With Paul's Eastern bent, he knew that change was the only constant, that it was inevitable, and that I might do better to accept some level of discomfort as part of life than to think I myself could change and become comfortable with change. All along, "letting go" had been a key to my therapy, relinquishing my need for such rigid routine and control. "Letting go" was the essence of our meditation sessions. And "letting go" was the cornerstone of our 12-step program. The only constant is change; resistance is futile.

Yet neither of us could have possibly been prepared for the biggest change that transpired between us. I was at a Cubs game in Chicago when I heard a voice-mail message that said my appointment with Paul for next week had been canceled, and that I should call his office. When I did, I was told little more than that I couldn't reschedule at this time, and, cryptically, that I should try again next week. And when I tried again, I was told he had retired.

How could he do this to me? I no longer needed therapy, or so I felt, but I still needed Paul. Or at least an explanation of what had happened, an explanation his office plainly wasn't giving out. As it turned out, he had been preparing his regular patients, the ones he saw weekly, for a few months now, and his colleagues knew that's where he was heading, into retirement. I suppose his friends did as well, but it had never been mentioned in our weekly meditation sessions.

When I returned to Des Moines, I saw him at our next weekly meditation session, and he seemed to be in spirits as good as ever. He acknowledged that he had been anticipating his retirement for a while now—we had discussed mine as well, the possibility of it, since I had reached the age where it was feasible but not likely—but then circumstances beyond his control had thrown everything out of whack.

A few months earlier, he had been suffering symptoms of what had been diagnosed as Parkinson's disease, which he initially controlled with medication. He had kept this development secret, private, so I'd had no idea. Maybe even his friends who weren't patients didn't. It wouldn't have surprised me either way, if there was an inner circle that knew him much better than I did, or if there was no such circle, for a man who had seemed so self-sufficient, so fully himself.

But then the medicine stopped working as well as it had, and the symptoms had intensified—the spasmodic jerks, the shakes, the roadblocks to speech making its way from his brain through his voice. All so uncharacteristic for a man so refined, so impeccable in dress and manner and speech. He still had stretches where everything seemed fine—like the day when we talked at the meditation meeting—but there were also spells when everything would be much worse. He couldn't predict or control these, so he had to suspend his practice, hasten his retirement.

So, we had reached a pivotal point in our relationship, one where he was no longer my therapist, or anyone's therapist. Typically, when therapy ends, so does the connection with the therapist. I might still see him every week at meditation, but who knew how long he might be able to continue leading those meetings, or even attending them? So I mentioned that we ought to go out for dinner sometime; he said he'd enjoy that. I asked for his phone number, and he gave it to me.

We never did go out for dinner. When I texted him about getting together, after a few meditation meetings without him left me increasingly concerned, he suggested that I come to his townhouse. When I did, he was dressed in sweat clothes, more or less my own usual preference for comfort wear, but otherwise his place was much as I'd expected from his office, our relationship, our meditation.

The walls were an off-white, the décor was spare but striking, the furnishings essential but impeccable. No trace of the clutter that dominated my own life. He had lots of CDs, and a Bang & Olufsen stereo system, a beautiful piece of design. He also had Alexa, the

Amazon personal assistant, which would play whatever he asked on a wireless speaker system.

He was glad to see me, and it seemed very natural to be sitting with him there, at the kitchen table, talking first about his Parkinson's and the quick progression of the disease, how it continued to outpace his attempts to medicate it.

"Parkinson's sucks!" he said with a laugh and a broad smile, knowing there was nothing he could do about it but manage the best he could. "If you have a choice, do not choose Parkinson's!" Again a joke, with Paul knowing that what had happened to him and whatever might happen would not be a matter of choice.

Once Paul had answered all my how and why questions about the disease and his retirement, the conversation switched its focus to me, what I was going through, the transition from summer to the semester. The transcript wouldn't have read much differently than one of our therapy sessions. And at the end of about an hour, the same length of one of our appointments or meditation meetings, it seemed to be natural to leave, that we'd had enough time together.

I was really glad I had visited with him, but I didn't get the sense that he was eager for a lot of company or missing the social activity. Nor did I feel like I should be checking in on him more regularly, even weekly, as had been our meditation routine. Once the semester was in full swing, I tended to put everything else to the side.

I visited Paul twice more at his townhouse over the next year. There were extended intervals, four months or more, between visits, even though I only lived a few miles from him. When school was on, I was always so busy it felt like I was on a runaway train, hanging on for dear life. Paul's life had become more basic than ever. First he quit driving, and on the rare occasions that he attended our meditation meetings, someone else would drive him. I had told him that I would be happy to drive him there, or anywhere else he wanted to go, but he never asked.

And if he was desirous of company more often, he never said. I would talk to others at the meditation meeting who had seemed close to him, maybe even closer than I was, though I had no idea whether he had ever been their therapist. Their impressions seemed a lot like mine—it was a shame what had happened to Paul, should visit him more often, seemed like he was doing as well as could be expected the last time, but that had been weeks or months ago.

Once the semester was finished, I texted him to set up another visit. There was some confusion about dates, confusion that seemed to me to be in his mind about when I was available and when I wasn't. Or maybe when he was or wasn't.

Anyway, we finally got together, and he again seemed very happy to see me. We hugged when I arrived, which was something we had never done when he was my therapist, nor did I do so much with my male friends, but people in recovery did it all the time. I had come bearing gifts, a blanket that my wife had crocheted for him. (She was power crocheting in these days, her routine against tedium, to ward off depression, and was always looking to give them away.) He loved the blanket, was effusive in his appreciation, and he asked for her number so he could thank her. And when I suggested that maybe she could join us on our next visit, he said that would be lovely.

The visit itself was much the same as the first, about an hour long, though no need to repeat the back story about what had led to his premature retirement. Always thin, he had become skeletal, and he said he had been through some rough patches with eating and sleeping. Changes of medications, changes of doctors. But he said he seemed to be rallying, feeling better. I told him what had been going on with me, with the transitions into and out of the academic semester, but there was nothing he didn't already know from our years of therapy. I was glad I had come to see him, and glad when the visit was over.

The next time would be the last time I would ever see Paul, though neither of us seemed to have any premonition of that at the time. I brought my wife, so Paul could thank her again in person, and so that we wouldn't be left to our own conversational devices. And he made sure that his girlfriend was there. She had by now become his caretaker, though they retained separate residences.

So this was like a double date, with Parkinson's. Aretha Franklin had died recently, and this gave us something different to talk about, and someone to listen to without talking. Everybody loved Aretha, and it was no surprise that Paul did. He didn't even disagree when his girlfriend insisted that Aretha had been a greater artist than Paul's beloved Prince. He played from the expanded edition of Aretha's monumental *Amazing Grace,* and the call-and-response gospel music had plainly penetrated so deeply into his atheist soul. He was dancing to it, sometimes jerking or flailing his arms, his own amazing grace at odds with his Parkinson's disease.

He seemed unaware of this awkwardness, which seemed to me a little dangerous because of his skin-and-bones fragility. Or maybe just unembarrassed by it. He himself would be dead less than six months later.

I didn't learn of his death until a few days after he had died. We had been in Austin, making an extended visit right after the semester ended, and, though we had made no plans, I had presumed I'd see him on the extended break between semesters. Check in on him. See how he was doing. That had become my routine, to make one visit during my breaks, sometime after the one semester ended and the next one started.

Even if I hadn't been in Austin and hadn't been away from my meditation meeting, the one that Paul had started and now never attended, I might not have learned of his death any earlier. I received a text from a friend, who had heard about it from a mutual friend, who was closer to a woman who had been closer than the rest of us to Paul and his girlfriend.

He had declined quickly, a couple of months after our previous visit. He had developed trouble breathing, gulping and gasping for air. And that's all I knew, or learned. He had wanted to leave with the lightest possible footprint. By his instructions, there was to be no obituary, no visitation, no services, no memorial celebration.

Have I violated the spirit of Paul's wishes by writing this? I don't think so, or at least I don't think Paul would mind, or feel violated. He knew that I was a writer, and we had often talked about how everything in my life was potential material, and how writing was the way I struggled to make some sort of sense out of my life.

He also knew I was writing a memoir about my unexpected turn toward sobriety, and he asked about it often, encouraging me. Without our ever discussing it, he knew he would play a role in that narrative.

What he didn't know was how soon he would be dead.

I suspect that the possibility that I might write something like this would have been the least of his concerns during his final weeks, probably never crossed his mind. But after struggling with his death for weeks afterward, I knew I had to write about Paul, to try to make some sense of our relationship, to pay some sort of tribute to what knowing him had meant to me and I suspect to so many others. Others who likely saw him as so much more than a therapist. Writing about him is the only way I can begin to let him go. And the paradox here is that if I had never met a person who had influenced me the way that Paul did, I would never have been able to let such a person go.

Gratitude List

As I mentioned before, a daily "gratitude list" is one of the tools some use to stay sober, a way of counting your blessings now that you don't drink. This is the first one I've actually written out, though I am thankful every day for the spiritual dimensions of my sober life. And for so much else. But in the case of this book, for these people in particular:

For Maria, without whom there would be no book. And no sobriety, no family, no second half of my life as rich and rewarding as the one I have shared with her. I sometimes joke in meetings about "my higher power, whom I chose to call Maria." This is what my dad used to call "kidding on the square."

For Kelly and Molly, and the unconditional love I feel toward both of them. I couldn't be prouder of our two daughters, and of all they have brought into our lives. Including Ryan, and then Max, the sons we never had. And Hailey and Paige, our two granddaughters from Kelly and Ryan, who give me all the more reason to live as long as I can, to see how it all turns out.

For Richard, Doug, David and Katie. And for our mother and father, Don and Joan McLeese. I suspect the experience and memories of my siblings occasionally differ from mine, and that their books would be different as well. Maybe even better. The life and love we've shared has flourished through senior citizenry in all of us, and now extends through spouses and offspring who do the bloodline proud. We remain a pretty close-knit family. I love them all. Mom would be happy.

For Lloyd Sachs and John Soss, who have been like brothers to me through decades, through the occasional drunken stumbles and the sober struggles with this book. Lloyd's critical reading of the early chapters helped sharpen the focus. John has been the sounding board for sharing so many of our mutual interests and challenges. We all connect over a passion for music, literature and so much more.

(John also shepherded this project through its final stages, providing the artistry and design for the book's cover and turning his diligence and eye for detail to final proofreading as well. I can't thank him enough.)

And for Jim "J.C." Moore, wherever he is. My longtime drinking buddy, I suspect he was an alcoholic. Maybe he suspected the same of me.

My former editor Keith Moerer provided some crucial early perspective on the first section of this manuscript, and went above and beyond the call of friendship in helping me with some market research.

My journalism colleagues in Chicago and Austin have provided support, connection and perspective throughout my career—as well as plenty of laughs—and I continue to learn and benefit from my students and colleagues at the University of Iowa (where I have now been employed twice as long as I was at either of my newspaper jobs, and still find that weird).

I am especially grateful for Steve Semken and his Ice Cube Press, the sort of publisher I'd been hoping to find when I embarked on all this, and then discovered somewhat by happenstance and serendipity. Story of my life. I'm fortunate to have had Steve midwife this project and feel grateful to be working with someone who shares these ideals and has made such helpful suggestions.

I'm also grateful for the final read by my brother Richard, for his meticulous eye for proofreading and his editorial instincts. I have long thought of him as my older brother.

As for those who "trudge the Road of Happy Destiny," in Big Book parlance, I'm grateful for your inspiration and thankful for your company. In Des Moines alone, I've met so many recovering alcoholics that I now consider friends. Their names could fill a book. But since this is a program of anonymity, I'll simply thank Mike B., Sam G., and the two Pauls here, and then the rest of you when I see you.

Finally, for all of you who read this and any of you who find yourselves in this book, I couldn't be more grateful.

The Ice Cube Press began publishing in 1991 to focus on how to live with the natural world and to better understand how people can best live together in the communities they share and inhabit. Using the literary arts to explore life and experiences in the heartland of the United States we have been recognized by a number of well-known writers including: Bill Bradley, Gary Snyder, Gene Logsdon, Wes Jackson, Patricia Hampl, Greg Brown, Jim Harrison, Annie Dillard, Ken Burns, Roz Chast, Jane Hamilton, Daniel Menaker, Kathleen Norris, Janisse Ray, Craig Lesley, Alison Deming, Harriet Lerner, Richard Lynn Stegner, Richard Rhodes, Michael Pollan, David Abram, David Orr, and Barry Lopez. We've published a number of well-known authors including: Mary Swander, Jim Heynen, Mary Pipher, Bill Holm, Connie Mutel, John T. Price, Carol Bly, Marvin Bell, Debra Marquart, Ted Kooser, Stephanie Mills, Bill McKibben, Craig Lesley, Elizabeth McCracken, Derrick Jensen, Dean Bakopoulos, Rick Bass, Linda Hogan, Pam Houston, Paul Gruchow and Bill Moyers. Check out Ice Cube Press books on our web site, join our email list, Facebook group, or follow us on Twitter. Visit booksellers, museum shops, or any place you can find good books and support our truly honest to goodness independent publishing projects and discover why we continue striving to "hear the other side."

Ice Cube Press, LLC (Est. 1991)
North Liberty, Iowa, Midwest, USA
Resting above the Silurian and Jordan aquifers
steve@icecubepress.com
Check us out on Twitter and Facebook.
www.icecubepress.com

Celebrating Thirty-One Years of Independent Publishing

To Fenna Marie—
A slippery smiling
good as it gets
gift to make
my life just right.

Carmel Clay Public Library
Renewal Line: 317-814-3936
carmelclaylibrary.org

Withdrawn From
Carmel Clay Public Library